Praise for *Informal Learning*

"Outstanding! Finally, a book that walks its own talk. Jay Cross forces us to look at informal learning in a new way—the right way—helping casual observers and seasoned practitioners understand how people truly learn. I've waited a lifetime for this book."
—Marcia L. Conner, author, *Learn More Now* and *Creating a Learning Culture*, managing director, Ageless Learner

"When you look back at your most powerful and deep learning, it's informal. It's in context. It has meaning. And it's guided by realities that rarely get addressed in formal training programs. Accepting this thinking is fundamental to designing learning and performance experiences realistically. Acting on it is necessary for success."
—Gloria Gery, author, *Electronic Performance Support Systems*

"Jay Cross understands learning like no one else. In *Informal Learning*, he taps a fabulous array of real-life examples to provide practical insights for individuals and organizations to learn and succeed in the knowledge economy."
—Ross Dawson, author and chairman, Future Exploration Network

"*Informal learning* is something a lot of people are talking about, but [that] no one quite seems . . . to get a grasp of. Jay Cross is putting the pieces of the puzzle together in his new book, whose direct and conversational style is perfect for the topic. Now you may object that a book is too formal a way to [teach] about informal learning. And Jay may even agree. When he lists the major sources of our learning, he mentions everyone from your sister to your boss, but he does not mention books. Well, don't believe him. Reading this one will prove that there is life yet for splendid learning in good old books."
—Etienne Wenger, CP Square

"Jay Cross is a brilliant writer, synthesizer of ideas, and advocate for optimizing the development of human capital. Organizational development professionals, human resource directors, people managers, those concerned with 'the social life of information,' read this book. It will cause you to think and act!"
—Edward L. Davis, author, *Lessons for Tomorrow: Bringing America's Schools Back from the Brink*

"Life is all about learning, and learning to learn is the most valuable investment an organization can make. If you are eager to learn how organizations can truly boost the potential of their high-performance individuals, *Informal Learning* is the first readable, nontechnical visual map to the fascinating journey of getting better at learning more."
—Robin Good, chief editor, Robin Good Online Publishing Network

"You'll learn more reading this book than sitting in lectures. Jay will make you think and worry. Those are good things, in my view."
—Allison Rossett, San Diego State University

"As usual, Jay has his finger on the pulse of trends in corporate learning. He combines a thorough and engaging review of the rationale and manifestations of informal learning with a compelling perspective on its value. This book is a must read for anyone in the learning field today."
—Brenda Sugrue, director of research, ASTD

"The world has been waiting for this book. Learning will never be the same again."
—Jane Knight, e-Learning Centre and Learning Light

"Jay Cross is one of the pioneers in the field, one of the first to understand how the Internet changes learning in the workplace. This book shows you how to improve learning in the workplace by working with, not against, new technologies and does so in an engaging and informative manner. A must for any corporate trainer's bookshelf."
—Stephen Downes, National Research Council of Canada

"Corporations are just beginning to warm up to what Jay Cross has known for a long time: The water cooler is the new corporate university, and idle chatter—the productive kind—should be encouraged, not stamped out. Read this book if you want to understand how the learning most people think of as unimportant and unproductive is probably the most powerful learning of all—and how to amplify that."
—Jerry Michalski, Sociate

"Jay Cross distills years of experience and timeless wisdom into simple principles for what really works. He gracefully blows away the cobwebs of popular myths and misconceptions so that we can see the truly effective and astonishingly easy ways we can best support collaboration and learning."
—Verna Allee, founder, ValueNet Works, author, *The Future of Knowledge*

"Learning happens on the job, in the break rooms and around the water cooler. As life and business get faster and more complex, informal learning is the only option. How can you design learning structures and environments that support informal learning? Ask Jay. He got e-learning before anyone else. Now he gets informal learning. He just plain 'gets it.' And now that he's written a book, you can get it too."
—Dave Gray, CEO, XPLANE

"During the many chats and exchanges I have had with Jay, I've always felt I learned a lot from his insights, wisdom, and wit. Therefore it seems almost a contradiction in terms that Jay is putting all his thoughts and observations on informal learning into a book, the container par excellence of formal learning as we know it. In between the informal chats with Jay, this book will do great for me now, until our next meeting!"
—Rebecca Stromeyer, managing director, ICWE, Online Educa

"Jay's book demonstrates that informal learning is linked to innovations in business management, employee motivation, communities of practice, and productivity. If you have been a hermit for the past few years, reading this book will quickly bring you up-to-date and push your thinking ahead to the coming decades."
—Curtis J. Bonk, professor, Indiana University, and president, SurveyShare, Inc.

"Learning cannot be left to chance! The skill sets required by the new business environment of the twenty-first century can no longer be served by the traditional training methods of the twentieth century. How we even think about learning must change. Jay Cross is right on target. Every learning and business executive should read this important book. It will raise your consciousness about informal learning as the most important component of an enterprise learning environment."
—Frank J. Anderson, Jr., president and chief learning officer, Defense Acquisition University

"We're moving into an age where informal learning is recognized for what it is—our greatest service provider! You want to know how we're going to get there. This book by emergent learning guru Jay Cross is here to help you."
—Peter Issackson, Intersmart, Paris

"In *Informal Learning,* Jay Cross presents, with dramatic clarity

- How and why people can learn at a lightning-fast pace, even in what seem to be the stodgiest organizations or environments
- How entire organizations can be transformed overnight
- How enterprises that understand learning, social networking, and the full potential of the Internet can position themselves to anticipate changes, leap on opportunities, and enjoy extreme success
- How to create conditions that nurture creative, responsive individuals who keep the organization flexible, dynamic, and thriving."

—Susan Smith Nash, http://www.beyondutopia.com, Leadership and the eLearning Organization

About This Book

Why is this topic important?

Workers learn more in the coffee room than in the classroom. They discover how to do their jobs through informal learning: talking, observing others, trial and error, and simply working with people in the know. Formal learning—classes and workshops—is the source of only 10 to 20 percent of what people learn at work. Corporations overinvest in formal training programs while neglecting natural, simpler informal processes. This book describes how visualization, impromptu conferences, organizational network analysis, conversation space, and communities of purpose fuel innovation and agility. In short, informal learning is generally more effective and less expensive than its formal counterpart.

What can you achieve with this book?

After reading this book, you should be able to:

- Recognize informal learning when you see it
- Apply informal learning practices in your organization
- Co-create a culture that nurtures natural learning
- Replace training events with learning environments
- Seed communities of practice for bottom-up knowledge dissemination
- Make your organization more agile, resilient, spirited, and open
- Focus on performance

How is this book organized?

This book is divided into four major parts. "Concepts" examines the incredible acceleration of time, a working definition of informal learning, how informal learning benefits organizations, and why learning ecosystems will crowd out training programs. "Learners" focuses on the individual and the skills and attitudes that make for a successful informal learner. "Cases" are stories of informal learning in action in a variety of companies. "Just Do It" advises how to bring informal learning into your organization. Additional material includes the "In a Nutshell" as Appendix A (because repetition improves learning), two other appendixes, a glossary, and a list of related resources. A Web site for the book, http://informL.com, contains supplemental material, updates, and links to community.

About Pfeiffer

Pfeiffer serves the professional development and hands-on resource needs of training and human resource practitioners and gives them products to do their jobs better. We deliver proven ideas and solutions from experts in HR development and HR management, and we offer effective and customizable tools to improve workplace performance. From novice to seasoned professional, Pfeiffer is the source you can trust to make yourself and your organization more successful.

Essential Knowledge Pfeiffer produces insightful, practical, and comprehensive materials on topics that matter the most to training and HR professionals. Our Essential Knowledge resources translate the expertise of seasoned professionals into practical, how-to guidance on critical workplace issues and problems. These resources are supported by case studies, worksheets, and job aids and are frequently supplemented with CD-ROMs, Web sites, and other means of making the content easier to read, understand, and use.

Essential Tools Pfeiffer's Essential Tools resources save time and expense by offering proven, ready-to-use materials—including exercises, activities, games, instruments, and assessments—for use during a training or team-learning event. These resources are frequently offered in looseleaf or CD-ROM format to facilitate copying and customization of the material.

Pfeiffer also recognizes the remarkable power of new technologies in expanding the reach and effectiveness of training. While e-hype has often created whizbang solutions in search of a problem, we are dedicated to bringing convenience and enhancements to proven training solutions. All our e-tools comply with rigorous functionality standards. The most appropriate technology wrapped around essential content yields the perfect solution for today's on-the-go trainers and human resource professionals.

www.pfeiffer.com

Essential resources for training and HR professionals

INFORMAL LEARNING

Rediscovering the Natural Pathways
That Inspire Innovation and Performance

Jay Cross

Pfeiffer
A Wiley Imprint
www.pfeiffer.com

John Wiley & Sons, Inc.

Published by Pfeiffer
An Imprint of Wiley
989 Market Street, San Francisco, CA 94103-1741
www.pfeiffer.com

For additional copies/bulk purchases of this book in the
U.S. please contact 800-274-4434.

Pfeiffer books and products are available through most
bookstores. To contact Pfeiffer directly call our Customer
Care Department within the U.S. at 800-274-4434, outside the U.S. at 317-572-3985, fax 317-572-4002, or visit
www.pfeiffer.com.

Pfeiffer also publishes its books in a variety of electronic
formats. Some content that appears in print may not be
available in electronic books.

Library of Congress Cataloging-in-Publication Data

Cross, Jay, date.
  Informal learning: rediscovering the natural pathways
that inspire innovation and performance/Jay Cross.
      p. cm.
  Includes bibliographical references and index.
  ISBN-13: 978-0-7879-8169-3 (pbk.)
  ISBN-10: 0-7879-8169-9 (pbk.)
  1. Organizational learning. 2. Experiential learning.
3. Non-formal education. I. Title.
HD58.82.C76 2006
658.3'124—dc22

                                        2006027162

Acquiring Editor: Lisa Shannon
Director of Development: Kathleen Dolan Davies
Developmental Editor: Susan Rachmeler
Production Editor: Rachel Anderson
Editor: Beverly Miller
Manufacturing Supervisor: Becky Carreno
Illustrations: Lotus Art

Printed in the United States of America

Printing   10 9 8 7 6 5 4 3 2 1

CONTENTS

PART FOUR: JUST DO IT

PREFACE

THIS IS A BOOK about knowledge workers, twenty-first-century business, and informal learning. I first heard the term *informal learning* from the late Peter Henschel, then director of the Institute for Research on Learning (IRL), who told me:

> People are learning all the time, in varied settings and often most effectively in the context of work itself. "Training"—formal learning of all kinds—channels some important learning but doesn't carry the heaviest load. The workhorse of the knowledge economy has been, and continues to be, informal learning.

For thirty years, I'd been designing, cost-justifying, and marketing formal training programs. Now this distinguished-sounding fellow was telling me that people learned more by accident. Back in California, Peter and I met at IRL to talk further about informal learning, communities of practice, anthropological research, and learning as engagement. I reflected on how I had acquired my professional skills: watching master performers, trial and error, bull sessions with friends, faking it, reading magazines, and, above all, just talking with others. Conversation was a more effective teacher than school.

Peter was right. Most learning about how to do a job is informal. If your organization is not addressing informal learning, it's leaving a tremendous amount of learning to chance. Is that okay? Not any longer. This is a knowledge economy.

Most corporations invest their training budget where it will have the least impact, as shown in Figure P.1:

> *Imagine a world where everyone was constantly learning, a world where what you wondered was more interesting than what you knew, and curiosity counted for more than certain knowledge.*
>
> **THE CLUETRAIN MANIFESTO**

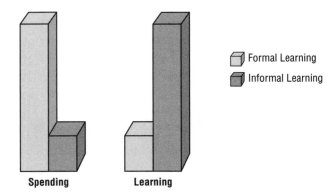

FIGURE P.1. The Spending/Outcomes Paradox

> *Informal learning, that's what we call the learning that takes place out of school.*
> **DON NORMAN**

In July 2002, a three-day event entitled Creating a Learning Culture rekindled my interest in informal learning. Convened by Marcia Conner at the University of Virginia's Darden School of Business in Charlottesville, it was clear from the start that this was not going to be the typical graduate school colloquium. Marcia told us *we* were the experts, so no one was going to be teaching at us from the front of the room. We were seeking discovery, not answers. Here are a few of the comments from the fifty assembled gurus and rebels:

> "Institutions suck the life out of people. I want to be fully alive, not just going through the motions."
>
> "Our DNA makes people so much alike. We should build on our similarities, not our differences."
>
> "You don't stop work to learn. Learning is the work."
>
> "People like change; it's exciting. People don't want to *be* changed."

> *Informal, adjective: casual, familiar, easy, congenial, simple, unpretentious.*
> **ALLWORDS.COM MULTI-LINGUAL DICTIONARY**

The Darden event encouraged me to think even further out of the box, and in 2003 I wrote a white paper entitled "Informal Learning, the Other 80 Percent," which described IRL's findings and added Marcia's and others' suggestions on what to do should an organization choose not to leave learning to chance. The following is excerpted from that white paper:

Learning is not what you think it is

Most of what we learn, we learn from other people—parents, grandparents, aunts, uncles, brothers, sisters, playmates, cousins, Little Leaguers, Scouts, school chums, roommates, teammates, classmates, study groups, coaches, bosses, mentors, colleagues, gossips, co-workers, neighbors, and, eventually, our children. Sometimes we even learn from our teachers.

Informal learning is effective because it is personal. The individual calls the shots. The learner is responsible. It's real. How different from formal learning, which is imposed by someone else. How many learners believe the subject matter of classes and workshops is "the right stuff"? How many feel the corporation really has their best interests at heart? Given today's job mobility, workers who delegate responsibility for learning to their employers become perpetual novices [p. 1].

Many people agreed with what I was saying but were at a loss as to what to do about it. A publisher approached me, and in early 2005 I began digging deeper into the concept of informal learning. I've since read eighty books, interviewed more than a hundred people, and visited heaven knows how many Web sites. I've concluded that we are on a journey from an industrial world ruled by certainty, precision, and logic to a natural world characterized by unity, unpredictability, and complexity.

The industrial age has run out of steam. A quick scan reveals unhappy workers, overcrowded cities, polluted skies, volatile economics, crumbling values, the eradication of leisure, and general malaise that too much is going on. These are the death throes of a model that has outlived its usefulness. It is time to close this chapter and head for new territory.

Join me in exploring how informal learning can boost your organization's performance and enable your workers to lead more fulfilling lives.

August 2006   Jay Cross
                                                          Berkeley, California

ACKNOWLEDGMENTS

HUNDREDS OF PEOPLE helped write this book, and I cannot name them all here. However, special recognition is due to a number of them:

- Busy people who gave their time to help me explore the world of informal learning: Don Norman, David Sibbet, Don Novello, Larry Prusak, Verna Allee, George Leonard, Tom Stewart, Steve Denning, Steve Rae, Rob Cross, Etay Gafni, John Sperling, Gloria Gery, Kevin Wheeler, Tony O'Driscoll, John Adams, Ned Davis, Craig Weber, Jerry Michalski, Ted Cocheu, Valdis Krebs, and Paul Duguid

- Bloggers who go beyond the call of duty to share their thoughts, help others, and make the world a better place, notably Don Clark, Don Clark (yes, there are two of them), Stephen Downes, Robin Good, Denham Gray, Harold Jarche, Maish Nichani, Mark Oehlert, Godfrey Parkin, Dave Pollard, George Siemens, Kevin Kruse, Dave Winer, and David Weinberger; you are my teachers and soulmates, and I thank you for your generosity.

- Others who shared their insights and shaped my perspective: Brenda Sugrue, Bill Bruck, Curt Bonk, Bill Mitchell, Brian Behlendorf, Chris Pirillo, Clark Aldrich, Dale Dougherty, David Grebow, Don Tosti, Doug Engelbart, Doug Kaye, Elizabeth Doti, Eugene Kim, Gary Dickelman, Herwig Rollett, Jim Schuyler, Lance Dublin, Lee LeFever, Loretta Daniels, Marc Rosenberg, Mary Hodder, Michael Spock, Mike Parmentier, Murray Gell-Mann, Paul Mace, Rob Hathaway, Ross Button, Ross Mayfield, David Weekly, Christian Bauman, Bruce Cryer, Bill Veltrop, Seth Kahan, Terri Griffith, Tom King, Tom Malone, Trace Urdan,

Vance Stevens, Tayeb Kamali, Will Wright, Soren Kaplan, Pele Rouge, Hobie Swan, Jaron Lanier, Leonard Pitt, John Hagel, Ben Watson, Bob Frankston, Dick Sethi, Jake McKee, and Wim Veen

- Clark Quinn, who gave me solid advice throughout the project, and the other members of the Meta-Learning Lab: Claudia Welss, Claudia L'Amoreaux, and Bill Daul
- Marcia Conner, an ageless learner who inspires me to think different
- The late Peter Henschel, who first turned me on to informal learning
- Jane Hart, who reviewed the entire manuscript and provided wise counsel
- Dave Gray and the other guys at XPLANE for helping me (and you) visualize what informal learning is all about
- Bob Horn, who makes genius look simple and is a true pioneer in the field of informal learning
- Smokey the Wonderdog, who was always cheerful, got me up mornings, never doubted that I would pull this off, and was a constant source of inspiration
- My darling wife Uta, for being there

INTRODUCTION

WORKERS LEARN MORE in the coffee room than in the classroom. They discover how to do their jobs through informal learning: asking the person in the next cubicle, trial and error, calling the help desk, working with people in the know, and joining the conversation. This is natural learning—learning from others when you feel the need to do so.

Training programs, workshops, and schools get the lion's share of the corporate budget for developing talent, despite the fact that this formal learning has almost no impact on job performance. And informal learning, the major source of knowledge transfer and innovation, is left to chance.

This book aims to raise your consciousness about informal learning. You will discover that informal learning is a profit strategy, that it flexes with change, and that it respects and challenges workers. You will see how hard-nosed businesses use organizational network analysis, conversation space, and communities of purpose to fuel innovation and agility. You will read stories of dozens of companies that have prospered by putting informal learning techniques to work.

Learning is that which enables you to participate successfully in life, at work, and in the groups that matter to you.

WHO SHOULD READ THIS BOOK

This book is first and foremost for decision makers. Informal learning is neither the training department's job nor a human resource function. Nurturing informal learning is an implicit part of every manager's job.

This book is for executives who know in their hearts that their organization's approaches are not sufficient to prepare their workers for the future. It is also for knowledge workers who are taking charge of their own learning.

Learning is like breathing, so much a part of our lives that we're unaware of it until a mentor or a book refocuses our attention. When you know what to look for, you can leverage it to your advantage.

Chief learning officers and training managers also will read this book because it proposes a framework for learning that is more spontaneous, cost-effective, and enjoyable than what has come before.

ORGANIZATION OF THE BOOK

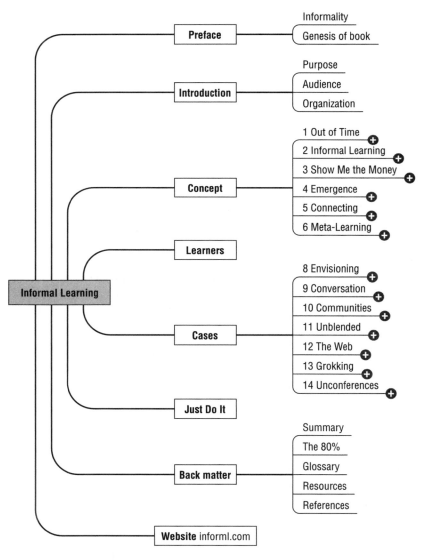

FIGURE I.1. Mind Map of *Informal Learning*

- The Concepts chapters examine the incredible acceleration of time, a working definition of *informal learning*, how informal learning benefits organizations, and why learning ecosystems will crowd out training programs.

- The Learners chapter offers short-cuts for skills that individuals must master to succeed as informal learners.

- The Cases chapters tell stories of informal learning in organizations.

- The Just Do It chapter advises how to bring informal learning into your organization. We look at governance and trust. Experience teaches the importance of envisioning opportunity, keeping it simple, and avoiding the pitfalls.

- At the end of the book are appendixes, a glossary, and resources for implementing informal learning.

The companion Web site at http://informl.com provides new developments, additional examples, and a community of interest.

Since we're going to focus on informal learning, we will not be dealing with compliance training or certification programs. Books on those topics crowd the shelves of your local library and bookstore. Four out of five companies that follow are American; your culture may vary. Finally, this book does not address schooling or how children learn.

OUT OF TIME

I AM OUT OF TIME. You bought the beta edition of this book. Things change so fast that all books are dated by the time they are published. Check the book Web site for extensions and updates (http://informl.com). Of course, the site is beta, too, but at least it is more recent. Nothing gets finished anymore. The world is moving too fast for closure. Our lives are in beta.

Everything is faster, more interconnected, and less predictable. Getting aligned with this new world is the road to profit and longevity for organizations, well-being and fulfillment for individuals. This book won't give you the answers, but it will set you on the right path.

THE HYPERINFLATION OF TIME

When I was growing up in Hope, Arkansas, a ticket to the Saturday afternoon double feature cost fifteen cents. A Pepsi cost a nickel. Penny candy cost a penny. Motel 6 once charged six dollars a night. It's not that everything in the old days was dirt cheap. Rather, the value of money has changed.

The same thing is now happening to time. More happens in a minute today than in one of your great-grandmother's minutes. Not only is more and more activity packed into every minute, the rate of change itself is increasing. Measured by the atomic clock, the twenty-first century will contain a hundred years. Measured by how much will happen, in the twenty-first century, we will experience twenty thousand current years (Kurzweil, 2005).

A plot of the acceleration of time resembles a hockey stick. We have just left the blade and are shooting up the handle. We cannot keep driving into

> *Two billion years ago, our ancestors were microbes; a half-billion years ago, fish; a hundred million years ago, something like mice; ten million years ago, arboreal apes; and a million years ago, proto-humans puzzling out the taming of fire. Our evolutionary lineage is marked by mastery of change. In our time, the pace is quickening.*
>
> **CARL SAGAN**

the future with the same old ox-cart; the wheels would fall off. The vehicle we ride into the future must be very responsive, for we are sure to encounter many surprises. There's no map to what's up ahead.

Everything flows. That's life. Now everything flows faster. Survivors will be those who are most responsive to change. Unlearning obsolete routines is the secret of long life. Anything that is rigid is probably a vestige of earlier, slower times.

TIME GUSHES FORWARD

When I was ten or eleven, Disney's nature movie *Living Desert* provided my first experience of time-lapse photography. A seedling sprouted, grew, bloomed, and died in a couple of seconds on the screen. Withered green disks of cactus plumped up and grew little buds, and the buds miraculously turned into fat red prickly pears. Living things were always growing. I'd failed to notice that before because they changed too slowly for me to perceive.

Stopping time has fascinated me ever since, be it Eadward Muybridge's photographs capturing a horse with all feet in the air or Harold Edgerton freezing a bullet in flight. Read Stewart Brand's marvelous book *How Buildings Learn* (1994), and you realize that a fifteen-second animation of a century of New York's Park Avenue would show buildings going up and coming down again and again, an immense railroad yard sinking beneath the earth, and mansions being replaced with gleaming skyscrapers, the scene morphing from cabin to brownstone to a Mies van der Rohe glass box.

Even the most permanent things are temporary when you shift to the long term and convert eons to seconds. A stream trickling across flat land carves the Grand Canyon. The floors of seas rise to form mountains. If dinosaurs get half an hour on screen, we humans get only a few seconds.

Three or four hundred years ago, a nanosecond in geological time, we adolescent humans convinced ourselves that we were the center of the universe, that we were in control, and that we could bend nature to our will. Descartes told us it was all in our heads. Newton explained how things moved (logically). Englishmen and Scots invented industry. Frederick Taylor told workers "You are not paid to think." Hierarchy flourished.

Those days of certainty are over. We no longer control the universe (actually we never did). We are simply another thread in the fabric of life. A hundred years after Einstein, everything is beginning to feel relative. The watchmaker has left the stage. Uncertainty is the rule. We are all in this together.

NETWORK EFFECTS

Networks are growing faster than vines in the rain forest, reaching out, and encircling the earth. Denser connections yield faster throughput. The exponential growth of networks is the underlying reason that everything is speeding up.

Social networks, computer networks, communications networks, and any other network you can think up are constructed of nodes and connectors and nothing more. Each new node of a network increases the value of the overall network exponentially because the additional node connects to all the preexisting nodes. Connecting networks to other networks turbocharges their growth.

New linkages distribute information and power, breaking down organizational boundaries and fiefdoms. Networks subvert hierarchy. Perhaps it took longer than we expected, but people were right when they said the Net changes everything.

Forty years ago, Intel cofounder Gordon Moore noted that the number of transistors on a chip doubled every year. Later, the rate slowed to doubling every eighteen months, and the exponential growth of computing power per dollar became known as *Moore's Law*. Moore's Law is why the laptop computer you bought not long ago is now selling for half what you paid for it.

Research has found that Moore's Law applies to many areas besides computing. Examples are fields like DNA sequencing, gross domestic product, manufacturing output, e-commerce, educational expenditures, magnetic data storage, wireless data devices, Internet hosts, bandwidth, and miniaturization.

Inventor Ray Kurzweil (2005) plots what fifteen thinkers and reference works consider "the key events in biological and technological evolution from the Big Bang to the Internet" (p. 19). They're taking place at a quicker and quicker pace. The speed of evolution itself is picking up. "Before the middle of this century, the growth rates of our technology—which will be indistinguishable from ourselves—will be so steep as to appear essentially vertical. . . . The growth rates will be . . . so extreme that the changes they bring about will appear to rupture the fabric of human history" (p. 30).

> *We are being propelled into this new century with no plan, no control, no brakes.*
> **BILL JOY**

ON A HUMAN SCALE

It's a safe bet that you don't have as much time as you used to. Things used to be simple. People had plenty of time. Suddenly everything is complex, life is out of control, nobody has time, and most workers hate their jobs. The world has changed, and we humans have not kept up.

You don't have to do the math to feel what's going on. Compare your e-mail to a couple of years ago. Are you in control of the situation? Does the incessant arrival of more and more stress you out? What if you receive twice as many e-mails and voice mails next year? Or four times as many the year after that?

People are so overwhelmed with incoming messages that they have little time to cover new ground. You say your company wants innovation? How can people innovate when they hardly have time to get their regular jobs done?

We all face a choice. The first option is to run faster and faster to keep up. A word of warning here: time management courses, self-improvement books, fancy calendars, personal digital assistants, spam filters, tickler files, discipline, and longer hours are not going to get you out of this one. At best they give you a temporary advantage. The second option is to get off the treadmill, admit that the world is not under your control, and embrace the chaos of change. That's what the remainder of this book is about.

In Figure 1.1, my son, three years old in the photograph, is not reading the technology catalogue in his hands. (It's upside down.) He is merely going through the motions. You may be in a similar state. If you are looking for an immediate quick fix to deep-seated organizational and personal issues without study and reflection, don't waste any more time reading here. Thumb through these pages, pluck out a few nuggets, and keep up with your helter-skelter schedule. There's a complete summary in Appendix A.

> *Life is either a daring adventure or nothing.*
> **HELEN KELLER**

FIGURE 1.1. Young Austin Cross, Going Through the Motions

To get the most out of this book, you must think outside of your comfort zone. You may find yourself nodding in agreement with many commonsense statements, only to reflect that adopting this approach wholesale will require a reversal of the corporate culture you are accustomed to. As Chairman Mao said, "You want to make an omelet, you break a few eggs."

KEEPING UP

When the job environment changed only slowly, corporate learning involved acquiring the skills and know-how to do the job. Now corporate learning means keeping up with the new things you need to know to do the job, maybe even daily. The traditional barriers separating training, development, knowledge management, performance support, informal learning, mentoring, and knowing the latest news have become obstacles to performance. They are all one thing and for one purpose: performance.

Learning used to focus on what was in an individual's head. The individual took the test, got the degree, or earned the certificate. The new learning focuses on what it takes to do the job right. The workplace is an open-book exam. What worker doesn't have a cell phone and an Internet connection? Using one's lifelines to get help from colleagues and the Internet to access the world's information is encouraged. Besides, it's probably the team that must perform, not a single individual.

The new learning means having great connections: sources that know, advice that helps, alerts to what's important, and ready answers to questions. Perhaps it's time to promote the chief learning officer to chief performance officer. Beyond running an in-house schoolhouse, the chief performance officer's concerns include the corporate news function, the architecture of the work space, the quality of communications, intranet structure, and organization development.

THE FUTURE OF WORK

At the Accelerating Change 2005 conference, MIT professor Tom Malone said, "New technologies are making it possible for the first time in human history to have the economic benefits of very large organizations and, at the same time, to have the human benefits of very small organizations, things like freedom, flexibility, motivation and creativity."

In *The Future of Work: How the New Order of Business Will Shape Your Organization, Your Management Style and Your Life*, Malone (2004) observes that all networks are alike in that they form and grow in similar stages. At first, nodes are unconnected. When communication becomes feasible, they evolve into a hub-and-spoke arrangement around a single source of power. As communication becomes cheaper still, all nodes begin to take on power. For example, early humans organized in bands of thirty to forty people (larger groups would have overhunted the local area). When spoken language and writing came on the scene, kingdoms formed. And when printing and mass communication appeared, democracies replaced them. (See Figure 1.2.)

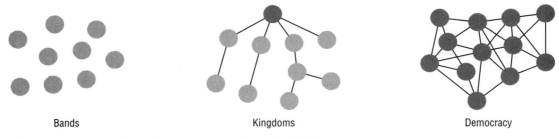

Bands   Kingdoms   Democracy

FIGURE 1.2. Human Organization over the Past 10,000 Years

Business went through a similar evolution, albeit in accelerated fashion. When I was a boy, if you needed a prescription filled, you walked to Cox's Drugstore and Mr. Cox filled your prescription. Then Rexall, Walgreen's, and Eckerd's took over the independents. When I buy drugs over the Internet now, I don't know who I'm dealing with any more (Figure 1.3).

 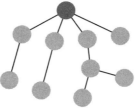 

Small, local business   Large, central corporation   Loosely coupled network

FIGURE 1.3. Evolution of Business in the Twentieth Century

I remember living through this pattern with computers, as shown in Figure 1.4. I wrote my first computer program in FORTRAN IV for an IBM 7094 Mod II at the Princeton Computing Center in 1966. That $11 million machine had 144 KB of memory and a cycle time of ¼ MIP. My IBM X40 ThinkPad cost one-five thousandth as much yet runs five thousand times faster. Price-to-performance has doubled twenty-four times in the last thirty-six years.

   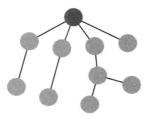   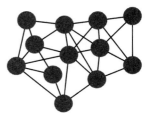

Standalone proprietary   Client/server LANS and WANS   On demand and Internet
mainframes

FIGURE 1.4. Evolution of Connectivity of Computers

The 7094 stood alone on a raised floor in a glass box, totally isolated. Twenty years later, top-down client-server networks became the rule. And now the Internet is the model of a completely distributed network.

Training is no exception to the rules of network evolution. In past times, training was individualized; people learned at grandma's knee or in the studio of a master craftsman. With printing came instructor-centric schools. As we enter an age of informal and workflow learning, authority is less centralized than ever before (Figure 1.5.) "Learning is best understood as an interaction among practitioners, rather than a process in which a producer provides knowledge to a consumer," says Etienne Wenger, a social researcher and champion of communities of practice.

   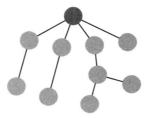   

One-on-one   Classes and workshops   Informal learning

FIGURE 1.5. Evolution of Learning

We've outgrown the definition of learning as the activity of an individual and moved back to an apprenticeship model, though at a higher level. We learn in context, with others, as we live and work. Recognizing this fact is the first step to crafting an effective learning strategy.

We humans exist in networks. We are part of social networks. Our heads contain neural networks. Learning consists of making and maintaining better connections to our networks, be they social, operational, commercial, or entertainment. Rich learning will always be more than a matter of bits flowing back and forth, but the metaphor of learning as networking gives us a way to describe how learning can be embedded in work itself.

Walter J. Freeman, speaking on the poetry of brains at the August 2005 meeting of the Future Salon, said we focus too much on the individual brain instead of on the collaboration of groups of brains. Working with one another is the essence of Doug Engelbart's goal of 1951: "As much as possible, to boost mankind's collective capability for coping with complex, urgent problems."

We're beginning to consider a new concept of worker. Think of a worker as the sum of employee and support systems, combining the strengths of each into a whole greater than the sum of the parts. The worker's dashboard appears on a phone, personal digital assistant, monitor, or head-mounted display. Bear in mind, however, that this is a two-way dashboard. It empowers the worker to give as well as receive, to collaborate with other people and to be contacted by others.

Business Week (12/19/05) calls a business where power is distributed an open-source workplace and notes that "the CEO is no longer omnipotent—and the truly effective ones don't want to be. The best ideas may evolve from the bottom up and sometimes from the outside in. New technologies such as private workplace wikis and blogs are disrupting command-and-control corporate structures. Any employee can create, edit, refine, comment on, or fix an idea. What some used to dismiss as a recipe for chaos is more likely a path to greater productivity."

THE WORK OF THE FUTURE

The work of the future is knowledge work. You're undoubtedly a knowledge worker yourself. See if you don't agree, as I do, with Tom Davenport's statement that knowledge workers "don't like to be told what to do, . . . work best when working with other people in social networks, and are better led by example than by explicit management" (2005, p. 14).

> *Knowledge workers are people who know more about their work than their bosses do.*
> **PETER DRUCKER**

I fit Davenport's description of knowledge worker well. I want to set my own schedule and choose where I work. I think for myself. No one will ever reduce what I do to a flowchart. I like to work on things I help create. I'm always building for the long term while getting today's work out the door. And if I don't feel good about doing something, I probably won't do it well. I work for me first and my organization second.

"What the mind can conceive, man can achieve," preached positive-thinking evangelist Napoleon Hill (1937), and while he was over the top, it's true that we live up (or down) to our expectations. Tell someone it will take her a week to do a report, and she will find a way to stretch the project to a week, even if she would otherwise have completed it in a couple of hours. Tell a group of students they are in the "slow group," and they'll perform at the slow-group level.

Slow and fast. We're accustomed to measuring the speed of production in terms of output per hour. How many sandwiches can the cook assemble? How many cakes can Lucy and Ethel put in boxes? How many phone calls can the telemarketer complete? How long should it take a third grader to learn to multiply?

This industrial mind-set has seeped into all aspects of work. If the average input operator keys in 100,000 digits per hour, we'd expect the range of performance to be in the 80,000 to 120,000 range. The slowest operator is not going to log, say, 10 strokes per hour, and the fastest is not going to enter 250,000.

Knowledge work doesn't have these physical limitations. The best worker may be hundreds of times more productive than her less effective peer. Following a speed reading course, the average reader goes from reading 90 words a minute to 150; high performers go from 350 to 2,900 words per minute. These people justify special handling.

Innovative knowledge work is a different beast. A knowledge worker may go months without having a great idea, but her one great idea more than makes up for the difference in frequency.

"The butterfly effect" is a popular metaphor for the potential asymmetry of results that occur from the interaction of complex systems. If a butterfly flaps its wings in Brazil, might it cause a tornado in Texas? The answer is, "Probably not, but it could happen."

The chief technical officer at Google believes a superlative engineer can be 250 times more productive than an average performer. Making a great performer better gives more bang for the buck than moving an average performer up a notch. It's a human butterfly effect.

Are you uncomfortable in your job? Seventy to eighty percent of Americans say they don't like their work. People enjoy change, but they don't like to be changed. We're struggling because we're attempting to serve two masters. Workers are straddling the gulf between business-as-usual and a new networked world.

Twenty years ago I had two secretaries. They screened my calls, prepared my correspondence, scheduled my appointments, and made my travel arrangements. Now I write my own letters, keep my own calendar, and schedule my own travel. No one screens my calls, unless you count cutting off the phone and letting the answering machine take messages. My inputs used to be phone calls, snail mail, and interoffice memos. Now I also get e-mail, voice mail, Skype and GoogleTalk calls, instant messages, Web feeds, listservs, and calls on four telephones.

This is why a third of all male knowledge workers clock more than fifty hours a week. Forty-three percent get less than seven hours sleep a night. Sixty percent rush through meals. Twenty-five percent of executives report that their communications are unmanageable (*Business Week*, Oct. 3, 2005). In Table 1.1, Verna Allee highlights the differences between the old world or work and the new.

TABLE 1.1. Traditional Thinking, New Thinking

Assumption	Traditional Thinking	New Thinking
Scientific foundation	Newtonian physics	Quantum physics
We understand by	Dissecting into parts	Seeing in terms of the whole
Information is	Ultimately knowable	Infinite and unbounded
Growth is	Linear, managed	Organic, chaotic
Managing means	Control, predictability	Insight and participation
Workers are	Specialized, segments	Multifaceted, always learning
Motivation is from	External forces and influences	Intrinsic
Knowledge is	Individual	Collective
Organization is	By design	Emergent
Life thrives on	Competition	Cooperation
Change is	Something to worry about	All there is

Source: Allee (1997). Reprinted with permission.

Shifting from hierarchies to network organizations has another ramification: there is no boss. This is a case of, "Be careful what you wish for." Workers aren't accustomed to having no superior to get instructions from, to fight for their cause, to listen to their complaints, or to ask for guidance. Instead of playing well-defined roles, workers become nodes that must respond to demands in real time.

SLOW DOWN

The author of *In Praise of Slowness* (2004), Carl Honore, read a newspaper item about One-Minute Bedtime Stories, a time-saver for harried parents. At first he was delighted with this swell idea. On reflection, he realized how screwy it was to cut corners on quality time with one's children. Who's calling the shots on this one? Carl digs into the subject, looking at the Slow Food movement, the Slow City movement, hours-long Tantric sex, the frenzied pace of work, and the diminution of leisure.

Each of us sets our own metronome. You can take time to smell the roses or you can zip right past them. This ties in to Bodil Jonsson's observation in *Unwinding the Clock* (2001), that "if I can fool myself into thinking that I don't have enough time, couldn't I just as well fool myself into thinking that I have plenty of time? So I decided to have plenty of time" (p. 48). So I decided to slow down for a spell.

There is more to life than increasing its speed.
GANDHI

When automobile drivers drive recklessly, they have accidents. When people rev out too high in their daily lives, they tear the fabric of everything that makes living worthwhile: family, relationships, values, community.

Fast and slow are attitudes, not absolute rates. "Fast is busy, controlling, aggressive, hurried, analytical, stressed, superficial, impatient, active, quantity-over-quality. Slow is the opposite: calm, careful, receptive, still, intuitive, unhurried, patient, reflective, quality-over-quantity. It is about making real and meaningful connections—with people, culture, work, food, everything. The paradox is that Slow does not always mean slow" (Honoré, 2004). Carl is about as subtle as a neo-conservative Amway sales rep, but he does make a strong case for checking your internal speedometer periodically.

If quality performance and a quality life are your goals, don't give in to someone else's ridiculous pace. Learning requires time to sink in. Don't let scrambling to meet the clock crowd out time for reflection.

UNLEARNING REQUIRED

Your brain is a trickster. It has to be. If your brain stopped filtering out 99.99 percent of the input bombarding your senses, your head would explode from sensory overload.

Most men pursue pleasure with such breathless haste that they hurry past it.
SØREN KIERKEGAARD

Every second, 14 million bits of sensory information slam into our cranial firewalls. The bandwidth of human consciousness is about 18 bits per second. We don't see things with just our eyes; we hallucinate images from low-resolution clues. It's like one of those pictures that's made up of large squares. When you're close, it's just a bunch of squares. Back up, and the picture becomes clear. Look at a painting by Monet up close and then twenty feet back to experience the same effect. Your brain connects the dots to show you something that's not there.

People who put on a pair of spectacles whose lenses turn everything upside down become totally disoriented, but after a while, their vision adjusts, and everything appears to be normal again—until they remove the glasses and again see an upside-down world. Lenses that show the left eye what the right normally sees, and vice versa, give a jarringly odd cubist vision, but the brain soon adapts to this too and flips back to normal when the glasses are removed.

The human brain is a trickster. Keep this in mind as we delve into counterintuitive material. Taking it to heart will require unlearning some long-held beliefs. Your mind will fight you on this.

Neuroscientists reported recently that fMRI tests confirmed what social psychologist Solomon Asch had reported fifty years ago (Blakeslee, 2005). Here's Asch's experiment. Eight people sit in a circle. They are handed a card with lines of varying length (Figure 1.6). The first person says the lines are the same length, as does the second, the third, and so on through to number seven. (The first seven were in on the ruse.) The eighth person? One in four of them answered incorrectly 50 percent of the time. fMRI studies showed that people sometimes actually *saw* what other people described rather than what was on the cards.

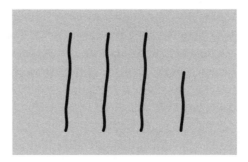

FIGURE 1.6. All the Same Length? Some People Thought So

Informal learning, which we dig into in the next chapter, is nothing new. It is a return to the natural way people learn: through conversations with one another, trying things out, and listening to stories. Learning is how people adapt to changing conditions, and things are changing faster than ever before.

By the way, the lines ahead are not all the same length.

A NATURAL WAY OF LEARNING

2

LEARNING IS THAT WHICH enables you to participate successfully in life, at work, and in the groups that matter to you. Informal learning is the unofficial, unscheduled, impromptu way people learn to do their jobs.

When faced with massive, inevitable change, and the hyperinflation of time certainly qualifies, living things adapt or die. Darwinian evolution is one form of adaptation, but natural selection is glacially slow; we don't have eons to wait. Living things also adapt by learning (Figure 2.1). Learning is any non-genetic adaptation one makes to interact more effectively with the ecosystems in which one participates.

> *Real learning is not what most of us grew up thinking it was.*
> **CHARLES HANDY**

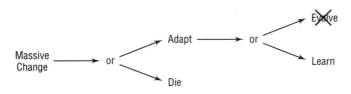

FIGURE 2.1. Learning Is Adaptation

Ask people what comes to mind when they hear the word *learning*, and many will say *school* or perhaps *training*. School is a time-consuming and generally ineffective way to learn; most corporate training is wasted effort.

Corporations would bypass learning altogether were it not politically incorrect to do so. Executives don't want learning; they want *execution*. They want the job done. They want *performance*.

> *All learning is
> self-directed.*
> **DAN TOBIN**

To a business manager, learning is a means to an end. If someone were to invent a smart pill that enabled workers to excel at their jobs without training, that person would make a fortune marketing smart pharmaceuticals, and most trainers would be out of work.

Let me reiterate: learning is adaptation. Taking advantage of the double meaning of the word *network*, "to learn" is to optimize the quality of one's networks.

INFORMAL LEARNING OR FORMAL?

Some people see the world in terms of dichotomies: yes or no, on or off. To them, everything is black or white and only rarely gray. Real issues contain gradations, maybes, what-ifs, emotions, mitigating factors, and other entanglements. Figure 2.2 illustrates a continuum of yes to no.

Yes   No

FIGURE 2.2. A Continuum of Yes to No

Formal learning and informal learning are both-and, not either-or. This book is focused on informal learning, but when you assess what will work for your organization, consider how informal learning might supplement what you are doing now rather than replace it.

THE SPECTRUM OF LEARNING

Formal and informal learning are ranges along a continuum of learning. Formal learning is accomplished in school, courses, classrooms, and workshops. It's official, it's usually scheduled, and it teaches a curriculum. Most of the time, it's top-down: learners are evaluated and graded on mastering material someone else deems important. Those who have good memories or test well receive gold stars and privileged placement. Graduates receive diplomas, degrees, and certificates.

Informal learning often flies under the official radar. It can happen intentionally or inadvertently. No one takes attendance, for there are no classes. No one assigns grades, for success in life and work is the measure of its effectiveness. No one graduates, because learning never ends. Examples are learning through observing, trial-and-error, calling the help line, asking a neighbor, traveling to a new place, reading a magazine, conversing with others, taking part in a group, composing a story, reflecting on the day's events, burning your finger on a hot stove, awakening with an inspiration, raising a child, visiting a museum, or pursuing a hobby.

Formal and informal learning both have important roles to play. Informal learning is not a cure-all, and were it not for formal learning, I would not be writing this book.

Most learning experiences blend both formal and informal aspects. Sometimes public transit is the best way to get somewhere; other times it's better to take one's own path.

SAP's Etay Gafni helped me conceptualize the split between formal and informal learning by describing the styles of his one-year-old son and four-year-old daughter. When his son is hungry, he wants food. Any food that Etay brings will suffice. He trusts Dad to deliver. His daughter is more discriminating. She wants rice, not potatoes, and the ketchup on her plate should never touch the rice. His son is analogous to a formal learner: he accepts what comes. His daughter takes control, as does an informal learner. In an ideal world, everyone will progress from passive, formal learner to creative, informal storyteller.

THE SPENDING-OUTCOMES PARADOX

People learn informally most of what they need to do their jobs. Although every situation is different, a common assertion is that 80 percent of learning in organizations is informal. The number is backed up by the Institute for Research on Learning, the Bureau of Labor and Statistics, the Education Development Center of Massachusetts, Capitalworks, the eLearning Guild, and Canada's National Research Network on New Approaches to Lifelong Learning. (See Appendix B for details.)

> Informal learning is effective because it is personal, just-in-time, customized, and the learner is motivated and open to receiving it. It also has greater credibility and relevance.
>
> **DICK SETHI**

Ironically, 80 percent of corporate spending goes to formal learning and only 20 percent to informal. To tell you the truth, I pulled this figure out of thin air; it feels right. I'm aware of how much corporations spend on learning management systems, instructional design, tuition reimbursement, instructor salaries, classrooms, and courseware. I don't know the tab for meetings, conference attendance, professional dues, pool tables, beer busts, expertise locator software, watercooler meetings, and other informal learning investments.

DELUSIONS OF CONTROL

A core business belief is that people are manageable. This is a comfort to managers. It implies that to get things done, all you have to do is tell people to do them. The real world doesn't work that way. To extract optimal performance from workers, managers must inspire them rather than command them. Antoine de Saint-Exupéry put it nicely: "If you want to build a boat, do not instruct the men to saw wood, stitch the sails, prepare the tools and organize the work, but make them long for setting sail and travel to distant lands."

Today's free-range learners are knowledge workers. They expect the freedom to connect the dots for themselves. Imagine the difference between a free-range (informal) learner and a (formal) high school student. The high school student is not allowed to take notes, books, or a cell phone into the room for the final exam. Happily for us all, life is unlike high school.

It is no longer useful to define learning as what someone is able to do all on his or her lonesome. This is not *Survivor*. Knowledge workers of the future will have instant, ubiquitous access to the Net. The measure of their learning is an open-book exam. "What can you do?" has been replaced with, "What can you and your network connections do?" Knowledge itself is moving from the individual to the individual and his contacts.

> Knowledge itself is moving from the individual to the net.
> **JAY CROSS**

High school also assumed that the curriculum was stable. One edition of a textbook would be in service for five years or maybe more. At work, the curriculum changes all the time. Nothing stands still. Learning new things requires unlearning old ones.

Learning is social, and social networks interconnect workers with families, circles of friends, neighborhood groups, professional associations, task teams, business webs, value nets, user groups, flash mobs, gangs, political groups, scout troops, bridge clubs, twelve-step groups, and alumni associations. In one sense, our worker is defined by who he knows. Our definition of learning must embrace the people the worker interacts with and the learning that comes from their interacting with one another.

GRAVITY ATTRACTS

As much as I favor letting things take their natural course, I don't mind rigging the situation for the best odds of success. Learners need to be attracted to learning experiences, or not much is going to happen.

> When we try to pick out anything by itself, we find it hitched to everything else in the universe.
> **JOHN MUIR**

IBM's Steve Rae posits three gravitational forces for informal learning. The first force is *access*. The learner has to know the opportunity exists, the costs are reasonable, and it fits her requirements. The second force is *quality*: production values, ease of use, what I was looking for. These two forces account for but 40 percent of the gravitational pull. The dominant factor is *walkaway value*. This includes what's-in-it-for-me, timeliness ("latency"), time savings, economic value, outside incentives, punishments for not doing it, and participation. Steve finds that these three forces can pinpoint the

Achilles heel of an informal learning initiative 80 percent of the time (personal communication, 2005).

ENGINEERING THE INDIVIDUAL'S LEARNING NETWORK

Learning originally meant finding the right path. Paths are connectors; people are nodes. The world is constructed of networks. We're back where we started.

In networks, connections are the only thing that matters. We network with people; we use networks to gather information and to learn things; we have neural networks in our heads.

Learning is optimizing our connections to the networks that matter to us. This satisfies both the community concept of learning (social networking) and the knowledge aspect (gaining access to information and fitting it into the patterns in one's head).

To learn is to adapt to fit with one's ecosystems. We can look at learning as making and maintaining good connections in a network. Cultivators of learning environments can borrow from network engineers, focusing on such things as:

- Improving signal-to-noise ratio
- Installing fat pipes for backbone connections
- Pruning worthless, unproductive branches
- Promoting standards for interoperability
- Balancing the load
- Seeking continuous improvement

Unfortunately, there are very few learning network engineers. No corporate function owns learning. Corporate learning involves information flows, corporate communication, customer relations, knowledge management, training, induction, debriefing, performance support, mentors and coaches, architecture and interior design, corporate culture, information technology, professional communities, social network optimization, rapid prototyping, storytelling, collaboration, meaningful meetings, and more. I raised this issue on my blog (http://internettime.com), specifically: "Learning Ecosystem Question, February 24, 2006."

A learner interacts with stuff through what I'll call pipes and with people through relationships. A net connection is one form of *pipe;* web pages and other information are *stuff.* Interactions with people and stuff lead to learning.

FIGURE 2.3. An Individual's Learning Ecosystem

The first draft of my book described how people can communicate effectively, calm their emotions, and be happy. My review team found these topics irrelevant. I am perplexed. I don't understand how building the worker's learning capacity can be excluded from the equation. Have I been drinking too much holistic, systems-theory Kool-Aid? Is it okay for a Chief Learning Officer to blow this one off with "That's not my department"? Send me an email or leave a comment below. I just don't get this.

Among the responses was this one:

CLOs will always blow it off; it is not part of their worldview. . . . It is seen as part of the personal, not the public, and however much mumbo jumbo is spouted, however much we can tout the benefits, if it doesn't clearly translate to shareholder value, it won't be bought. . . . You are talking about treating people as people. This is very radical.

Boundaries define formal learning, but informal learning is unbounded. We'll look at the payback of informal learning in the next chapter and address governance in the last chapter.

UNIVERSALS

Informal does not mean lackadaisical. Formal, informal, or in between, people learn best when they:

- Know what's in it for them and deem it relevant
- Understand what's expected of them
- Connect with other people
- Are challenged to make choices
- Feel safe about showing what they do and do not know
- Receive information in small packets
- Get frequent progress reports
- Learn things close to the time they need them
- Are encouraged by coaches or mentors
- Learn from a variety of modalities (for example, discussion followed by a simulation)
- Confront maybes instead of certainties
- Teach others
- Get positive reinforcement for small victories
- Make and correct mistakes
- Try, try, and try again
- Reflect on their learning and apply its lessons

HUMAN POTENTIAL

George Leonard, one of my heroes, coined the term *Human Potential Movement*. He has studied aikido for nearly thirty years and is the author of four inspiring books: *Ecstasy and Education, Mastery, The Way of Aikido,* and *The Life We Are Given*. He is a past president of the Association of Humanistic Psychology and of Esalen Institute. "We all have the potential for genius within us," he told me. "Learning has been my whole life," he said, eyes gleaming. Encouraged by his parents, George collected reptiles, became a ham radio enthusiast, had a lab for his zany chemistry projects, studied modern American literature, played the clarinet (after hearing Benny Goodman on the radio), and formed his own swing band, all before turning eighteen years old. None of this took place in a classroom.

When I asked George what advice he would offer people who want to improve their learning, everything he mentioned involved informal learning:

- Stay open to possibilities. The world is feeding you opportunities all the time. Keep your eyes open and you will see them.
- You need instruction to get the basics, but after that, watch closely and see what works. Don't try to change everything at once—that doesn't work.
- Learn from accidents. Learn from mistakes. Capitalize on them. Celebrate the unexpected.

NEXT UP

The former Monty Python comedian John Cleese has said that in the faster, faster, faster culture of business today, stopping to reflect on a situation almost feels like laziness. Research has found that creative people aren't particularly smarter than others; they simply spend more time mulling things over. Discovering one's true feelings and sleeping on it take time. Short-cuts are false economies.

Someone asked Cleese where he got his ideas, and he replied that the ideas arrive every Monday morning on a postcard from a little old man in Skelton. Why can't people use common sense instead of following mindless rules?

My postcard this morning said that you are intrigued by informal learning but you aren't buying it until you understand how you will benefit from it. That's the topic of our next chapter.

SHOW ME
THE MONEY

INFORMAL LEARNING IS THE PATH to organizational capability, agility, and profits. It also respects workers and challenges them to be all they can be.

"Fine," you say, "but my company is not going to go for any of this unless I can show them a solid return on investment." Tell them about the examples of informal learning in this chapter, which we'll explore in more detail in chapters ahead.

> Learning is not compulsory but neither is survival.
> **W. EDWARDS DEMING**

GETTING DOWN TO CASES
Sales Force Readiness

A global technology leader is moving at a fever pitch, acquiring a new company on average once a month. The company maintains its competitive advantage by providing its sales force and customers with instant access to case studies, product specs, sales tools, and insight into future trends. Company thought leaders in twelve strategically important areas meet regularly in person to update one another, talk with customers, and discuss what's new in their field. The firm says they "Google-ize" this content, making it as easy to search as with Google but also retrievable as video-on-demand, podcast, presentation, or text The result is a better-informed sales force, more competence on sales calls, more cross-selling, better presentations, and ease in bringing partners up to speed.

Access to Expertise

Knowledge workers waste a third of their time looking for information and finding the right people to talk with. Frequently they spend more time recreating existing information they were unaware of than creating original material.

Expertise locators direct workers to people with the right answers. Organizational network analysis pinpoints bottlenecks and poor connections. Bottom-up systems provide exception-handling workarounds and rules of thumb. Instant messaging accelerates information flow. Reduced search times, streamlined organizational processes, and finding people faster can increase worker productivity 20 to 30 percent.

> *It's an immutable law of business that words are words, promises are promises, but only performance is reality.*
> **HAROLD GENEEN**

Transformation

In three years, a major semiconductor company transformed itself from near bankruptcy to record profitability. It used group graphics to develop and communicate a new strategy throughout the organization. Ninety-five percent of employees could explain the strategy and how they contributed to it personally. No formal training took place.

 Many companies that nurture communities of customers provide an on-ramp for new customers and fresh ideas for old hands.

Innovation

Times of change require new approaches, and conversation is the parent of innovation. Organizations are redesigning the work space to encourage meaningful conversation. Mind maps and visualization tools accelerate discussion. Concept prototyping multiplies the volume of new ideas generated by work groups. Online collaboration and discussion software spark innovation among far-flung groups that share common interests. Formal learning promotes a curriculum; informal learning encourages thinking about opportunities.

Increase Information Technology Flexibility

An organization that brings Internet technology and Internet culture inside the firewall reduces total cost of ownership. Workers do not need to learn a new interface to participate. They already know how to search, blog, navigate, and add features. Software improves incrementally instead of in disruptive new editions. Modular Web services replace brittle, hard-coded monolithic systems and flex with change.

> *It's like arguing in favor of the plough. You know some people are going to argue against it, but you also know it's going to exist.*
> **JAMES HUGHES**

Increase Sales

The more people know about a product or service, the more likely they will buy it. Many companies that nurture communities of customers provide an on-ramp for new customers and fresh ideas for old hands. The company provides the platform—space at a trade show, for example, or directions on building a group Web site; the customers provide the content. Loyal customers are great salespeople. Beyond that, they are often the source of new product ideas.

Improve Work Processes

In a knowledge-based economy, said Shell Oil's Arie De Geus, "The ability to learn faster than your competitors may be the only sustainable competitive advantage." Nonetheless, when it comes to learning, most companies are akin to the lumberjack who was too busy chopping down trees to sharpen his axe. Learning is a skill, not a given. Meta-learning, that is, helping people learn to be better learners, underpins continuous improvement across organizations. Improving worker process skills such as speaking and writing opens up the circuitry through which knowledge flows.

Reduce Stress

Job stress has been implicated as a factor in heart disease, stroke, diabetes, ulcers, depression, serious accidents, alcoholism, and hypertension. It also devastates work performance. Three out of four American workers report stress on the job. Health care expenditures are nearly 50 percent higher for workers who report high levels of stress. Attacking the problems associated with stress head-on and giving workers more control over decision making yield dramatic improvements. One organization reported reducing tension by 65 percent and aches and pains by 70 percent. Participants were 65 percent less angry, 70 percent less worried, 87 percent less fatigued, and 68 percent happier. There was a 44 percent decrease in their desire to leave the company and a 52 percent decrease in the desire to quit their jobs (Institute of HeartMath, 2004).

▷ ▷   *Formal learning historically targets newly hired employees and novices. Midcareer high performers don't have time for it.*

Unlock Worker Potential

The role of management used to be telling workers how to do their jobs. "You're not paid to think," Frederick Taylor told workers. That's history. Today, people *are* paid to think. Formal training is deemed successful if everyone passes the test or demonstrates enough to get by. In contrast, informal learning helps people be all that they can be. It also appeals to young workers who are accustomed to learning from small chunks of information and snippets of conversation.

Optimize Return on Investment

In the knowledge economy, a superlative performer is not just 20 percent more effective than average; she can easily be ten times as productive. Seasoned workers, the big middle between young workers and senior staff, generate most of a firm's profits, yet formal learning historically targets those newly hired and novices. Midcareer professionals don't have time for classes, and their learning is haphazard and unmanaged. If you were starting with a clean slate, you would focus the training budget less on novices and more on high performers.

Increase Professionalism

Workers develop professional expertise in loose confederations of like-minded individuals. For example, engineers with an interest in optical computing might meet for beer after work to swap stories about breakthroughs and what's on the horizon. Security experts come together when facing a common threat. Corporations that support these communities of practice by providing workers time to participate and technical support to capture and distribute their conversations stay on top of new developments, foster camaraderie, and avoid the unnecessary step of requiring subject matter experts to explain things to instructional designers.

Self-Service

As business removes the labor content from services, often service improves while costs go down. We enjoy the convenience of the ATM, pumping our own gas, and ordering merchandise over the Net. Informal learning brings the same benefits to acquiring knowledge: greater user convenience and lower overall cost.

Improve Morale

Knowledge workers balk at being told how to do their work; they see it as micromanagement and an insult to their abilities. People enjoy conversation and learning; they do not relish listening to pontification from the podium. Formal training is top-down. By contrast, informal learning trusts the worker with the decision of how to master new knowledge and skills, which increases morale while lowering turnover.

Impromptu Meetings

Companies invest heavily in annual sales meetings and other galas under the big tent. Lead time for large events is six months or more. Often 90 percent or more of the airtime is devoted to presentations. I'm not one to complain about occasional celebrations or parties, but they are a poor way for people to learn anything. Participatory sessions, conducted as needed and often impromptu, cost less and get more across.

Conversations

Conversation is the most powerful learning technology ever invented. Conversations carry news, create meaning, foster cooperation, and spark innovation. Encouraging open, honest conversation through work space design, setting ground rules for conversing productively, and baking conversation into the corporate culture spread intellectual capital, improve cooperation, and strengthen personal relationships.

Keeping Up

San Franciscans know that when the ground shakes, rigid structures crumble and flexible ones roll with the punches. The acceleration of time, globalization, outsourcing, software interoperability, open sourcing, supply chains, and more are rattling the foundations of business. As we'll see in the next chapter, business is going from push (rigid, conforming, monoliths) to pull (flexible, innovative, small pieces). Training programs are push; they are top down, teach the standard, and difficult to revise. A learning platform is pull—dynamic, always responding to change. What is the return on investment of survival?

EVALUATING INNOVATION

Successful businesspeople make decisions based on reasonable expectations of future returns. In general, the more senior the leader is, the further out the time horizon. The further in the future, the less precise is the expectation. Great leaders have vision, not exactitude.

The investment community is, misguidedly in my opinion, fixated on quarterly results. But wisdom tells us that perpetually focusing on short-term numbers is not a prescription for long-term success. Given a choice of now or later, senior managers want both. How can we deal with this conundrum? I'll suggest that we adopt the perspective of a supremely successful businessperson, someone like Andrew Carnegie.

Carnegie rose from abject poverty to unimaginable riches through enlightened management and sound investments. He quit at the peak of his game, sold his holdings to J. P. Morgan, built himself a castle in his home town in Scotland, and spent the rest of his days giving his fortune to good causes. As a businessman, he did not put up with foolishness.

When you're evaluating an investment of time or money or a new approach such as informal learning, ask yourself, "What would Andrew Carnegie do?" Ask yourself the questions he'd ask. Get to the heart of it: Does this project feel right? Is this the best use of your hard-earned money? Will this pay us back for taking a risk on it?

If a learning project—make that *any* project—does not make business sense, don't do it. If the return on investment is not so obvious that you can sketch it out on the back of a napkin, do something with a higher return.

By the way, Carnegie favored informal learning. He was convinced "that much of that which is taught in the schools is of no value whatsoever in connection with the business of earning a living or accumulating riches. He had arrived at this decision, because he had taken into his business one young man after another, many of them with but little schooling, and by coaching them . . ., developed in them rare leadership" (Hill, 1932, p. 66).

WHAT DO WORKERS WANT?

Knowledge workers demand respect for who they are. They expect to be treated fairly. They thrive when given the freedom to decide how they will do what they're asked to do. They rise or fall to meet expectations.

This is hardly new. They want life, liberty, and the pursuit of happiness. What's new is that if they don't get those opportunities, they will work for someone else. Talent is scarce and getting scarcer.

Ask yourself about your workers. Are they happy? Are they proud of what they do at work? Do they lead the lives they want to lead? Are they preparing themselves for the work of the future? Are they progressing in ways that increase their economic value? Do you think they feel that they're doing their part to make the world a better place? Are they satisfied with their jobs or looking for the quickest escape route?

Psychic income is real. I just read a note from someone who attended my first day-long workshop on informal learning. (If you really want to learn something, teach it.) The students were Chinese knowledge workers and professors. I was not confident that I'd gotten my message across. Then I found this on the wiki I'd left behind for follow-up.

> One message I got from Jay's speech is the exponential acceleration of, not only the learning evolution, but the evolution of intellectual humankind. I feel enlightened and liberated. I am reminded of Plato's Cave. Imagine humankind finally taking away the chains on their legs and necks, turning around to see that the traditional learning contents are but the shadows of the puppets manipulated by marionette players [instructors? Unfortunately I am one of them.] Will we, among the first released prisoners (thanks to Jay), become one of the intrepid pioneers to walk toward the light from outside of the cave, and "dive in" the realities of the world?

Now I am walking on air. Everyone should feel this good. You don't receive rewards like this unless you have the latitude to make your own choices.

HOW CAN I TELL IF IT WORKS?

"How do I know that a graduate of one of these off-campus programs has learned anything?" snarled an accreditation official in the early days of distance education. "And how do we know if a Stanford grad knows anything?" came the retort of my boss, the future founder of the University of Phoenix.

He and I both knew academia's deep, dark secret: outside of the school system, grades are meaningless. In fact, it's hard to find a more random variable. Grades do not predict wealth, happiness, income, health, social standing, home ownership, optimism, or professional standing. The only place grades matter is at other schools and for professional credentials. So if grades make no difference to a graduate's well-being, are students learning anything at school?

Traditional schools take attendance. That must count for something, right? Actually, the literacy rate in America was higher before we made schooling compulsory.

I talked with Don Novello (who plays the character of Father Guido Sarducci) about his routine, the Five-Minute University. In five minutes, you learn everything the typical college graduate remembers after five years. Where did he come up with the idea? "It's all true, man," he replied.

When I was championing the advantages of eLearning at the end of the last century, many people questioned whether self-directed learning could ever be as effective as a live training session. I questioned whether it could be worse:

- Forty percent of American adults (upward of 70 million people) did not know that Germany was our enemy in World War II (Davis, 2005).

- Fifty percent of high school students were unaware of the Cold War, and 60 percent of the same group had no idea of how the United States came into existence (Davis, 2005).

- Sixty percent of adult Americans claim never to have read a book, 50 percent believe in UFOs, and 42 percent cannot find Japan on a map (Berman, 2001).

In school, a student "learns to sit still, to line up in orderly rows, to take instructions, to feel guilt for his natural impulses—and perhaps to do a few simple things that he could learn to do one-fiftieth—yes, one-fiftieth—of the time it usually takes him" (Leonard, 1968).

Formal Training Has Scant Impact

Training managers have complained for years that senior managers don't understand the value of training. That's why training is often the first area to get the axe when business is bad. And that's also why training managers don't get to sit at the table with the organization's decision makers.

 Maybe the executives do understand the value of formal training. They've determined that in its present form, it's not worth much.

Several years ago, researcher Sam Adkins (2003) posted this item to the Learning Circuits Blog:

We Are the Problem: We Are Selling Snake Oil

I read these long tortuous posts bewailing the malaise of our educational systems. The problem is not "out there." We are the problem. We are selling snake oil. We now have ample data to show that:

- Training does not work.
- eLearning does not work.
- Blending Learning does not work.
- Knowledge Management does not work.

Sam expected vigorous protests but was surprised to find that most people, almost all training and development professionals, agreed with him. Perhaps it's because he set out some of these findings:

Only 10 to 20 percent of training transfers to the job.

"At least 90 percent of American industry's spending on training fails to result in transfer to the job" (Ford & Weissbein, 1997).

". . . Less than 20 percent of training transferred to the job" (Brinkerhoff & Gill, 1994, p. 22).

"Most of the investment in organizational training and development is wasted because most of the knowledge and skills gained in training (well over 80 percent by some estimates) is not fully applied by employees on the job" (Broad & Newstrom, 1992).

". . .More than 10 percent of the expenditures [on job training] actually result in transfer to the job" (Baldwin & Ford, 1988).

Training is a necessary but insufficient means of changing worker performance. The leading human performance authorities "have all demonstrated that most performance deficiencies in the workplace are not a result of skill and knowledge gaps. Far more frequently, they are due to environmental factors, such as lack of clear expectations; insufficient and untimely feedback; lack of access to required information; inadequate tools, resources, and procedures; inappropriate and even counterproductive incentives; task interferences and administrative obstacles that prevent achieving desired results" (Stolovitch & Keeps, 2002, p. 1).

Rummler and Brache (1995) determined that training accounts for only about 10 percent of the potential for changing performance on the job. (Other factors are incentives and rewards, information and feedback, support and resources, individual capacity, and motives and expectations.)

As we've seen, training departments manage only the 20 percent of training that is formal, assuming that informal learning is not in their charter.

Working with averages can be tricky. (You can drown in a river that's an average of six inches deep.) Nonetheless, even if we beef up the numbers to compensate for double-counting, the impact of formal training is at best a drop in the bucket.

Do the math: 20 percent × 20 percent × 10 percent = 0.4 percent. This implies that formal training is responsible for less than 1 percent of the potential change in performance on the job.

▷ ▷ *Tragically, many firms have mistaken measuring activity for measuring results.*

At least half of most companies' investments in training is wasted because the training occurs too far in advance of its application. You lay down a great bottle of wine, leave it undisturbed, and open it a dozen years later to discover ordinary wine has become extraordinary wine. Bottle your great knowledge, leave it undisturbed, and when you open it a dozen weeks later, the bottle will be empty.

Maybe the executives *do* understand the value of formal training. They've determined that in its present form, it's not worth much.

Don't Get Fooled Again

You cannot manage what you cannot measure is one of the oldest clichés in management, and it's either false or meaningless. It's false in that companies have always managed things—people, morale, strategy, etc.—that are essentially unmeasured. It's meaningless in the sense that everything in business—including people, morale, strategy, etc.—eventually shows up in someone's ledger of costs or revenues. Measurement, in other words, is a worldview, not just a scorecard. It is a means of thinking and acting, as well as measuring.—TOM STEWART

Businesses exist to create value, and the source of value resides outside the learning function. As the late Peter Drucker (1993, p. 5) pointed out, "Neither results nor resources exist inside the business. Both exist outside. The *customer* is the business."

Tragically, many firms have mistaken measuring activity for measuring results. Training directors measure participant satisfaction, the ability to pass tests, and demonstrations. They don't measure business results because they don't own the yardstick by which business results are measured. Elaborate learning management systems track who has attended what, courseware distribution, workshop schedules, test scores, and online course completion but not business metrics.

Especially egregious is the advice from consultants to measure performance using traditional accounting rules. This gives the false precision of hard numbers. Unfortunately those numbers are almost always off because they attribute no value to intangibles. Invisible assets such as intellectual capital, customer relationships, brand image, and business intelligence are worth far more than plant and equipment, but they do not appear on a traditional balance sheet.

People have told me that intangibles do not count because they are impossible to measure. It's as if what you cannot see is not really there. Tell it to Wall Street. Google is worth $3 billion on paper (using traditional accounting measures), but investors value Google's stock at $125 billion. That's more than the value of Disney, the *Washington Post*, the *New York Times*, the *Wall Street Journal*, Amazon.com, Ford, and General Motors combined. Where is the missing $122 billion? It's invisible stuff like brand, culture, and a team of people that investors expect to keep minting money for them. Intangibles are real. You can't see air either, but you can't live without it.

The appropriate measure of learning is how good a job one is doing. Training metrics should be business metrics.

Paying attention to pragmatic end measures will bring informal learning to prominence, but the switch is only now starting. In the next chapter, we'll look into what's just emerging.

EMERGENCE

FIVE YEARS AGO, the words *training* and *learning* were interchangeable, but these days learning is honored and training is disdained. What's the difference? Training is something that's pushed on you; someone else is in charge. Learning is something you choose to do, whether you're being trained or not. You're in charge.

Many knowledge workers will tell you, "I love to learn, but I hate to be trained." Learning is in keeping with the democratization of the workplace spawned by the network revolution. Decision making is passing from the manager to the worker, and part of the deal is that learning is crowding out training. (See Table 4.1 for a comparison.)

TABLE 4.1. Traditional Versus Emergent Learning

Traditional	Emergent
Training	Learning
Management in charge	Worker in charge
Often formal	Often informal

Emergence is the key characteristic of complex systems. It is the process by which simple entities self-organize to form something more complex. As training converges with bottom-up self-organizing systems, network effects, and the empowerment of individuals, it morphs into emergent learning.

FROM PUSH TO PULL

John Seely Brown and John Hagel (2005) persuasively argue that the business world is shifting from push to pull. *Push* and *pull* were originally marketing terms. The telemarketer who calls you at dinnertime is push (and maybe pushy too). The store with the great window display pulls you in (perhaps with a pulley?). Table 4.2 contrasts push and pull.

TABLE 4.2. Characteristics of Push and Pull

Push	Pull
Assumes you can predict demand	Assumes world is unpredictable
Anticipates	Responds
Rigid, static	Flexible, dynamic
Conform, core	Innovate, edge
Monoliths, components glued together	Small pieces, loosely joined
Program	Learnscape

In a nutshell, Brown and Hagel tell us that a complex, interconnected world is unpredictable. Because you don't know what to expect, planning is folly. It's wiser to be as responsive as possible when the future arrives. Gone are the days of tweaking systems to get the last ounce of performance out of them. The fast response time we need comes from keeping options open and creating an organization sufficiently flexible to roll with the waves.

Business used to concentrate on executing core processes well. Future businesses will focus on being sufficiently innovative to swap in new core processes for old in response to changes in the environment.

Empowering the worker changes how we look at training and development. If you're going to be nimble, the six-month course development cycles of the past aren't going to be good enough—not that lengthy courses fit today's go-go business environment anyway. Take someone away from cell phone and e-mail cold turkey to attend a class, and you'll see the agony associated with heroine junkies. Pluck salespeople out of the field, no matter how green and in need of new skills they may be, and the sales vice president will say you're the reason she didn't make quota.

People who already know the lay of the land don't want a curriculum. That's someone else's opinion of what they need to know. It undoubtedly contains lots of things they either already know or have no interest in finding out. They prefer to cherry-pick what they need in the easiest way available to them.

Learning something at the moment of need couples learning and application and has more lasting effects.

Courses are dead. Who's got the time? Courses are almost always separate from work, and that goes against the trend of integrating learning and work. Hence, learning from performance support fits better with today's workplace.

A training program is the same as courses, except often more time is robbed from work. Since most learning is social, wouldn't it be more effective to put workers in touch with others so they can learn from one another?

A busy person detests being told to make time for something to convenience someone else. Self-service learning is more convenient and more economical. I don't go to the bank during banking hours much any more. It's more convenient to bank in the evening. The ATM doesn't mind what I'm wearing or whether I say hello.

Learning things in advance, "just in case," is a losing game. Until the case arrives, the worker suspects the subject matter won't be relevant. And when the case does come along, the knowledge acquired in advance is probably long gone. Knowledge, like muscle tissue, deteriorates when it's not used. But learning something at the moment of need couples learning and application and has more lasting effects.

When you cannot predict the future and emergence is unpredictable, you can't build training programs in advance because you don't know what you'll need.

Those who are charged with developing an organization's talent must rise above the level of training programs. Static programs do not fare well in a dynamic world. Instead, we should focus on setting the right conditions for learning. Sometimes there will be a course thrown in; at other times, a loose collective exercise will prompt learning, and often we'll just get out of the way and let learning happen on its own. Table 4.3 summarizes this discussion.

TABLE 4.3. The Emergence of a New Form of Learning

Push	*Pull*
Training	Learning
Curriculum	Discovery
Courses	Performance support
Training program	Collaboration platform
Mandated	Self-service
Just in case	Just in time

FROM TRAINING PROGRAMS TO LEARNSCAPES

Formal learning takes place in classrooms; informal learning happens in *learnscapes*. A learnscape is a learning ecology. As the environment of learning, a learnscape includes the workplace. In fact, a learnscape has no boundaries. No two learnscapes are alike. Your learnscape may include being coached on giving effective presentations, calling the help desk for an explanation, and researching an industry on the Net. My learnscape could include participating in a community of field technicians, looking things up on a search engine, and living in France for three months.

How would you build a learnscape for emergent learning? People who say that content is king would probably start there, with lessons to be learned. Others would point out that content out of context is meaningless, so they would start by putting some sort of infrastructure in place.

The truth is that content and context are inseparable. They are like inside and outside: you can't have one without the other. You have to have faith that if you add a mixture of content and context into your organization, good results will emerge. The whole is more than the sum of the parts. You have to begin with a vision.

XPLANE is an information design firm that develops visual maps and stories to make complex business issues easier to understand. (It created the nifty images you find throughout this book.) Envisioning a learning platform begins with a sketch. I'm working with XPLANE on just such a sketch of a learnscape as I write these words. Here is what I see thus far.

The primary image is an immense learnscape, floating atop a stormy sea of blur, business process automation, information overload, outsourcing, globalization, Web as platform, broadband, pervasive interoperability, and Internet time. A great wave of network tangle is crashing over the back of the platform. At the front are business results, talented people, and continuous improvement of each.

Nodes are born when needed, visuals speed up understanding, and workers learn from one another. These nodes and other activities are all connected; if we were creating a time-lapse film, we'd show the network continually connecting to new nodes and becoming more tightly interwoven, with work flowing through it ever faster.

This is but a mental model. An organization comprises thousands of nodes with immeasurably complex connections. Not only that, but the connections reach out to suppliers, customers, and partners, as well as its own workers.

The old way of learning used workshops, training programs, role plays, lectures, readings, tests, practice assignments, group discussion, homework, self-study, computer-mediated lessons, job rotation, assessments, and on-the-job training. The emergent way of learning is more likely to involve community, storytelling, simulation, dynamic learning portals, social network analysis, expertise location, presence awareness, workflow integration, search technology, help desks, spontaneity, personal knowledge management, mobile learning, and co-creation.

We aim to create a learnscape where workers can easily find the people and information they need, learning is fluid and new ideas flow freely, corporate citizens live and work by the organization's values, people know the best way to get things done, workers spend more time creating value than handling exceptions, and everyone finds their work challenging and fulfilling.

▷ ▷ *Knowledge lives in people's heads, not in mere words. You can no more capture true knowledge in a repository than you can trap lightning in a box.*

The typical starting learnscape hosts noxious weeds. Workers spend more time searching for the right information and the right people than creating value. Poor work space hampers effective learning. Bad architecture stifles innovation. Corporations give lip-service to values but have no place to celebrate them.

Companies never work as depicted on their organization charts. A shadow organization really runs the show. Unless x-rays of the underground organization in the form of an organizational network analysis are available, people will be unaware of how to get things done productively.

Most of the network diagrams I've seen show every node connected and all connections of the same quality. Most of the organizations I've analyzed look more like the illustration in Figure 4.1.

Let's look at some connections, going clockwise around this picture. Our hypothetical worker is at the center of the network from this perspective:

- To the right is a productive connection, just what we're looking for. I have a person at the end node, but it could just as well be an intranet or the Internet cloud.

- The next node is linked by a thin connector; there is not much information or emotion going back and forth here. This could be because the worker inhabits a different silo, or the other person does not have a broadband connection, or maybe they work in different time zones or don't speak the same language.

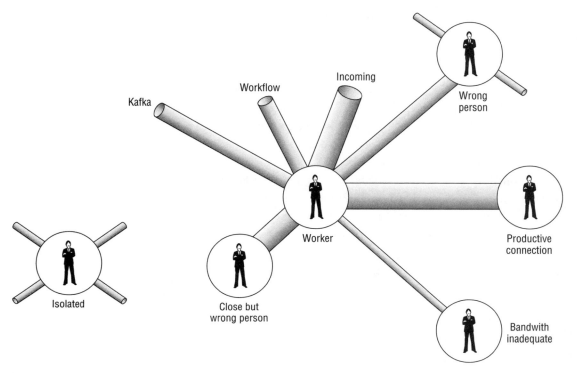

FIGURE 4.1. Hypothetical Network Connections

Note: The width of the connections—thin, medium, and fat—is relevant. The wider the line, the higher the bandwidth.

- At seven o'clock is someone with high bandwidth, because this person is in the next cubicle. Neighbors are the first people most workers turn to when they are seeking the answer to a question; unfortunately, they are rarely the best person to ask.

- The isolated person is not a member of our worker's network and is unaware that a connection would be beneficial.

- The connector to Kafka stands for entering the labyrinth of links that lead to nowhere. Perhaps it's a Web search gone wrong, where one link leads to another useless link and so on ad infinitum, or when you're looking for a person in another organization and can't figure out the phone tree, much less where the function you're looking for might reside.

- The connection to work flow is vital, for without it, the worker doesn't know what's going on.

- The node marked "incoming" is the fat pipe delivering e-mail copies, spam, memos you don't want to read, junk mail, junk faxes, junk letters, and junk phone calls.
- The wrong-person node is the individual you finally reach after fifteen tries, only to find out this is not the person you're looking for. You've got to talk with Sally instead.

An in-house directory, expertise location, instant messenger, presence awareness, and an informal in-house knowledge repository will go a long way toward making this network functional again.

MAKE SPACE FOR LEARNING

A group of training managers at Hewlett Packard told me they felt helpless to influence things outside the bounds of authorized training programs. "What can we do?" they asked. Every bit of floor space except narrow hallways was chock-a-block with cubicles designed to fence off individual work spaces. This was in HP world headquarters, not a hundred feet from the CEO's office. There was no space for people to get together. Most of the cubicles were empty, for people found it more comfortable to work from home and meet at restaurants.

What could HP do? I suggested replacing a quarter of the cubicles with sofas and pool tables. Put in espresso machines and a few whiteboards. Encourage people to work together. Let nature take its course. Productivity and morale inevitably would go up.

At a Microsoft conference, the stark glass buildings offered no space for informal get-togethers. A visiting group pointed out that Microsoft was not getting its money's worth by relying entirely on PowerPoints delivered by vice presidents with ten-minute breakouts to engage the visitors. In the evening, the group went to a restaurant with the developers. That's where the conversation flowed. The Microsoft developers said they got more ideas there than at any previous meeting.

And in the days when the IBM ship was sinking, John Akers chastised a group of engineers huddled around the watercooler, telling them to get back to work—and failing to realize that talk around the cooler *was* the work.

Form is supposed to follow function, but you'd never guess it by looking at most corporate work spaces. Tom Davenport (2005), heir to the title of best knowledge work guru now that Peter Drucker is no longer with us, says:

The workspace improves or hinders performance. Work space design must take into account:

- Knowledge workers prefer closed offices, but seem to communicate better in open ones.
- Knowledge workers congregate in particular geographical areas.
- Knowledge workers move around in the course of their work.
- Knowledge workers collaborate.
- Knowledge workers concentrate.
- Knowledge workers work in the office.
- Knowledge workers communicate with people who are close by.
- Knowledge workers don't care about facilities gewgaws [pp. 165–170].

Creating Learning Spaces at MIT

Buildings at MIT must support learning communities. Social spaces (cafeterias, nooks, atriums, and other public spaces) are much in demand. In fact, demand is high and getting higher for informal, multipurpose spaces. Demand for private offices and cubicles is dropping.

An effective learning space combines push and pull. The push is to create fringe spaces where disciplines overlap; this is a prerequisite of innovation. The pull is the portability that goes with a wireless connection. Staff used to meet in an office surrounded by books, files, and phone. That's no longer necessary.

Building in these fringe spaces seems like a no-brainer, but it's hard to do. For one thing, you must fight obsolete metrics. A traditional measure is the net-to-gross ratio, that is, the proportion of the building that's productive. The problem is that social space is defined as unproductive, but in fact the most unproductive space you can find is an empty office, where nothing is going on.

Another vestigial metric is the surface-to-volume ratio. Less is more, unless you care about people, who want windows, corners, nooks, and other things that create more surface, not less.

Many have compared MIT's old Building 20 to the Media Lab. Building 20 was totally informal, the ultimate in flexibility. By contrast, the Media Lab is quite formal, in a way that deters collaboration. Bill Mitchell, chief architect at MIT, notes that people forget that Building 20 was also cold, rat infested, falling apart, and loaded with asbestos.

An open plan floor space is flexible. It physically breaks down the walls and barriers, replacing them with undefined boundaries. You can see what others are up to; their work becomes transparent, enabling people to inter-act. Not everyone likes that idea. As Tom Davenport said, they want their privacy. They see open plan architecture as social engineering, and they have a point. Most find that they like openness once they become accustomed to it. It takes courage to fight for the new, but the results are worth it. In the new data center, robots are running around, and you see things going on. It's an exciting space.

You need to build support from the bottom up. Architect Frank Gehry's approach to designing MIT's Ray and Maria Stata Center, home to engineering and computer science faculty, is exemplary. Gehry began by engaging the community. He'd put a model on the table. When they said that wasn't it, he created another prototype. This was important to gain commitment; he put physical things out there. This fostered more discussion and more mutual understanding. Rather than fearing the tension, he welcomed it as a means of making progress.

Of course, highly charged atmospheres can create misunderstandings. Gehry challenged the faculty to rethink their conception of the relationship of offices and work space. He suggested they think of a village of orangutans: at night, they sleep apart, way up in the trees. In daylight, they form a community on the ground. Maybe the new MIT building should work like an orangutan village. The faculty complained to Bill Mitchell, "He called us orangutans."

Knowledge workers need spaces for:

- Thinking and conceiving
- Designing
- Presenting
- Collaborating
- Debating and negotiating
- Implementing
- Practicing
- Sensing
- Operating

Two mind-sets are required when we set about constructing new learnscapes:

- *Realizing* that learning is about situated action, collaboration, coaching, and reflection, not study and reading
- *Thinking* buildings as the beginning of an evolutionary process in a state of permanent flux and iterative change

(Brown & Hagel, 2005).

John Seely Brown is married to an architect, so he has seen many architecture studios. Picture the drawing boards side by side in a big, well-lit, airy room. You can peruse one another's work. You see how projects take shape. You eavesdrop, you lurk, and you learn what's going on. It makes one wonder why business isn't more transparent. You can learn a lot by looking over someone's shoulder.

iWork at Sun Microsystems

Location matters. The design of the workplace is an important component of productivity, yet all too many businesses are blind to its impact. Architects are creating corporate buildings today with hierarchical floor plans and grid layouts from a previous era. Corporate efforts to reduce one-time costs and maximize usable space backfire because they hamper the work of the building's inhabitants for as long as it stands.

Since 2002, the iWork program at Sun Microsystems has improved employee satisfaction, cut turnover, and saved the company a quarter-billion dollars in real estate costs by designing work spaces that suit the work. "The iWork program has revolutionized the way people work," says Eric Richert, vice president of Sun's iWork Solutions Group. Originally the space planning and design group, the team designs Sun offices to optimize what future occupants need to do to accomplish their core deliverables—the eight to twelve essential service factors on which their performance was measured. After surveying the work group's culture and management practices, the team would investigate three aspects of their work in great detail. One person designed the information technology (IT) architecture, another examined human factors, and the third worked on the space.

Following confirmation through a series of focus groups, the iWork team used a software model to develop four or five scenarios to present to the work group. Not mere drawings, each scenario included predictions of the work group's performance, cost estimates to build out the scenario, and the individual impact of the IT, human, and space considerations.

When the team designed the layout of a new sales and service center in Atlanta, they found that many employees spent significant time on the road, so 60 percent of the facility was dedicated to shared space. An itinerant employee would check in at a front desk (as if in a hotel) and be assigned a work space according to his or her needs. Since office time was filled with debriefings and coordination meetings, the team designed four-person and two-person spaces, as well as individual workstations and meeting rooms. To accommodate work styles, tables in the cafeteria were fully wired for Net connections.

The work situation at Sun's offices in Detroit was much the opposite. Sun's major client was Ford Motor Company, which was right next door. People used their offices to quickly check e-mail and prepare reports before returning to the client's site. In Detroit, the work groups wanted individual cubicles to work in.

Sun's hardware design group had entirely different requirements. Overhearing conversations was an important component of their work. The team designed an office space that resembled the lounge of a country club, with carpet and lots of sofas and easy chairs. Whiteboards on wheels could be rolled in to support impromptu conversation.

The iWork Solutions Group pioneered flexible working hours and telecommuting. Nearly all Sun employees have the option of working from home or using flexible work spaces. The flexibility helps workers balance life and work. Sun set up drop-in centers that save the average commuter ninety minutes a day in drive time. Sun research finds that about sixty of those ninety minutes go into additional work for the company.

An employee might work at home during the morning, drop the kids at soccer practice in the afternoon, stop by the drop-in center, and finish up at home in the evening. As a side benefit, work-at-home and drop-in centers eliminated the need for seventy-seven hundred cubicles and workstations. A facility in the United Kingdom implemented a flextime plan that expanded the capacity of the building from 130 to 250 employees with no loss of productivity or morale.

Sun lives up to its credo: "The network is the computer." Four out of five employees log into servers instead of standalone PCs. They insert a smart card (a "Sun Ray"), and their custom environment appears on screen no matter where they log in from.

Since 1994, the iWork Solutions Group has studied best practices for getting people together over long distances without having to travel. A virtual team may have members spread around the world. As anyone who has been on the wrong end of a misconstrued e-mail can attest, seeing gestures and expressions adds a lot of meaning to a conversation, so collaboration and video-conferencing tools are a standard part of the iWork package.

Monitoring Productivity

Many people at Microsoft's Redmond, Washington, campus have two or three monitors on their desks: one for their immediate project, another for the Web, and perhaps another for mail and news (see Figure 4.2). Did this improve performance?

FIGURE 4.2. The Internet Time Group Command Center

Volunteers were placed in front of fifteen-inch monitors; researchers clocked their performance in a variety of challenging tasks. Then they replaced the fifteen-inch monitors with immense forty-two-inch plasma screens. On average, productivity increased 10 percent. Some people were as much as 44 percent more productive. The big screens enabled workers to view a variety of applications simultaneously. They could watch certain processes with peripheral vision, rather than by changing applications. People begged to take the large screens home with them (Thompson, 2005).

You do the math. Take a knowledge worker with an annual salary of $100,000 who costs the company $150,000 when benefits are added. This individual better be turning out $300,000 a year in value or wouldn't have a job in Redmond. A forty-two-inch plasma monitor costs about three thousand dollars. The monitor pays for itself in less than one quarter, and that doesn't count the smiles on workers' faces or the buzz that brings new talent to such a forward-looking company.

The Knowledge Campus at Novartis

Swiss pharmaceutical giant Novartis is converting a manufacturing neighborhood on the Rhine in Basel into a $27 billion knowledge campus. Its goal is to stimulate creativity and innovation among disciplines. Forty or fifty industrial buildings are being converted into an environment designed to foster interaction. To promote openness, communication, and aesthetics, the first project completed was a walled garden and meeting place. Campus planners are keen to avoid "desktop isolation."

The Knowledge Campus, as it is known, will be open to the public, to encourage interaction with visitors from Basel's universities and research centers. Inviting plazas, walkways, and technology-rich collaboration spaces are planned, as are auditoriums and social networking spaces. Novartis's Web site describes it this way:

> An initial milestone in the transformation of the Novartis St. Johann site from an industrial complex to a place of innovation, knowledge and encounter has been achieved: the completion in June 2003 of a courtyard garden at Building 200, after nine months of construction. It is a natural, green space that is meant to be both pretty and practical, with symbolic as well as social value.
>
> "The garden consists of three parts," explains landscape architect Peter Walker, whose California-based firm led the design effort that started two years ago. To the north is a birch grove, to the south is a circular lawn rimmed by Hornbeam trees, and in-between is a reflecting pool that connects the two. Illumination comes mainly from the sun or from the neighboring building, but there also are lights at ground level. Modeled after Mexican luminarias—decorative candles in sacks—these can be shone in any color and at varying intensity to create different moods."
>
> The layout is meant to be attractive to observers in offices above, but also inviting to people at ground level. Chairs and tables are spread about, ready to host a quiet coffee or an informal business meeting. A large bench serves as both a waiting and meeting point for people getting together. "The garden is meant to be used," Walker notes, "not just looked at. The circular lawn—which can accommodate up to about 50 people—may be used more formally, for parties, award ceremonies and small meetings. This is a natural way of giving such events more light and air, when weather permits."

At a more subtle level, the garden also presents a symbolic narrative. A cross formed by white-marble footpaths and the birch trees are emblematic of Switzerland. The trees, the water and again the cross are representative of pharmacy, medicine and restoration in general. And the geometric forms suggest the precision of science.

Novartis would like to recreate the ancient agora on the banks of the Rhine. Internationally renowned architects are planning aesthetically pleasing buildings and plants to go hand in hand with their innovative functionality. Art is on display to encourage innovative thinking.

Corporate Values on Display

When I meet with out-of-towners to discuss business, we generally end up at the San Francisco Museum of Modern Art. It's a more inspiring place to chat than any office.

Mike Spock has been designing museum spaces for half a century. As a youngster, he compensated for a reading disability by learning from radio and movies and simply roaming around. Most museums were free at the time. Taking a break from roller-skating in Central Park to drop by the Egyptian antiquities section of the Metropolitan Museum of Art was a routine. Ancient mummies and tombs lead a boy to think about the meaning of death and other weighty matters. Later, Mike's time at Antioch College reinforced the validity of learning by venturing out into the real world.

His unconventional learning style shaped Mike's work at the Children's Museum and the Field Museum of Chicago. Museums offer an invitation to experiment. Visitors learn by interacting with the exhibits, mentally or physically. The dialogue between visitor and object is the essence of the experience.

The Monterey Bay Aquarium is a marvelous experience because it was designed from the start as an experience, not a series of exhibits. The labels on the exhibits tell you just what you want to know, as if a friend were excitedly describing the scene. Look! Notice! See that! The visitor becomes a participant.

The Exploratorium in San Francisco begs you to get involved. You have to play, and the interaction of visitor and exhibit is co-created. You collide with neat, challenging bits of science and walk away understanding science rather than memorizing it.

The Oakland Museum of California is beautifully orchestrated. The space draws visitors in. The dioramas in the natural history section are lifelike; the chirping of birds and whisper of the wind lull you into feeling you're really in nature. The art section walks you from idealist paintings that introduced the rest of the world to the beauty of the American West to the rebellious, free-spirited art that represents California today. The history section is pure magic, as you can see in the faces of children mesmerized by the gleaming (all original) fire wagon, the snazzy custom motorcycles, a real Wells Fargo gold assay office, and a 1940 kitchen.

You can't go to one of these museums without learning. If you want guidance, a docent will show you around, pointing to important lessons along the way. Many exhibitions offer a recorded program. Museums accommodate all sorts of visitors: adventurers (who like to explore), strategic browsers (who study floor plans so as to miss nothing worth talking about), and people who visit once a generation.

All of this makes me wonder why corporations do not have in-house museums to celebrate their heritage, their strengths, their accomplishments, and their famous failures.

Twenty years ago, *In Search of Excellence* highlighted the importance of corporate culture (Peters & Waterman, 1982). If culture is so important, isn't it curious that corporations have few cultural institutions? Wouldn't creating a cultural center perpetuate the organization's values?

When I visit the headquarters of powerful public companies, I frequently see a glass display case. Old-time companies display bowling trophies; hipsters showcase award plaques from suppliers and industry associations. Pure financial operations show the little Lucite blocks that investment bankers hand out when a deal is consummated. I wonder, *Is this the best you can do?*

I'm not proposing a museum with static displays. Museums that do not change don't draw repeat visitors. They gather dust. Rather, I envision a vibrant conversation space. Nooks, crannies, cushy sofas, indirect lighting, some small tables, a few shelves of interesting books, and a refrigerator with assorted waters and soft drinks. A few rooms will suffice. Perhaps a time line of the history of the organization and its industry lines one wall and an ever-changing array of notes, memos, and mementos is posted to another wall with magnets. A wall of blank whiteboard encourages participation.

Google has two thirty-inch whiteboards for cartoons, jokes, and corporate graffiti. Google's workforce doubles in size once a year. The firm's director of communications says that "when new hires see the boards they get a quick, comprehensive snapshot of our personality."

The in-house museum is for employees, not the general public. While preserving echoes of the past, it encourages conversation that creates the future. It would beat trying to envision a grand future in a cubicle.

People learn more from mistakes than from things that go right. A room in the in-house museum might be the Hall of Mistakes We Do Not Want to Repeat: stories and artifacts of the dozen greatest mistakes in the company's history and what it will take to ensure they never happen again.

PAIN AND PLAY

In *Engaging Learning* (2005), Clark Quinn writes, "Learning can, and should, be *hard fun*. It's fun, in the sense that you're engaged, there is a story that you care about, and you have the power to act; it's hard in that it's not trivial—there is sufficient challenge to keep you on your toes. Here, *engagement* is the word used to describe the situation when learners are captured, heart and mind, in learning—or to use formal terms, are cognitively and affectively connected to the learning experience" (p. 10).

> *It is the child in the man [woman] that is the source of his (her) uniqueness and creativity, and the playground is the optimal milieu for the unfolding of his [her] capacities and talents.*
>
> **ERIC HOFFER**

America's grouches do not agree. They feel that work should just be hard. No fun. It's like the worst-tasting medicine being good for you. This is a vestige of the dour Puritan fathers and of the strict oversight of manual jobs. Here's sociologist Max Weber (1904) giving the Calvinist viewpoint on work:

> Waste of time is thus the first and in principle the deadliest of sins. The span of human life is infinitely short and precious to make sure of one's own election. Loss of time through sociability, idle talk, luxury, even more sleep than is necessary for health . . is worthy of absolute moral condemnation. . . . [Time] is infinitely valuable because every hour lost is lost to labor for the glory of God. Thus inactive contemplation is also valueless, or even directly reprehensible if it is at the expense of one's daily work. For it is less pleasing to God than the active performance of His will in a calling [p. 104].

This is a heavy legacy to shuck off. Douglas Rushkoff (2005) notes that "establishing a playful career or company isn't as easy as it looks. It doesn't require expensive consultants, trips to the woods, or the reinvention of a company's culture based on some abstract ideal. But it does mean going against much of what we've been taught about competition and survival—not just in business school, but for the past five centuries!" (p. 108).

The times demand that free-range learners work playfully, for play is the source of innovation. Play permits one to push at the boundaries of convention. In *Serious Play*, Michael Schrage (2000) argues that fresh ideas arise from prototypes. For Schrage, a prototype can be physical or mental so long as it's placed in a shared space for discussion and comment, to be criticized without criticism of its originator. The more prototypes there are, the more innovation.

The Institute for Play (2000) reports on its Web site that

> the components of play—curiosity, discovery, novelty, risk-taking, trial and error, pretense, games, social etiquette and other ever more complex adaptive activities—are the same as the components of learning. Humans are designed by nature to play, and have played throughout their evolution.
>
> What do most Nobel Laureates, innovative entrepreneurs, artists and performers, well-adjusted children, happy couples and families, and the most successfully adapted mammals have in common? They play enthusiastically throughout their lives. What common denominator is shared by mass murderers, abused children, burnt-out employees, depressed mothers, caged animals, and chronically worried students?
>
> Play is rarely or never a part of their lives.

In the world of ideas, playful creativity has a palpable return (Naiman, 2000):

- The *Wall Street Journal* reported that a two year in-house creativity course at General Electric resulted in a 60% increase in patentable concepts.
- Participants in Pittsburgh Plate Glass creativity training showed a 300% increase in viable ideas compared with those who elected not to take the course.
- At Sylvania, several thousand employees took a 40 hour course in creative problem solving. ROI: $20 for every $1 spent.

The world labor market is facing a talent shortage of immense proportions. Free-range workers are choosing their employers instead of vice versa. Do you think they'll choose a workplace where people have fun—or a sweatshop?

Serious play is not an oxymoron; it is the essence of innovation.
MICHAEL SCHRAGE

A FUN PLACE TO WORK

Engineers at Google get one day a week to prototype whatever they feel like. It's hard to dislike a company with a corporate philosophy that says, "You can make money without doing evil. You can be serious without a suit. Great just isn't good enough. Always deliver more than expected. Google does not accept being the best as an endpoint, but a starting point. Through innovation and iteration, Google takes something that works well and improves upon it in unexpected ways."

One day I joined some Googlers (as employees are known) at the Googleplex (headquarters) in Mountain View, California, for lunch. Most people were sitting outside, noshing on barbecue and listening to live music. Here are some items from the company's official description of the Googleplex:

- *Lobby Décor*—Piano, lava lamps, and live projection of current search queries from around the world.

- *Hallway Décor*—Bicycles and large rubber exercise balls on the floors, press clippings from around the world posted on bulletin boards everywhere. Many Googlers standing around discussing arcane IP addressing issues and how to build a better spam filter.

- *Googler Offices*—Googlers work in high density clusters remarkably reflective of our server setup, with three or four staffers sharing spaces with couches and dogs. This improves information flow and saves on heating bills.

- *Equipment*—Most Googlers have high powered Linux OS workstations on their desktops. In Google's earliest days, desks were wooden doors mounted on two sawhorses. Some of these are still in use within the engineering group.

- *Recreation Facilities*—Workout room with weights and rowing machine, locker rooms, washers and dryers, massage room, assorted video games, Foosball, baby grand piano, pool table, ping pong, roller hockey twice a week in the parking lot.

- *Google Café*—Healthy lunches and dinners for all staff. Stations include "Charlie's Grill," "Back to Albuquerque," "East Meets West" and "Vegheads." Outdoor seating for sunshine daydreaming.

- *Snack Rooms*—Bins packed with various cereals, Gummi Bears, M&Ms, toffee, licorice, cashew nuts, yogurt, carrots, fresh fruit and other snacks. Dozens of different drinks including fresh juice, soda and make-your-own cappuccino.

- *Coolest stop on the tour*—A three-dimensional rotating image of the world on permanent display on a large flat panel monitor in the office of the engineer who created it. What makes it special is the toggle switch that allows you to view points of light representing real time searches rising from the surface of the globe toward space, color coded by language. Toggle and you can see traffic patterns for the entire Internet. Worth a trip to the second floor.

Google has created an environment that encourages conversation and speaks volumes to its commitment to employees and experimentation.

DIGITAL NATIVES

The 2004 eLearn International Conference in Edinburgh was a conference with a difference: the delegates focused on four potential scenarios for the future of learning ten years out.

To connect past and future, the first speaker was a professor of moral philosophy whose chair dated back more than five hundred years. Unwittingly, he exemplified why the academic model is dying. In a haughty tone, he asked if anyone really expected to receive a quality learning experience using computer. After all, his own attempts to put his material into a learning management system had failed. Did we appreciate that learning is more than serving up content? This erudite fellow was talking through his hat, so wedded to the way things were done on campus that he could only see eLearning as an inferior version of his real stuff that had stood the test of time.

Don Clark, founder of the largest eLearning firm in the United Kingdom, followed with a commonsense, crystal-clear description of the future of learning. If we lived in a world with no schools, what would we build in their place? Would we rebuild remote medieval colleges?

Clark showed photographs of his twin boys learning. These digital natives are autonomous learners. They learn from the Internet. With frameworks obtained from computer games, they ask their father about military strategy. The twins do not have patience for the stand-and-talk model of teaching.

What is a university anyway? The Internet offers more information resources than any university library. Faculty members come and go. The students are booted out where their time is up. What remains? In this age of digital abundance, the university is no more than a brand.

Learning has been a form of punishment, and it's time to end schooling's two thousand years of slavery. That gave us plenty to talk about among ourselves during the ensuing coffee break. Most people went easier on the professor than I did. No one disagreed with Clark.

Is there hope for those of us who did not grow up amid computers and networks? Yes, but we'll have to rip our blinders off and develop our skills.

A group of teenagers who had spent months exploring e-learning and the future of the school gave the penultimate presentation at eLearn International. Ten of them took the stage and acted out their messages, something no adult had even considered. Instead of showing a PowerPoint slide about learning styles, they asked everyone to complete a personal learning styles inventory.

In a truly lovely moment, a student gripped the podium and put on a schoolmarm's critical gaze. Someone in the audience snickered. "You there, what's so funny?" she growled. That drew laughter. She shushed us with a penetrating frown of disapproval. Learning through intimidation. Remember it? There *is* a better way.

Eighteen months later, a presentation by Wim Veen at Online Educa in Berlin, helped me appreciate what's going on with the generation now entering adolescence. This goes well beyond the tired observations about "how kids do their homework." It's true that what I used to spend hours trying to get through with paper and pencil alone at my desk is now a community experience involving multiple instant messaging windows, listening to music, and phone calls. It's not that they've found some new concentration technique; rather, they've become adept at synthesizing discontinuous thoughts.

Youth have grown up amid networks. When I was growing up, Europe, Asia, and Africa were concepts, more places where history happened than real geographical locations. Not so for the kid who plays War in the World with pals in Brazil, Morocco, and Finland. What was abstract to me is the home of Paolo, Ali, or Eero for my son.

"It's all so superficial," chide the skeptics. On the other hand, wouldn't you enjoy having the ability to run twenty projects simultaneously in your head? Such is life as an active node.

When he was eighteen years old, I interviewed my son Austin. What if he had landed a job as head of a game design team at Electronic Arts? Instead of taking the two-week orientation for new employees, he would be able to take the brand-new two-hour e-learning version. What do you say to that? "Sucks," he said. "I don't want anyone telling me what to do."

Veen brought a student rap band to the stage. Its message was clear: we're not taking any of your stuff. It's my way or the highway. Another professor wondered how this generation will get along with the establishment when it exerts its control over them. My answer is that we're entering an age of talent scarcity. Reading the manual, working alone, and not being plugged in will be anachronisms. We will change to meet their needs, not vice versa.

Veen is writing a book about Homo Zappiens, the generation for whom learning is playing. Veen projected a Calvin and Hobbes cartoon on the big screen. What game do they want to play? Anything but an organized sport. How about Calvinball? "No sport is less organized than Calvinball," says

Hobbes. Calvin replies, "New rule! New rule! If you don't touch the thirty-yard base wicker with the flag, you have to jump on one foot!" Calvinball is going to be everybody's favorite game.

WORKFLOW LEARNING

In the 1970s at Aetna Insurance, a trainer saw workers struggling with arcane, data-centric mainframe systems. The default solution to their frustration was training, but training generally camouflaged bad interface design. Ironically, the training often cost a lot more than designing the application for performance in the first place. The trainer saw the folly in this and said, "We must give up the idea that competence must exist within the person and expand our view that whenever possible it should be built into the situation" (Cross & O'Driscoll, 2005).

Thus began the notion of performance-centered design and the consulting career of Gloria Gery. In her 1991 book *Electronic Performance Support Systems*, she wrote, "Learning must be reconceived to influence the primary purpose of organization: to perform effectively and efficiently." The goal is "to enable people who don't know what they are doing to function as if they did" (p. 34).

These views are common wisdom now, but fifteen years ago, it was as if Gloria were screaming that the emperor had no clothes. She told us to give up the idea that competence must exist within the person and expand our view that whenever possible, it should be built into the situation. The question is, "How do we get people what they need at the moment of need, and what form should it be in?"

"A fusion of learning and doing is on the way," Gloria told participants at the Online Learning Conference in Anaheim in 1999. "Training will either be strategic or it will be marginalized." Combining work and learning is the foundation of performance-centered design and work flow learning.

At the Online Learning Conference in San Francisco six years later, Gloria and I gave a joint keynote on the debut of work flow learning. We defined this learning as real-time performance support connecting the worker and the current state of the work. Gloria said, "Workflow learning is performance support on steroids, magnified, with a much higher impact. The workflow is the context, the magic filter through which we will be able to filer content, against which we have to compare default tactics."

The logo I designed for the presentation in San Francisco shows a zipper. On the open end, the two sides are labeled *work* and *learning*; on the closed end, the mesh is labeled *work flow learning*. The concept is no different from what Gloria came up with at Aetna; what's new is that we have software and systems to carry out her vision.

Smart software is capable of monitoring work flow in real time, alerting the worker to a suboptimal condition, perhaps an emergency situation. When the worker does not know what to do, smart prompts or mini-simulations show how to accomplish the task. If the worker still lacks the know-how to proceed, she is referred to someone currently available who is likely to have the answer.

Is this informal learning? It is not scheduled; rarely is the training department involved in its implementation. Or is it formal learning because many of the interventions are canned? I sense that work flow learning is teetering at the middle of the continuum from formal to informal.

A SHARED SPACE

Creative relationships are more important for invention and innovation than creative individuals (Schrage, 1999). Marcia Conner (2001) interviewed Michael Schrage about his notion that the key to creative relationships is a shared space:

> *Conner:* What is the learning that takes place? How is that different from, for instance, one person just telling someone something, as opposed to two people working through it together?
>
> *Schrage:* I address this in the prologue of *Serious Play*. Consider a conversation. In a diagram, the conversation is represented by a dotted line going back and forth between the sender and receiver. The interaction changes dramatically when you add a shared space. Most of us have had the experience of getting into a friendly discussion over lunch with a friend or colleague, when you pull out a pen and begin writing on a napkin or a piece of paper, and the other person says, "No, no, that's not what I mean." Then they take the pen and paper from you and mark it up to modify what you were saying, and you begin conversing around the images on the paper. If a waiter were to come by and remove that paper, the conversation would go away. You are no longer talking to or with that other person. You are talking with the other person through a medium, a reference point or shared space that becomes like a little capture device, a little reflector of the conversation. It changes the point of reference for what is going on. The shared space fundamentally transforms the dynamics, not

just of the representations, but also of the interaction between people. It changes the ecology of the interaction.

Conner: It's not simply that the people have this shared space. It's that the shared space becomes the medium through which they are working.

Schrage: Exactly. If you don't have a shared space, you're not collaborating. You can put out a table, cutlery, and fine china, but if you're not serving food, you don't have a meal.

An organization that seeks more innovation should encourage its people to build shared spaces in which to work on prototype ideas. This concept of a shared space is both physical and behavioral. This chapter has focused on physical architecture. Now we will turn to people, mapping their relationships and social networks.

CONNECTING

5

MARC ROSENBERG IS A pioneer in the field of training and design, a former president of the International Society for Performance Improvement, a captivating public speaker, and author of *eLearning* and *Beyond eLearning*. I asked Marc how he learns. "I ask somebody," he replied.

Anything else? "Cultivate the right people to ask."

Ah-hah.

Knowledge workers spend 40 percent of their time looking for information. Many of them ask a colleague in the next cubicle or whoever is in the coffee room. That's why they don't get the answer they're looking for half the time and why a third of the answers they receive are dead wrong: they are asking the wrong people.

Building a network of reliable sources helps illuminate the field you're searching in. Consider IBM. It has a third of a million people spread over 170 countries. Half of them have been with the company less than five years. Forty percent of them work from their homes. On more than one occasion, I've found myself introducing one IBMer to another: they see one another only at conferences and when they share projects.

Everyone who works for IBM is listed in its *Blue Pages*, the online directory that includes information like employees' prior work history, papers they have written, patents they have received, customers they have worked with, and competitors they know. Imagine I'm in a client meeting and need some advice on financial security protocol in Czech banks. I tap in a few codes and up come the names of IBMers who fill the bill. Not only that, *Blue Pages* tells me how to contact them by phone, cell, e-mail, or IM and whether they're currently online. When you see someone use this, it's like magic.

FINDING THE RIGHT INFORMATION

Corporate life is like the old Sufi story of the fellow on his hands and knees searching the sidewalk in the glow of a streetlight in front of his house. A passerby asks what he's looking for: "My keys. I can't find my keys." The newcomer offers to help and asks where the fellow thinks he lost them. "Around the corner," comes the reply. Why are you looking here? "Because the light is better here."

What would you think of an assembly line where workers didn't know where to find the parts they were supposed to attach? Absurd, you say. Heads would roll. Yet for knowledge workers, this is routine. Consider a knowledge worker stymied by a lack of information, hardly an uncommon situation. In many professions, knowledge workers spend a third of their time looking for answers and helping their colleagues do the same.

How does our knowledge worker respond? She's five times more likely to turn to another person than to an impersonal source such as a database or a file cabinet. Often she asks whoever happens to be close by—the denizen of the next cubicle or someone getting a cup of coffee. Half the time, this person doesn't have a clue.

Only one in five knowledge workers consistently finds the information needed to do their jobs. This happens to knowledge customers too, half of whom never complete online orders. Other studies have found that knowledge workers spend more time recreating existing information they were unaware of than creating original material.

All this slows the pace of the enterprise, burns out the workforce with busywork, reduces responsiveness to customers, and increases job dissatisfaction. Reinventing the wheel, looking for information in the wrong places, and answering questions from peers consume two-thirds of the average knowledge worker's time. Slashing this waste time provides a lot more time to devote to improving the business, reducing payroll, or, more likely, a bit of both.

Knowledge workers waste a third of their time looking for information and finding the right people to talk with. This amounts to several hundred billions of dollars worth of time in the United States alone. Good architecture and space planning help people find the information they need. Organization network architecture helps connect the right people by spotting bottlenecks and opportunities for integration.

This knowledge productivity problem is destined to get worse before it gets better. The haystack is getting bigger exponentially. Corporate information doubles in volume every eighteen months. Half of the recorded information in the entire world has been created in the past five years.

Specialists used to keep their heads above the floodtide of incoming knowledge by knowing more and more about less and less. In today's interconnected world, boundaries between disciplines are becoming porous. Everything is multidisciplinary. We have to know more and more about more and more.

Successful organizations connect people. Learning is social. We learn from, by, and with other people. Conversation, storytelling, and observation are great ways to learn, but they aren't things you do by yourself.

The first need is to help knowledge workers find the answers they need. Rob Cross and others describe many ways to go about this in a marvelous book, *Creating Value with Knowledge*, edited by IBM's Eric Lesser and Laurence Prusak (2003). If people are going to go to others for answers, make it easy for them to get to the people who know. (Get them to look for their keys where they're likely to find them, not where the light's better.) Set up help desks to support new product rollouts and organizational initiatives. Have the help desk apply the 80/20 rule and document the common queries in a mercifully short frequently asked question (FAQ). Then, tier responses by triage. First query the FAQ, then ask the help desk, and if those don't work, contact the prime subject matter expert.

Learning a new software release is a special case. Since a release generally builds on an existing foundation, workers more often need answers to specific questions than the sort of overview that workshops and courses provide. Trial-and-error is an effective way to learn as long as there's a way to deal with roadblocks. Since the release is new, learners won't find answers in-house. In this case, outsource mentoring to a firm that does have the answers.

Web standards and smart software can monitor work flow to provide lessons or contacts precisely when they are needed.

KNOW-WHO

Knowledge management (KM) is no longer the intellectual high ground it once was, by and large because it didn't work. In spite of the old saw that you need executive support for success, the fact that KM entered many organizations as a management fad sold by high-priced consultants to CEOs on the golf course started KM off on the wrong track. The idea was to codify important knowledge and put it into a database for easy retrieval by all.

Unfortunately, knowledge doesn't work this way. The nuggets of wisdom loaded in from the top end often turn out to be generalities that lose meaning when taken out of context. The velocity of information gives knowledge a short usable life. Most important, knowledge lives in people's heads, not in mere words. You can no more capture true knowledge in a repository than you can trap lightning in a box.

▷ ▷   *The informal organization is how most business gets done,*
       yet executives miss it because they can't see it.

Ted Kahn (2001), leader of DesignWorlds for Learning, says that since knowledge resides not just in people's heads, "know who" trumps "know how." He has come up with seven Knows that contribute to learning (Kahn, 2001):

- *Know-who*—social networking skills, locating the key people and communities where competencies, knowledge, and practice reside—and who can add the greatest value to one's learning and work
- *Know-what/Know-not*—facts, information, concepts; how to customize and filter out information, distinguish junk and glitz from real substance, ignore unwanted and unneeded information and interactions
- *Know-how*—creative skills, social practices, tacit knowing-as-doing, experience
- *Know "What-if . . . ?"*—simulation, modeling, alternative futures projection
- *Know-where*—where to seek and find the best information and resources one needs in different learning and work situations
- *Know-when*—process and project management skills, both self-management and collaborative group processes
- *Know/Care-why*—reflection and organizational knowing about one's participation and roles in different communities; being ecological and socially proactive in caring for one's world and environment

Researchers at the National Supercomputing Center in Urbana, Illinois, extend the know-who concept until it resembles the infinite reflections you see in barbershop mirrors on opposite walls. It would be nice to know who knows who knows what well and also knows what you know. You get the idea.

WHAT YOU DON'T SEE

In the movie *Bullitt*, Steve McQueen chases the bad guys up and down the steepest hills in San Francisco. Intersections become ramps that lift all four wheels of Steve's Mustang off the ground. Cars hop and screech at blazing speed for what seems like miles. The first dozen times I saw the chase, I could taste adrenalin.

Bullitt is a popular rerun in the San Francisco Bay Area, and the chase from the top of Pacific Heights to the Marina would always hijack my attention. About five years ago, the rush disappeared in an instant when my wife asked me, "What about the Volkswagen?"

When Steve's green Mustang is chasing the bad guys' black Charger down the steepest part of Fillmore Street, they each pass the same Volkswagen again and again. If you're wrapped up in the action, you don't notice it, but once someone points it out, it's impossible to erase from view.

The formal organization is like Steve's Mustang. It's got a name, a charter, goals, owners, officers, managers, departments, property, financial statements, money in the bank, lawyers, contracts, and factories. It's rigid; change does not come to it naturally. The formal organization is a machine for making money.

The informal organization is the green Volkswagen. It's a separate shadow organization that runs the show through an undocumented series of personal and professional relationships. It is a living entity with a mind of its own. The informal organization is forever changing, evolving, responding, and adapting. The informal organization is a community: it runs on life's rules. You can influence it but not manage it; it's not for sale.

The designed structure of the formal provides unparalleled efficiencies and magnificent feats. The flexible network of the informal learns and adapts.

As Fritjof Capra writes in *The Hidden Connections* (2002), "The issue is not one of discarding designed structures in favor of emergent ones. We need both. In every human organization there is a tension between its designed structures, which embody relationships or power, and its emergent structures, which represent the organization's aliveness and creativity" (p. 121).

Many executives refuse to see the Volkswagen. The informal organization is how most business gets done, yet executives miss it because they can't see it.

Optimizing connections enables learning to flow. Network effects provide outsize rewards. Visualizing how people interact maps potential opportunities and likely breakdowns.

Organizational network analysis (ONA) blueprints the interactions of the informal organization. Most shadow organizations give allegiance to a "core group." Members of the core group make the decisions, exchanging the gift of direction to workers in return for their loyalty that legitimizes the group. They are not necessarily all senior managers.

Art Kleiner's marvelous book *Who Really Matters* (2003) tells the story. Totally undocumented, the core group's perceived needs, desires, and priorities give the rest of the organization its marching orders. Mapping social networks makes the pattern clear.

DISCOVERING WHO MATTERS

If you join a large organization and you're not plugged into the social network, you won't know what you need to know to do your job. You'll be about as effective as a car with no gas.

Organization network analysis pioneer Valdis Krebs told me about an early application. In the early 1990s, he worked in TRW's Space Park facility in Redondo Beach, California. The goal of the lab was to prepare proposals for satellite projects. He asked the staff of 180, many of them rocket scientists, "Who do you go to for expertise and advice when preparing a proposal?"

In a matter of days, he was posting a map of who connected to whom on the wall of the manager's office. The lab manager squinted at the network diagram and said that something was off. This fellow Charlie connected to only two other people. Was Valdis certain of his findings? Yes.

Charlie was a retired U.S. Air Force officer who had been hired because he understood proposals from the client side. He was knocking down a six-figure salary because he was supposed to help win deals. Yet no one talked with him. The manager asked his staff for an explanation. After a lengthy silence, one courageous soul piped up, "Charlie's a jerk." Ask Charlie for help, and he'd tell you he was busy or that you'd asked a stupid question. Hence, no one talked to Charlie.

The lab manager noticed another anomaly. Just about everyone relied on advice from Mary. "Mary Johnson?" [not her real name] he asked. Yes. He was stunned. It seems that Mary was pleasant to be around. She'd been with TRW for a long time, and she was happy to answer everyone's questions about their proposals. She'd tell Joe what NASA was looking for and explain to Jill the nuances of air force procurement. Mary had seen and learned it all. Had she left the organization, quality would have degraded instantly. Mary received a way-above-average merit increase and recognition from the lab manager.

Imagine the payback of Valdis's organization network mapping project. For an all-in cost of twenty-five thousand to thirty thousand dollars had Valdis been an external consultant, TRW was able to cut its losses on a nonperforming asset (Charlie) and justly reward a vitally important employee.

Most managers presume they know what's going on in their organizations, but when you map the actual knowledge exchanges, you find that they really don't. Like everyone else, they can see only so far. Key dynamics may be happening beyond the manager's horizon into the network.

Paradoxically, the less important a worker's contribution is, the more attention is paid to evaluate it. Corporations have established precise measures of the performance of lower-level employees, like business process redesign and quality control, but the precision vanishes in going up the ladder into the executive ranks. Mapping the relationships of executives is one of the few objective measures of their performance.

WEAK TIES

A couple of years ago, I met Stanford sociology professor Mark Granovetter. While a graduate student, he had studied how people landed new jobs. The job-hunting books are right: people find job opportunities through personal contacts, not by answering ads and mass-mailing résumés.

▷ ▷ *It's not who you know that's important; it's who they know.*

To double-check his findings, Granovetter fed back what he'd heard. "You found the job through a friend." Well, no, not exactly. Almost every time, the job came from a personal contact who was more a friend of a friend. Your immediate circle know the same people and organizations you do, so they're not much help when you're searching for something new. The circles of your friends, however, include people who are tied into other networks. You have weak ties to these people, but they link to your friends through hobby groups, sports, clubs, bridge parties, swap meets, wine tastings, and professional groups.

Granovetter is now famed for recognizing the strength of weak ties. It's not who you know that's important; it's who they know. This holds true in the functioning of organizations too, but until recently, few people had mapped out the relationships of their people, and you generally can't see the second-tier folks.

Reflect on your relationships at work. Sure, you can come up with the people you deal with face-to-face, but how far down the chain of contacts can you go? If you're like most of us, you're not that aware of the membership of your potential network.

Organizational network analysts talk of nodes and connectors, but it quickly becomes more complicated than that. Social networks are dynamic, shifting in response to changes in contacts, job requirements, and strategies. Not only that, but what comes out of a person differs from what went in. Remember the children's game where you whisper a sentence from one child to another? The end result is always a surprise. Imagine doing this amid the turf wars and hidden agendas at the office.

Why do companies invest in making the invisible work visible? Because it facilitates execution of strategy, supports alliances, improves the quality of decisions made, promotes innovation, assists integration after a merger, and nurtures communities of practice.

Think of the dark side as well. Some organizations discover that business units are not talking with one another. Employees working out of their homes may not feel like employees at all. Information hoarders deny others the opportunity to benefit from what they know. Bottlenecks hinder the progress of entire departments. The departure of a single individual may break vital relationships within the organization and with customers as well.

What's a manager to do? First, contemplate where the invisible empire's network may be in danger of breaking down. If you're in a smaller organization, you can probably feel the heat of the friction already. For larger groups, where the potential payoff is larger, surveying workers, 360 degree analyses, and automated e-mail analysis tools can map social networks, highlighting potential trouble spots. Search natural fault lines for dislocations in the social network. Check for broken communication links among natural divides: new recruit–veteran, male-female, young-old, low status–high.

Physical distance may seem trivial, especially when people work in the same office. A study of interactions among scientists at seven different laboratories found that the likelihood of communicating began to decay noticeably when two people were more than three feet apart. Place them thirty-three feet apart, and interaction was squeezed to a trickle (Stewart, 2003). Now I understand why my staff seemed so distant when I had a snazzy office thirty-five feet from where they sat.

Then what? If two groups are not connecting, bring them together and have them work on joint projects. Don't simply put them in a room together: we are all inclined to hang out with our friends.

Face-to-face meetings are effective for kicking off a relationship. After trust is established in person, a relationship can coast on electronic contact for quite some time.

A dozen years ago, Bruce Tognazzini (1995) designed a workstation ten years into the future for Sun. This was a thought leadership dream piece, along the lines of Apple's Knowledge Navigator scenario or IBM's recent Future of Learning Vignettes. Starfire was a prototype of what computing might look like far into the future, all the way to 2004.

The work spaces served by Starfire were online collaboration booths with wraparound displays showing real-time images of coworkers and customers. Resolution would be so high that talking with a colleague would be like talking with her through an open window.

If someone on my screen looks exactly like he or she is there in the flesh, will our interaction be as powerful as face-to-face? Science has yet to pin down what makes being there in person so compelling. Some think it's micromovements of the eyes; others attribute it to smell. I am baffled, but instinct tells me not to expect confusing the real person with a copy during my lifetime.

Being with other people is here to stay, but often it's quite expensive. Once formed in person, relationships that are nurtured will persist. If you were setting up a global project team to work on a year-long project but could afford to bring them together only once, do it early in the project. People will bond, and it will be easier for them to partner remotely since they know one another from meeting face-to-face.

Conversation is an incredibly productive means of communicating and learning. If you read a verbatim transcript of an informal conversation, you'll be surprised at how disjointed it seems. What's going on is a swirl of interaction that's driven more by emotion, body language, and context than the words being said.

Tom Stewart told me about researching the secrets of General Electric's success for a *Fortune* article published in 1989. He attended many meetings, and the secret he uncovered was that "they all knew each other." GE rotated managers through different divisions, enabling them to build companywide networks.

Robin Good, the guru of distance learning software, told me about sessions he ran for the World Bank. He would set participants loose to explore the jungle or soak in the pool while contemplating a problem. The group developed a shared passion around the issues. Alumni were motivated to continue working with one another. This doesn't happen by accident.

Every organization has people who leave you feeling inspired. Their enthusiasm boosts your energy level. Unfortunately, the enthusiasts are usually counterbalanced by toxic workers—folks who sap your strength. Pull the plug on them.

ORGANIZATION NETWORK ANALYSIS

Rob Cross is professor of business at the University of Virginia in Charlottesville. He is also founder and research director of the Network Roundtable, a consortium of forty learning organizations working with UVA faculty to apply network techniques to critical business issues. The Roundtable's member list reads like a who's who of business thought leaders from firms like Boeing, BP, Chevron Texaco, Fuji Xerox, Goldman Sachs, Herman Miller, HP, IBM, Intel, Merck, Microsoft, Raytheon, and Schlumberger (R. Cross, 2005a,b).

Cross is looking to optimize organizations, not individuals. His work goes far beyond simplistic analysis of who e-mails whom. He asks if you are an energizer or a deenergizer. When he and his coauthor Andrew Parker (2004) posed this question, they were surprised to find that most people hadn't thought systematically about their impact on their colleagues. Energizers think about both task and relationship; deenergizers are all task driven. Relationships fuel business. To prosper, pay attention to how you relate to others, and don't make the mistake of thinking that getting the task accomplished makes it okay to ignore other people.

The Network Roundtable's Web site is a cornucopia of research results, presentations, and explanations. With Cross's permission, I have cherry-picked information from the Roundtable Web site (R. Cross, 2005a,b) and from his home page.

Organizational network analysis x-rays the inner workings of an organization, a powerful means of making invisible patterns of information flow and collaboration in strategically important groups visible.

Cross conducted an ONA of executives in the exploration and production division of a large petroleum organization. This group was in the midst of implementing a technology to help transfer knowledge across drilling initiatives and was also interested in assessing its ability as a group to create and share knowledge. As can be seen in Figure 5.1, the network analysis revealed a striking contrast between the group's formal and informal structure.

Three important points quickly emerged from the ONA. First, the ONA identified midlevel managers who were critical in terms of information flow within the group. A particular surprise came from the central role that Cole played in terms of both overall information flow within the group and being the only point of contact between members of the production division and the rest of the network. If he were hired away, the efficiency of this group as a whole would be significantly diminished as people in the informal network reestablished important informational relationships. Simply categorizing various informational requests that Cole received and then allocating ownership of these informational or decision domains to other executives served to unburden Cole and make the overall network more responsive and robust.

Second, the ONA helped to identify highly peripheral people who essentially represented untapped expertise and underused resources for the group. In particular, it became apparent that many of the senior people had become too removed from the day-to-day operations of this group. For example, the most senior person (Jones) was one of the most peripheral in the

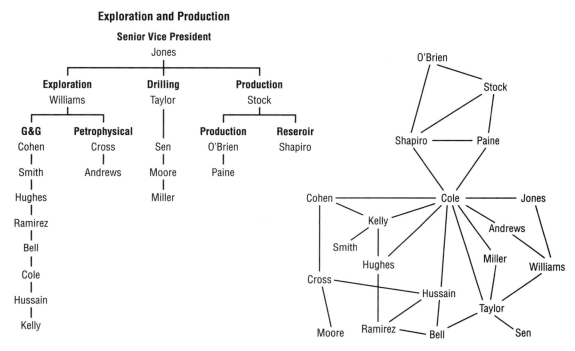

Exploration and Production

FIGURE 5.1. Using Organizational Network Analysis to Pinpoint the Vulnerability of the Informal Organization

Source: Rob Cross. Reprinted with permission.

informal network. This is a common finding. As people move higher within an organization, their work begins to entail more administrative tasks that make them both less accessible and less knowledgeable about the day-to-day work of their subordinates. However, in this case, our debriefing session indicated that Jones had become too removed, and his lack of responsiveness frequently held the entire network back when important decisions needed to be made.

Third, the ONA demonstrated the extent to which the production division (the subgroup on the top of the diagram) had become separated from the overall network. Several months prior to this analysis, these people had been physically moved to a different floor in the building. On reviewing the network diagram, many of the executives realized that this physical separation had resulted in loss of a lot of the serendipitous meetings that occurred when they were colocated. Structured meetings were set up to help avoid operational problems the group had been experiencing due to this loss of communication between production and the rest of the network.

Network analysis can benefit organizations in many ways:

- Supporting partnerships and alliances can tell executives whether appropriate points of connectivity exist across organizations and whether governance is restricting collaboration.
- Ensuring strategy execution allows executives to determine if the appropriate cross-functional or departmental collaborations are occurring to support strategic objectives.
- Collaboration and decision making in top leadership networks help assess connections within a top leadership team and also reveal how information is entering and leaving this group.
- Integrating networks across core processes or expertise provides a diagnostic assessment of information and knowledge flow both within and across functions critical to a core process.
- Promoting innovation can be accomplished by assessing how a group is integrating its expertise and the effectiveness with which it is drawing on the expertise of others within and outside an organization.
- Ensuring integration postmerger or large-scale change. Particularly in knowledge-intensive settings, large-scale change is fundamentally an issue of network integration. ONA, done before a change initiative, can help inform the change process as well as central people within the network that a sponsor might want to engage in design because of their ability to convey information to others. ONA can also be done as a follow-up six to nine months after implementation. Often these assessments reveal significant issues that leaders need to address for the initiative to be successful.
- Developing communities of practice begins by identifying key members of the community as well as assessing overall health in terms of connectivity.

Lest traditionalists reject ONA as just a thought experiment from the ivory tower of academia, I'll share a few excerpts from a case study of supporting communities of practice at Halliburton.

Halliburton employed ONA in building nineteen communities of practice across a variety of lines of business and technical services. Proud of its entrepreneurial roots, the $20 billion organization is hard-nosed. The CEO describes the workers as gritty and determined. Hundreds of them have taken bullets in Iraq. Senior management demanded that its communities of practice show measurable results linked directly to financial performance. For example, one community of practice demonstrated its performance by:

- Lowering customer dissatisfaction by 24 percent.
- Reducing the cost of poor quality by 66 percent.

- Increasing new product revenue by 22 percent.

- Improving operational productivity by more than 10 percent.

- Targeting actions to improve social network effectiveness instead of taking a "more is better" approach.

- Identifying overly connected people to spread the load, delegate answering of questions, helping people connect directly with one another to solve problems, removing mundane queries from time-constrained experts, and opening bottlenecks.

- Bridging invisible network silos to share best practices. One division had cut the annual cost of poor quality by 50 percent, while other divisions experienced a 12 percent increase over the same period of time. ONA spotted breakdowns in knowledge transfer among divisions.

- Creating awareness of expertise distributed through the network through a concerted effort to share who knows what.

- Identifying and drawing in peripheral network members and engaging them to help solve problems outside their areas of operations.

Activities like these don't require the infrastructure available to a company of Halliburton's size (100,000 employees working in a hundred countries). The logic of optimizing an organizational network can be implemented in small steps. If two groups have important things to share but aren't aware of what the others are doing, the first step is to involve their members in joint activities, seat their people next to one another in meetings, engage them in joint projects, and encourage them to share their members successes and challenges. Good connections are good business. The next chapter looks at learning as a process and the continuous improvement strategy of learning to learn.

META-LEARNING

META-LEARNING TREATS learning as a process. Learning is a skill, like playing golf. The more you practice, the better your performance becomes, but if golfers followed the pattern of businesspeople learning, they would arrive for a match without ever having thought about the game or touched a club. Hence, meta-learning begins with raising awareness of learning, listening for feedback, praising advancement, and getting lots of practice. This is how one learns to learn.

Meta-learning also embraces a variety of conditions that interfere with the learning process, such as mismatch of the form of learning and the maturity of the learner. The commitment of the learner is involved, for without it, the doors to the mind slam shut. People need communication skills to participate in the knowledge economy. Stress and poor health are frequent obstacles to learning. All of these factors and others are under the meta-learning umbrella.

> *Everyone takes the limits of his own vision for the limits of the world.*
> **ARTHUR SCHOPENHAUER**

THE META-LEARNING LAB

Bill Daul is what Malcolm Gladwell (2004) calls a *connector*. IBM executive Jim Spohrer describes Daul as "human glue." Daul brings people together. In 2002, he encouraged a small group of us who shared an interest in innovative approaches to adult learning to gather for lunch.

Four of us continued our dialogue, calling ourselves the Meta-Learning Lab. Claudia L'Amoreaux conducts learning conversations, highly focused coaching sessions designed to help people expand their capacity for learning and leadership. Claudia Welss is researching the cultivation of intuition aided by technology and is on the faculty of the Institute of Noetic Sciences. Clark Quinn is a cognitive psychologist who designs educational games, mobile learning applications, and intelligent learning systems and is the author of *Engaging Learning: Designing e-Learning Simulation Games* (2005). I round out the group with a background in training, software, group dynamics, and marketing.

> *A knowledge worker needs one thing only: to learn how to learn.*
>
> **PETER F. DRUCKER**

Discovering we each believed in the untapped potential of learning to learn, we met to become better acquainted and talk things out under the redwood trees in Berkeley's Tilden Park. We continued meeting at one another's houses off and on for years. Through dialogue, we co-created the vision of meta-learning that follows.

> Learning is so integral to human nature that it's often overlooked. We have to rise above the day-to-day to recognize its presence.

Here's how we described meta-learning to a meeting of the eLearning Forum:

> Walk with me up the stairs to the balcony. Rise above everyday rules, conventions, and sacred cows. Let's find a vantage point that enables us to see what's really going on. Look at the people in the plaza below.
>
> One man reads a book, two women debate, a dozen people listen attentively to a politician, a bearded man describes the old days to his grandchildren, a baby stares into her mother's eyes, three cigarette-smokers talk about the news, the gardener shows his apprentice how to plant a tulip, a teacher tells her students how acorns grow into oaks, a boy demonstrates how to blow a bubble with bubble gum to his little sister. All of these people are learning.
>
> From the balcony, we see elaborate social exchanges where roles and status and self-image come into play. Some learning is planned; other learning just happens. Some learners are active, others receptive. Some are gaining information, others pick up new skills, and yet others are developing something deeper, beliefs. Teachers learn. Learners teach. The activity on the plaza stimulates some but distracts others. Some are adept at learning, others not. From a distance, we see patterns. We are looking at meta-learning.
>
> The balcony's proprietor has put a variety of telescopes on the large wooden table to help us focus on what's happening down below. These are magic spyglasses. Each lets us watch the people in the plaza through the eyes of a different discipline.

I pick up the marketing spyglass. The learners look like customers shopping for knowledge and abilities to add to their repertoire. They love to buy but they hate to be sold. No matter how good the price, relationships are more important. They trust word of mouth more than advertisements. The people are not really shopping for lessons. They "buy" learning based on their expectations of how it will make them feel. In the end, all purchase decisions are emotional.

Next I bring the motivation spyglass to my eye. Some learners are enthusiastic; others are wallflowers. The gung-ho learners know what's in it for them and deem it relevant. They understand what's expected. They enjoy doing things their own way. They learn from teaching others. They're not afraid to screw up.

Lack-lustre learners show up unprepared. They fear looking stupid and are afraid to experiment. They don't seem to know how they're doing. They feel that learning is being imposed upon them.

The anthropology telescope helps me watch how folks in the plaza are behaving. Some are attending classes. Others are chatting by the fountain. Several old men tell jokes as they puff fat cigars. The scope filters out the static, and I notice that the people chatting in small groups are learning twice as much as those who are attending class.

HOW DOES META-LEARNING IMPROVE THE LEARNING PROCESS?

For an individual, learning how to learn improves performance. It includes such things as:

- Self-empowerment (attitude, self-confidence, understanding—what Peter Senge calls "personal mastery") (Senge, Kleiner, Roberts, Ross & Smith, 1994)

- Knowing and choosing the best way to learn (individual, group, debate, or triage, for example) and the best sources of information

- Personal knowledge management (capturing and reflecting on one's tool kit)

- Forming powerful relationships (with mentors, colleagues, and information sources)

- Continuous reflection (double loop, goal of self-improvement)

- Moving to a reinforcing learning environment

For an organization, improvement is influenced by culture, organizational support, manager roles, and other areas that extend beyond what an individual can do:

- Supportive organizational culture (tolerance of mistakes, vision of learning's import)
- Sense of community (common mission and values, linkages)
- Networking and communication infrastructure
- Respect for learning (and time and incentive to do it)
- Appreciation of the return on investment of learning
- Helping individuals sharpen their learning skills
- Helping mentors help individuals sharpen their learning skills
- Implementing programs with sound meta-learning design (for example, situated, timing right, discovery, fun, or mass customized)

LEARNING TO LEARN

You optimize people's learning and doing the same way you optimize other business processes: you review the process, looking for opportunities to improve it, and then you benchmark against best practices. You do the same for learning and problem-solving processes, only they're somewhat harder to document and examine.

We know a lot about good learning and doing. We also know how to improve skills. For example, research has shown how self-explanation of the steps in a process improves retention, how re-representing a problem facilitates solution, and how individuals process information in different ways. Setting people up to learn how to learn ignites a process of perpetual self-improvement. Once people's consciousness is raised, many of them will become aware of their own learning and take responsibility for improving it. They probably need help destroying myths about what they can't change about themselves and what they can, but after that, enlightened self-interest kicks in.

The ultimate goal is to optimize an individual's ability to *do*. Consider the practice of note taking. Many people take notes at meetings. It's a habit you acquired in school, and you reread the notes at least the night before the exam. People continue to take notes after school. Surprisingly, they don't reliably reread the notes. So the question arises, why do they bother to take notes?

The answer is that taking notes is a valuable form of processing information, a trick known to increase the likelihood of understanding and remembering material. If the notes are not exact transcriptions but instead are rephrasings or mind maps or include drawings that capture some of the expressed relationships between ideas, they help cement the experience into memory.

But most people probably haven't explicitly thought about developing such techniques; they haven't thought about learning to learn. It's not what they have been conditioned to do in the workplace, and it's rarely taught. It has to be deliberately acquired by systematically reviewing one's own learning activities, comparing oneself to best practice, and applying tactics to alter well-practiced but inefficient behaviors. This meta-learning process of review, comparison, and intervention can become habit.

Reflection is usually accomplished by listening to the internal dialogue within one's head. When experts were asked to repeat what was going through their minds while learning, they described linking new understandings to old, searching for missing pieces when confronted with mental puzzles, and other active processes.

Because our inner voices are rarely shared, their thinkers don't receive direct feedback from others. One's internal dialogue may be inappropriate, illogical, narrow-minded, or culturally biased yet never stand corrected. Learners may not realize they have the power to shape the voice that columnist Herb Caen used to call the "drunken monkey."

The members of the Meta-Learning Lab consider it particularly valuable for learners to get to know themselves by telling others how they're thinking. John Bransford (2000) relates that "reciprocal teaching, for example, is a technique designed to improve students' reading comprehension by helping them explicate, elaborate, and monitor their understanding as they read."

Facilitators can accelerate the discovery process by modeling their personal strategies for learning new material, solving problems, and allocating their time and effort. Different subjects call for different approaches to learning. Questions that lead to understanding physics differ from those for learning written composition, or history, or math problems, although meta-learning has improved performance in all of these subjects.

There's another factor at work that makes things learned at informal events more memorable than planned presentations and workshops. Repetition spread out over intervals is more likely to stick in long-term memory than repetition all at once. For example, if I hear a new concept at a presentation, then hear it in conversation at lunch and in conversation at the bar, it's unlikely I'm going to forget it.

Spaced repetition is more effective than nonspaced repetition, observes research psychologist Will Thalheimer (2006). Spacing minimizes forgetting:

"One way to utilize spacing is to change the definition of a learning event to include the connotation that learning takes place over time—real learning doesn't usually occur in one-time events."

Compressing learning events into fifty-minute presentations works against long-term remembering. Unconferences, events that put the audience in charge, make room for things worth remembering to bubble up time and time again. Furthermore, just as random reinforcement keeps pigeons in a Skinner box tapping the bait bar furiously, random repetition cements remembrance.

THE RIGHT STUFF

Every generation has its own ideas about what's important to learn. It used to be information to memorize, and now it's how to find things when you need them.

Back in the 1960s, students used slide rules in science class because electronic calculators had not been invented. A college graduate was expected to know basic philosophy (Descartes, Hume, Kant), literature (Shakespeare, Dostoevsky, Camus), history (revolutions, colonies, wars, inventions, dates), science (elementary physics at least), and lots of other stuff that had been piling up over the past half-millennium. This core knowledge was expected to last a lifetime. It was the close of an era where a learned person could know it all. Now many of those topics are going the way of the slide rule: useful but unnecessary.

"In your career, knowledge is like milk," says Louis Ross, chief technology officer of Ford Motor Company. "It has a shelf life stamped right on the carton. The shelf life of a degree in engineering is about three years. If you're not replacing everything you know by then, your career is going to turn sour fast."

As a teenager, I could recite the kings and queens of England, the books of the Bible, and the names and capitals of every country in the world. Now that this information is but a few keystrokes away, it is pointless to memorize them. (And of course I've forgotten them.) In place of memorization, today's learners need search skills, conceptualization, analysis, reasoning, decision making, and emotional intelligence.

Here are my personal meta-learning practices:

- Daily reflection.
- Be mindful and alert.
- Talk with my inner voice.
- Take notes and reflect on them.
- Mental feng-shui and spring cleaning.

- Think holistically; take frequent trips to the balcony.
- Set learning goals and monitor progress.
- Keep a journal and blog.
- Seek process improvements.
- Make and maintain good connections.
- Recognize and shut down bad connections.
- Hold on to what's important, and improve those memories.
- Continually ask, "Does this matter?"
- Discard the negative, the inconsequential, the clutter.
- Share my learning insights with others.
- Reinforce concepts by teaching others.
- Maintain an optimistic vision of the future.
- Find and spread joy in learning.
- Revere serendipity.
- Always expect miracles.

THE WORKER LEARNING LIFECYCLE

To everything there is a season. We are born, we play, we work, we teach, we die. How we learn changes as we mature. A baby's every waking moment goes into figuring things out. Babies are the ultimate free-range learners. Child's play for preschoolers is learning in disguise; they devote most of their time to experimenting, discovering, making connections, and understanding their world.

School children attend formal classes and do assignments to learn foundation knowledge and skills. The structure of school accelerates children's learning the 3 Rs, cultural artifacts, and social norms—to fill up their empty heads. The quality of the school experience is open to debate, but few would argue that children should have to invent, say, multiplication rather than have it taught to them in school.

Children weave a mental tapestry of understanding; adults patch holes in the fabric. Upon escaping the confines of school, most people go to work. Just as the high school graduate descends from the top of one heap to the bottom to become the entering freshman, the college graduate starts over as a new employee.

Most people arrive at adulthood having built the foundation skills and mentality to function in the world, but they know neither the ropes of their employer's organization nor many work skills. Granted, most of us are novices in some areas but expert in others, but new recruits need more foundation than experts almost by definition. They are weaving their work tapestry.

Marketers divide customers into segments in order to treat them differently. Pampers targets young parents, Home Depot appeals to do-it-yourselfers, and *Vogue* is edited for women. When we divide the workforce into segments, we find that we've often been trying to sell people the wrong thing.

Think of the demographics of the knowledge workers in your organization. How many are green? How many know the ropes? What fraction has the wisdom to teach others what to do? If yours is like most other organizations, old hands outnumber new recruits ten to one. Your top performers are the mature workers in the middle.

Many traditional training departments concentrate almost all of their energy on providing training to novices. Sometimes the justification is that then everyone will be able to understand it. In truth, the more mature learners are going to skip it entirely or become disgruntled.

In Chapter Two, I likened formal learning to riding on a bus and informal learning to driving a car or riding a bicycle. Training departments are adept at creating bus routes; often they have little to do assisting drivers and bikers (Table 6.1).

TABLE 6.1. Three Segments of Learners with Three Different Modes of Learning

Novice Worker Directed	Mature Worker Self-Directed	Senior Worker Helping Others
Class	Discovery	Coaching
Course	Searching/search engine	Mentoring
Teacher	Trial-and-error	Storytelling
Test	Collaborating	Giving feedback
Grades	Asking	Nurturing
Curriculum	Skimming	Modeling
Listening	Observing	Reflecting
Instructions	Conversing	Connecting

Imagine a seasoned executive who transfers from New York City to Paris. Her business skills rank as mature, perhaps senior, but she is a novice in speaking French. Most workers are riding the bus in some subjects and driving the car or riding the bicycle in others.

High performers usually fall in the center column, where learning is the most haphazard. Since they know better than any outsider what they need to learn, they actively resent trainers who tell them what they need. As Winston Churchill said, "Personally, I'm always ready to learn, although I don't always like being taught." The learning designer's responsibility is to make it as easy as possible for these workers to link to others, make discoveries, locate experts, and so forth.

Senior workers not only learn; they also teach. The firm's advisers, coaches, and mentors often come from their ranks. Most workers from now on will live well beyond retirement age. Tapping the knowledge of a firm's "alumni" by keeping them on as personal coaches is a win-win solution compared to the impending loss of know-how that otherwise exists when the baby boomers clean out their desks and hand over control to the next generation.

From a meta-learning standpoint, organizations stand to gain when they serve the organization's mature workers by investing more heavily in self-directed, informal learning. Currently, many companies approach training as if everyone will benefit from kindergarten.

SELF-SERVICE LEARNING

Former New York schoolteacher John Taylor Gatto (2003) wrote, "After a long life, and thirty years in the public school trenches, I've concluded that genius is as common as dirt. We suppress our genius only because we haven't yet figured out how to manage a population of educated men and women. The solution, I think, is simple and glorious. *Let them manage themselves*." The same advice can work in a corporate setting.

SAP is the world's leading provider of enterprise software, with thirty thousand customers in 120 countries. As recently as 2003, SAP was a closed company. Fifteen thousand developers shared information in-house, but what they discussed was behind the firewall, as if their fortress were surrounded by a moat. Then a visionary executive lifted the wall and invited users to join in. Soon the users were telling stories of how they implemented SAP. They answered one another's questions. They described things SAP hadn't thought of. SAP began keeping score, awarding points for the best blog and discussion postings. Success fed on success, and activity skyrocketed. Today the user community creates most of the information shared among SAP software developers.

Information that comes directly from users is compelling: no vendor can be as forthright as a customer. A few rough edges lend credibility. Sometimes SAP edits an entry—not to censor the content, for anything is fair game as criticism, but for clarity because English is often not the writer's primary language. You can't mandate community. The best you can do is to establish the context, provide a purpose, and nurture the group.

SAP customers have become self-service learners.

COMMITMENT

In *Good to Great* (2001), Jim Collins describes long-term enterprise transformations, which involve a major strategy shift and culture change, such as Citibank's commitment to be number 1 in global finance and Stanford University's drive to become the "Harvard of the West." To succeed on this scale, stakeholders must believe in the cause; they must take it to heart, embracing the transformation as the new paradigm.

Training that accompanies enterprise software installations is often too software specific. Put-this-item-in-this-field training isn't enough. Workers need to understand why, not just how. They need to comprehend the flow and impact of the new processes and the way the new system changes their relationships with customers, suppliers, manufacturing, accounting, and others. Success flows to those who embrace the knowledge and build a mental model of the transformation in their heads, learning how their new roles interact within and across the organization.

In operational transformations, mastering new skills is often paramount. Operating a new point-of-sale system doesn't take much faith; conceptualizing how it works doesn't require a course. However, the operator had better have learned how to operate the system to record or reverse a sale. Learning new skills and how to use new tools effectively is transformation of the hands.

Learning in support of transformation calls on many types of learning. The nature of the learning varies with the nature of the transformation. When developing a transformation strategy, you need to select learning methods to support the special requirements of the transformation at hand (Table 6.2). Enterprise transformations focus heavily on building beliefs and cultural change. Operational transformations require proportionally more emphasis on building skills. Process transformations fall roughly in between.

TABLE 6.2. Enterprise Learning for Culture, Knowledge, or Skills

	Nature of Learning	*Common Learning Methods*
Head	Processes	Communities of Practice
	Abstractions	Informal learning, peers
	Understanding	Knowledge management
	Knowledge	Simulation
Heart	Beliefs	Small group interaction
	Emotional intelligence	Outward Bound
	Soft skills	Alumni network
	Values	Storytelling
Hands	Procedures	Formal instruction
	Hard skills	Drill and practice
	Facts	Experimentation
	Muscle memory	Search learning

Imagine a brewer telling his workers to leave every sixth beer bottle un-filled because they've got to cut costs. The situation is absurd because it would come back to haunt them in short order.

Now imagine a senior executive telling her transformation team to chop back on training because they've got to cut costs. That's clearly penny-wise and pound-foolish too, yet it happens all too frequently. Training is easy to overlook or shortchange if it's just a number. The consequences of cutting become apparent when you think about what you're proposing to eliminate.

Which of the three areas we've talked about would you be prepared to do without?

- People who believe ("heart") that this is the way to go and embrace the change; project managers who automatically do the right thing because they have internalized the new.
- Workers who understand ("head") the project and know what to do.
- People who can operate ("hands") the new system with ease.

Learning will support the initial transformation and long-term, sustained innovation from the transformation. It will help ensure that people have the right skills, methods, and mind-set to embrace the transformation. Learning accelerates adoption of new technology and processes, fosters culture change, and is an integral component of effective human capital management.

INTUITION

Many people are skeptical of hunches because they lack the rigor of logical thought. Horror of horrors, your gut feel might be wrong (as if logic doesn't lead us astray as well). With awareness, you can learn to trust your feelings.

Few snap decisions are that. Ideas that seem to just come to you have often been brewing in your subconscious. When you're facing a difficult choice, take a deep breath and ask yourself, "How do I feel about this?"

Intuition is often more effective than logic because it calls on whole-body intelligence. It is born of relationships and patterns; draws on the power of the unconscious mind to sort through meaningful experience as well as the immediate situation; and addresses tacit, unspoken knowledge.

My good friend Claudia Welss is on the leading edge of research into the power of intuition. She senses that intuition and informal learning are inseparable. They both work by perceiving a greater whole, which might be the greatest whole, according to at least one interpretation of quantum physics (which challenges the basic assumptions of classical physics): that all of reality is an undivided whole where everything is deeply interconnected. An intuitive intelligence capable of accessing this quantum field of information would be unlimited.

She suggests intuition can be viewed as a learning skill and can be enhanced by getting "A CLUE":

> **A**cknowledge the legitimacy of your inner voice, even if you feel it has disappointed you in the past.
>
> **C**ultivate an environment of engagement, as in "seeking the acquaintance or goodwill of" by creating environments that engage intuition.
>
> **L**isten attentively, legitimizing feelings and hunches, beyond not disregarding the intuitive voice, to developing an attention to it.
>
> **U**nderstand how the inner voice may be filtered through prejudices: desires, fears, learned responses, worldviews, and cultural assumptions; learn to distinguish between what's real and what has been filtered.
>
> **E**xercise through practice—calibrate your intuition.

Commit to act on intuition in relatively safe ways at first, recognizing that intuition is a skill that can be strengthened by calibration through confirming or disconfirming evidence from other sources.

Sometimes failure is not an option. When a malevolent megalomaniac threatens to vaporize your empire, you send in your James Bond, not a raw recruit. Knowing what to do is second nature to 007.

In business, when it's vital to break into a complex new market, you send in a veteran who knows the territory to close the deals. You rely on an expert who has been there because he knows how to spot the signs and figure out what's going on as if by second nature. Until recently, extensive experience was the only way to become an expert. It took decades to develop and hone one's craft. It could not be taught in a classroom. That's about to change.

Singapore depends on establishing healthy trade relationships with China. A design group in Singapore had been commissioned to help small and medium businesses become experts in doing business in China.

Foreign businesspeople new to China have an extraordinarily difficult time learning to sense and respond to the culture's complexities. They don't need more information; instead, they need to be able to understand what's going on so they will know how to use the information they have. For a long time, no one could figure out how to transfer the insight of experienced foreign entrepreneurs.

What separates novices from experts is the way they size things up. Experts assess a situation with less new information than novices. In *Blink* (2004), Malcolm Gladwell calls this capability "thin-slicing" or "rapid cognition."

Designers tackling the sizing-up-China program started by teasing out the "thin slices" that experts pay attention to when making rapid decisions. They elicited narratives from China hands, focusing them on context rather than conclusions. The narratives fell into six themes: strategy, environment, people, culture, law, and fraud.

Next, the designers conducted extensive confidential interviews with seasoned professionals. They asked them to imagine challenging but typical scenarios and to display them on a table using small figures and props to represent roles and relationships. The experts explained the relationships displayed (that is, the social context). They also played the scenarios forward and backward, answering questions such as, "Let's imagine it turns out well [badly]. What would the situation look like then?"

The designers poured this content into six shell scenarios. They included representative businesses going into China (trading companies, manufacturing companies, and service companies), the situational themes, and a variety of geographic regions. Narrative techniques created by consultant and master storyteller Dave Snowden helped transform the raw material into realistic stories. Methods borrowed from screenwriting brought the stories to life. The result was a game pack of scenarios, each containing dozens of unfolding vignettes.

A half-dozen novices can work though the scenarios collaboratively, making individual judgments along the way and learning from what their colleagues deem important. One game takes a moderately experienced group three hours or more to complete, but the game is best played with diverse levels of experience. Forcing the group to agree on their reading of the situation before moving on requires them to explain their divergences, which in itself provides a high level of complex, highly contextualized knowledge.

These decision games, as pioneered by decision-making expert Gary Klein (2004), repeatedly test people's judgment and knowledge while they engage with business colleagues in a complex and ambiguous environment. While they are learning about a particular domain, participants also gain insight into the perspectives, styles, and capabilities of their colleagues.

Exposing novices to multiple ways of seeing and sizing up situations is how expertise is built. Switching the focus from teaching content to challenging contexts intensifies learning. Participants become so involved they don't even break for coffee.

Decision games have become a preferred method of developing experts in the U.S. Marines. These high-impact scenarios are also used to accelerate the decision-making capabilities of high-tech sales stars.

Chief learning officers recognize that training the corporate SWAT team takes more than traditional training. Expect to see more programs for high-potential performers that use thin slicing to build expertise fast.

"The key to using intuition effectively is experience—more specifically, meaningful experience—that allows us to recognize patterns and build mental models," says Gary Klein (2004, p. 36). Thousands of decision makers from the military, fire departments, and business have engaged in deliberate practice to hone their ability to size up situations quickly, have confidence in the first option that springs to mind, sense what will happen next, remain calm in the face of pressure, and find alternatives when plans fail (Klein, 2004).

Klein's *The Power of Intuition* (2004) is a cookbook of approaches for making tough choices, spotting problems before they get out of hand, managing uncertainty, sizing up situations, communicating your intuitions, and recognizing patterns. Here are some tips from the book that come in handy for almost any sort of decision making:

- The first option you think of is likely to be the best.
- Use analysis to support your intuitions.
- Put more energy into understanding the situation than in deliberating over what to do.
- Think ahead.

- Uncertainty adds excitement to decision making.
- Consult the experts.

Developing deep expertise requires accumulated experience. In short, you learn by doing. But how can you accomplish this without continually reinventing the wheel? How can you speed up learning without losing the nuances that are so important?

Some organizations are looking for help from experts who are designated as knowledge coaches. Knowledge coaches tell stories and ask Socratic questions. For the lessons to stick, the novice "needs to discover the expert's know-how through practice, observation, problem-solving, and experimentation" (Leonard & Snap, 2004).

TAKE STOCK

Before we go there, take a look around your workplace:

- Where do you see informal learning taking place?
- Is there room for improvement? How?
- How could your layout better encourage conversation?
- Could you improve how people find answers to their questions?
- Does everyone understand how the shadow organization works?
- Does the environment encourage casual meetings with customers, partners, and suppliers?
- Do high performers receive the same treatment as novices?

The next chapter zooms in from the organizational to the individual. We'll look at skills and attitudes one needs to be an optimal informal learner and offer some shortcuts for acquiring them.

LEARNERS

EMPOWERING WORKERS produces results only when workers have the will and the ability to use the power they are granted. Taking responsibility for one's learning and one's work requires passion and skill. These reside in the worker, not the organization.

Learning is one component in a business ecosystem. If something improves the overall value of the ecosystem or the welfare of the individual worker, I'm in favor of it. This includes helping the worker build personal strengths and overcome personal obstacles. My critics take a narrower view. They don't think it appropriate to interfere in the worker's personal life. You can deal with dress codes, zany behavior, and funky odors, but you are not allowed even to consider what goes on inside the worker's head.

I don't understand how a chief learning officer can say, "It's not my department," when it's obvious that a worker's mental health, physical fitness, emotional balance, outlook on life, authenticity, and social skills have a tremendous impact on work quality, not to mention personal satisfaction. These personal issues are vital to effective informal learning.

Steve Jobs, in his June 2005 commencement address at Stanford University said, "You've got to find what you love. And that is as true for your work as it is for your lovers. Your work is going to fill a large part of your life, and the only way to be truly satisfied is to do what you believe is great work. And the only way to do great work is to love what you do. If you haven't found it yet, keep looking. Don't settle. As with all matters of the heart, you'll know when you find it. And, like any great relationship, it just gets better and better as the years roll on. So keep looking until you find it. Don't settle."

> *There can be no knowledge without emotion. We may be aware of a truth, yet until we have felt its force, it is not ours. To the cognition of the brain must be added the experience of the soul.*
>
> **ARNOLD BENNETT**

You need to participate in the new business ecosystem to keep up and to create value. Let's go over some things your workers should be able to do to stay in top form and you right in there with them. Top managers can often benefit from mastering what's ahead too.

KNOW WHERE YOU ARE GOING

What do you want to do with your life? The answer comes to some people easily; I envy them. Once this advice helped me home in on my life's purpose: "Write your obituary." Try it. What do you want to be remembered for?

If you enjoy wallowing in self-exploration, pick up the latest version of *What Color Is Your Parachute?* (2005). Bolles has said that his perennial bestseller is a self-help book masquerading as a job hunting manual. *Parachute* will help you review what you've enjoyed in the past, what sort of people you want to hang out with, and whether you want to work with people, places, or things. It's a great resource. One word of caution: don't forget that your goal is to find yourself, not to spend weeks answering all the questions in the book.

My current favorite find-yourself aid is the 43 Things (43things.com) Web site. This is from the home page:

Write Down Your Goals

People have known for years that making a list of goals is the best way to achieve them. Why is that? First, getting your goals in writing can help you clarify what you really want to do. You might find you have some important and some frivolous goals. That is OK. You've got space for 43 Things on your list. Not every one of them has to change the world (but save room for the ones that might).

Get Inspired

What do you want to do with your life? It is not an easy question to answer—and you shouldn't have to answer alone. Browse 43 Things to find out what others want to do. You might find some goals you share. Click the "I want to do this" button to add a goal to your list. Got an idea for a new goal? Just type it in the text box on the homepage or at the bottom of any page on the site. Bam. Now, it's your thing.

Share Your Progress

We all have stories about what we care about. Writing down your progress on a goal can help someone else learn about something you both want to do. When you see a goal you've achieved, click on the "I've done this" button and share a story about how you did it.

> *You cannot mandate productivity; you must provide the tools to let people become their best.*
> **STEVE JOBS**

I particularly like 43 Things because it lets users figure things out incrementally, and I can track my progress. It's less lonely than doing the *Parachute* exercises, just you and the kitchen table. Give it a whirl; it's free.

FIND YOUR CALLING

A couple of years back, I attended an evening session around a fire that tapped into ancient roots. Richard Leider challenged us to think about "what makes you get up in the morning?"

> *If I am not for myself, who will be? If I am only for myself, who am I? If not now, when?*
>
> **TALMUD**

Leider has spent his time on earth as a "student of the second half of life." Most of us were clearly in the second half (those in the first half were probably in the pool, dancing, getting new tattoos, or doing things that defy description in a professional book, even an informal one). When Leider asks oldsters what they'd do differently if they could relive their experiences, they tell him:

- More time for reflection. Grow whole, not old. Come closer to the magic of the fire. Stare into the flame. Join the village elders in the front row.

- Courage. Take more risks in work and love. "What do you intend to do in your wild and crazy life?"

- Purpose. Everyone wants to make a difference, to leave a dent in the world.

SYSTEM CHECK

You will have a difficult time learning in any environment if your basic mental systems are out of whack, for you may be working extra hard just to cope. I was beyond my fortieth birthday when I discovered I had attention deficit disorder (ADD) and sleep apnea. I had recognized my clinical depression much earlier but didn't meet up with the appropriate treatment until later.

Don't say "Not me" quite yet. Denial is part of the routine. This isn't some sort of stain on your reputation. ADD didn't keep me from graduating from Princeton with honors; I think of it as attention deficit advantage. If the shrink asks you what you see in an inkblot, you run out after six or seven things. I'll keep going until he has to leave for the day.

Depression is often accompanied by blaming yourself and self-loathing. Friends suggest you can pull out of it if you just try hard enough, but they don't get it. They think your missed opportunities, poor health, withdrawal, and dangerously zany sense of humor are just you being a jerk. If that's the case, how might they explain that one tiny pill a day alters your brain chemistry and blows all the symptoms away?

If you find yourself easily distracted, get a copy of *Delivered from Distraction* (2005) by Edward Hallowell and John Ratey. See if you recognize yourself in the first couple of chapters. Author Thom Hartmann (2005) calls ADD a gift. He asserts that "having ADD in the gene pool was both essential to the survival and success of early humans, and is one of the driving forces for change, invention, and innovation in the modern world." He posits that the characteristics of ADD are what made prehistoric hunters successful. After farmers took over the world, the hunters seemed unruly and out of place.

FEELINGS

It's popular in Western business culture to act as if human feelings are inconsequential. We are supposed to check our humanity at the door when we arrive at the office. Business should be rational, not emotional. It's as if emotion taints decision making and blocks the pathway to performance. Yet emotion adds zest to life; emotion is the root of enthusiasm.

When John Adams joined the training group at Sun Microsystems in 1996, he brought with him an integrated stress and wellness program he had developed over the course of three decades, including a postdoctoral fellowship with the National Institutes of Health. A war for talent was raging, so Sun offered an incredible array of programs. While at work, Sun would have employees' laundry done. People in the parking lot would detail their cars. Staff could take meals home from the company cafeteria to microwave in the evening. Their mental well-being was another matter.

A major Oracle implementation with tight deadlines was driving staff up the wall, but Adams was told not to offer stress management training. It wasn't mission critical, he was told. CEO Scott McNealy ("Eat lunch or be lunch") decreed that two words he did not want to hear were *personal* and *process*. Adams offered optional stress management lessons under the table. Disguised as "high-performance seminars," he offered clandestine courses when bedraggled managers pleaded with him.

Denying a fact doesn't make it untrue. Humans are emotional beings. You can't lead an organization without touching people's hearts as well as their minds. Several economists have won Nobel prizes for exposing the folly of the rational economic man, which is the foundation of classical economics.

Human thought is always a blend of reason and feeling. Antonio R. Damasio (1999), a polymath brain researcher, reports that emotions grab people's attention, and this in turn motivates them to focus on issues rationally. He says people who do not feel emotions perform poorly as decision makers.

When David Maister (1997) studied 139 professional service firms covering fifty-five hundred people in fifteen countries, he discovered that margins, profit per employee, and profit growth are directly linked to employee satisfaction and happiness.

Daniel Goleman's three books on emotional intelligence (1995, 2000, 2001) are full of examples of ordinary people who achieved extraordinary results because they were emotionally aware and stable. He reports that "for star performance in all jobs, in every field, emotional competence is twice as important as purely cognitive abilities. For success at the highest levels, in leadership positions, emotional competence accounts for virtually the entire advantage" (2000, p. 161).

Richard Boyatzis (Boyatzis & McKee, 2005) notes that "people have to be grabbed by their values, their goals, their dreams of what's possible for them. If you focus at the outset on people's values and visions, on what they want to do with their life, then they see themselves as using the training opportunity for their own development—not just the company's."

Years ago, a customer service representative in Boulder, Colorado, asked me if I was with the firm that developed the sales training for his bank. When I said yes, he shook my hand and thanked me profusely. Applying the course's model of negotiating had saved his marriage, he said. We must all take on the task of developing the whole person.

"At the moment it is experienced, enjoyment can be both physically painful and mentally taxing; but because it involves a triumph over the forces of entropy and decay, it nourishes the spirit," wrote Mihaly Csikszentmihalyi, the author of *Flow* (1991). People aren't lazy; they are underchallenged. The same technology that lets us deal at the microlevel of work enables us to help at the macrolevel of holistic development.

SONY was built on a foundation of creating flow, not on dreaming up cool gadgets. Its founding purpose was "to establish a place of work where engineers can feel the joy of technological innovation, be aware of their mission to society, and work to their heart's content." Rather than forgetting the works of Herzberg, Maslow, McGregor, Mayo, and, more recently, Marty Seligman and David Cooperrider, we need to make them part of the system.

Evolution can take us places design cannot reach. Evolution knows no bounds; it doesn't top out once the problem is solved (Figure 7.1). In fact, it doesn't recognize the existence of problems. What is, is.

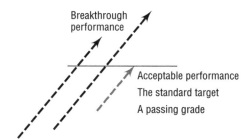

FIGURE 7.1. Aim for Breakthrough Performance, Not Adequacy

It should come as no surprise that workers don't like training. Most training is built on the pessimistic assumption that trainees are deficient. Training is the cure for what's broken. Consequences include:

- Negative reinforcement (correct what's wrong, take the test, do this or else) instead of positive (Great job!)
- Unmotivated learners (Who wants to accept that they are inadequate?)
- Learner disengagement, unrewarded curiosity, spurned creativity (Because the faculty implies, "My way or the highway")
- Training (we do it to you) instead of learning (co-creation of knowledge)
- Focus on fixing the individual rather than optimizing the team (because the individual trainee will submit to being fixed but the organization is reluctant to join in group therapy)

▷ ▷ *Everybody wins if the starting point is, "Be all that you can be."*

THE FUTURE IS GOOD

Years ago at an author reading at Black Oak Books in Berkeley, California, someone asked a seemingly negative writer why he appeared to be so optimistic. Without missing a beat, he replied, "Because optimism works better."

"Seek and ye shall find." If you believe you'll find a parking place in San Francisco or Manhattan, you're more likely to find one than if you don't expect to. This isn't because some higher spirit decided to give you a hand. Rather, you see what you expect to find. If you believe the open parking spot is waiting for you, you're more likely to find it.

Marty Seligman (1991) says that "the defining characteristic of pessimists is that they tend to believe bad events will last a long time, will undermine everything they do, and are their own fault" (p. 2).

Raise a dog in a box with a glass top that he hits off when he tries to get out of the box, and after a while he'll stop trying. Seligman calls this "learned helplessness," and its hallmark is believing that nothing you do matters.

People who catastrophize events, blowing them out of proportion and assuming they will last forever, become depressed. Depression is so common today that psychiatrists know it as the "common cold of mental illness."

No one should settle for good enough when best is an option. People are fulfilled by meeting challenges, not by just getting by. Informal learning is a continuing quest to improve. Also, innovations don't appear in the formal curriculum because they consist of the undiscovered and unexplored.

You may have the best thoughts in the world but if you don't communicate them effectively, they won't help you or anyone else. I'm thinking about how you converse, tell stories, speak in public, and write.

Learning is not soaking up information like a sponge. Learning is born from interactions. You put something out there and gauge the response. Or someone else offers up an idea and learns from your response to it.

I enjoy chatting, writing, and presenting ideas so much that it's what I've taken up for a living. It wasn't always this way. For many years, I was too shy to engage in conversation at parties. My writing was listless and without emotion. Public speaking terrified me. Myers Briggs pegged me as very, very "I" (for introvert). If you feel you'll never be really good at speaking and writing, get over it. You might be like me. The secret of success is to be who you are.

SPEAKING

Given a choice, many people would choose death over speaking in public. Call it stage fright, fear of speaking, or performance anxiety; it is said to be the number one dread in America. Symptoms may include shortness of breath, words that won't come, a shaky voice, trembling, rapid heartbeat, sweating, and nausea.

This form of social phobia often comes from fear of being humiliated in public. Sufferers can recognize their fears are irrational, but that doesn't stop them. They often believe that it's just them, that somehow everybody else makes perfect presentations. Susceptibility to social phobia is inherited. You've got to know what you're up against. Try some low-risk practice, and join Toastmasters.

Life is not fair. It's not fair that tall guys receive more promotions, beautiful women earn higher salaries, and some people are natural and compelling speakers. You can't change your height, but you can dramatically improve your presentations. Some great speakers are born, but most of them are made. Giving presentations can make or break your reputation. Poor presentations suffocate good ideas.

When I graduated from business school, I was an awful speaker: rushed, nervous, shaky, sweaty palms, quavering voice. My job required me to make presentations to groups in Silicon Valley, most often fifteen to sixty people huddled together after work in an auditorium or the company cafeteria. I read Dale Carnegie and Dorothy Sarnoff. Before long, I looked forward to speaking, and I got good at it. My sessions led to successes at NASA, IBM, Fairchild, Memorex, Ford Aerospace, Atari, Stanford, Berkeley, Shugart, Aeroject General, McKesson, Fireman's Fund, and Bank of America.

As my career progressed, I had the opportunity to take a two-day course on presentations with video feedback. I enjoyed it, and it stayed with me for a while. Several years later, I fell off the track. Colleagues told me my presentations were confusing and rushed, even a bit strange. The low point came after a presentation I made at Training in the mid-1990s. Afterward, my co-presenter told me that if speaking in public were important in my chosen career, I had a lot of work to do. He said I had drained the energy out of the audience and that I'd even turned my back to them while fiddling with my computer. I mumbled.

Friends told me not to worry. My companion was a highly regarded presenter, a former instructor at Harvard Business School and Boston Consulting Group consultant, but I knew he was right. I took his advice to heart and studied how good presentations are constructed. With two major speaking engagements directly ahead, I went back to my sources and practiced on anyone who would listen. While I hiked in the hills, I thought about how to engage my audience and get my ideas across. What came to me were these:

- Tell stories, not what appears on a PowerPoint slide.
- Use pictures—graphics and mental images—to convey the message.
- Put yourself in the listener's shoes first, last, and always.
- Practice, practice, dry run, practice, revise, practice, edit, practice.
- Never read a speech.
- Talk with one member of the audience at a time.

Some other excellent techniques I use comes from others:
- Present a series of objects, not a fully structured presentation; let the listener choose the sequence (Thank you, Gordon MacKinzie [personal communication, 1998].)

- Before the presentation, ask individuals in the audience what they want to or expect to hear (Thank you, Lance Dublin [personal communication].)
- Put the questions at the beginning, not just the end. (Thank you, Eric Vogt [personal communication].)

In the late 1980s, I managed marketing and customer service for a wholesale financial services start-up. To increase the odds that our chairman and CEO would be successful in raising funds, our venture capital backers brought in Jerry Weisman, the famed pitchman who had taught hundreds of high-tech honchos how to pitch their companies to investors. In an earlier television career, Weisman used to prepare questions for Mike Wallace to ask. Some people call his current business "CEO Charm School." I was preparing the slide deck for the road show, so I got to attend.

Weisman told us to pay utmost attention to the "3 V's," verbal, vocal, and visual, because style is more important than substance. He played videotapes of Ronald Reagan delivering a content-free but compelling presentation to make his point.

The visual lessons are to maintain eye contact, adopt a comfortable and open stance, smile, and keep your hands out of your pockets. Vocally, you must present at the right volume, inflection, and rate. The visual and vocal must be in sync with the verbal because contradictions confuse the listener. A videotape of the elder Bush was a great example of this.

Weisman had other advice as well:

- Silence is not deadly; wait it out.
- All groups are essentially the same.
- Don't ask yourself, "How am I doing?" Rather, ask "How are *they* doing?"
- Connect with your audience.
- Create empathy.
- Solicit their feedback. Use the power of projection.

Before uttering a word at any presentation, I take a deep breath, scan the crowd, and silently repeat these mantras I learned from Dorothy Sarnoff (1989):

- I'm glad that I'm here.
- I'm glad that you're here.
- I know that I know.
- I care about you.

The Decker Communications Program I attended in 1987 suggests there are six signals all audiences want to hear:

- I will not waste your time.
- I know who you are.
- I am well organized.
- I know my subject.
- Here is my most important part.
- I am finished.

BODY LANGUAGE

I'm losing my hearing. It's not like someone turned down the volume knob. It's more like the sliders on my mental audio mixer are set to drop out a few frequencies. A sound in an otherwise quiet room is crystal clear, but a voice in a crowded room fades into the generalized noise. This got me to thinking about nonverbal communication and how much I might be missing by not hearing the words.

Albert Mehrabian (1972) has pioneered the understanding of communications since the 1960s. He established that when we speak with one another face-to-face, 7 percent of meaning is in the words that are spoken, 38 percent of meaning is in the way words are said, and 55 percent of meaning is in the facial expression of the speaker. To take this into account when speaking with others, pay attention to your tone of voice since it carries five times more meaning than the words. Play your voice as a musician plays an instrument. Look at one another's face and body language; use video images if you're at a distance. Pay attention to the other person's moment-to-moment changes in expression.

Make a recording of yourself speaking and listen to it, even if you hate it. You're accustomed to hearing rich, resonant, deep tones because your skull is vibrating, not because that's really the way you sound. I do dry runs of presentations using Adobe Breeze. I can review rough spots and also get a record of the precise time dedicated to each portion of the talk.

WRITE TO THE POINT

My first assignment as a brand-new lieutenant at Headquarters U.S. Army Europe in Heidelberg was to write a set of instructions on how to process a personnel roster about to be sent to eight divisions and personnel service companies. *How hard could this be?* I thought. After all, I'd earned a bachelor's degree in social science less than two years before. I dashed off the instructions and soon received a call to report to the commanding officer.

Colonel Brannock had covered my two pages with so much red ink I could hardly read them. *Who does he think he is?* I thought to myself. But I came to my senses before saying anything. He was the authority. If he said red was black, my response should be, "Yes, sir!" His criticism sank in. He was right: my writing was bloated, confusing, flowery college-speak. My instructions were twice as long as necessary, and they wouldn't have gotten the job done. I began learning to write that day. I had to unlearn a lot of claptrap I'd picked up in college, a style of writing meant to sound sophisticated rather than to get the message across.

Each of my three favorite books on writing offer simple yet profound advice:

- Find your voice and write in it, from *Write to the Point* (1991) by Bill Stott
- Writing is a process; you can get better at it, from *On Writing Well* (1976) by William Zinsser
- Get in the spirit, from *Bird by Bird* (1995) by Anne Lamott

If you encounter writer's block, simply write down what you'd tell an imaginary friend, whatever it is. You can always delete it. Sometimes the first sentence is the toughest part of writing, so write whatever comes into your head. Failing that, steal someone else's first line and go from there.

Natalie Goldberg offers crazy wisdom that makes me laugh but delivers the goods. This advice is from *Writing Down the Bones* (1986):

Composting. Our bodies are garbage heaps: we collect experience, and from the decomposition of the thrown-out eggshells, spinach leaves, coffee grinds, and old steak bones of our minds come nitrogen, heat, and very fertile soil. Out of this fertile soil bloom our poems and stories. But this does not come all at once. It takes time.

The problem is we think we exist. We think our words are permanent and solid and stamp us forever. That's not true. We write in the moment. Every minute we change. At any point, we can step out of our frozen selves and our ideas and begin fresh. That is how writing is. Instead of freezing us, it frees us.

Timing your writing adds pressure and helps to heat things up and blast through the internal censor. Also, keeping your hand moving and not stopping add to the heat, so a beautiful cake may rise out of the mixture of your daily details [p. 49].

You can't write if you can't listen. The father of chef Alice Waters offers this advice (McDonald, 1983):

If you're really listening, you should be able to:

- Repeat the essence of what has been said.
- Repeat the feeling with which it was said.
- Sum up what you have heard to the satisfaction of the person who was talking.

Don Norman (2004) writes:

It has become commonplace to rail against the evils of PowerPoint talks; you know, those dull, boring never-ending ordeals where the speaker—or should I say "reader"—displays what appears to be a never-ending progression of slides, each with numerous bulleted points, sometimes coming on to the screen from unexpected directions in unexpected ways, each one being slowly read to the audience. PowerPoint should be banned, cries the crowd. Edward Tufte, the imperious critic of graphic displays has weighed in with a document entitled "The Cognitive Style of PowerPoint," in which, among other things, he credits poor PowerPoint slides with contributing to disaster with NASA's space shuttle Columbia (Tufte, 2003).

I respectfully submit that all of this is nonsense. Pure nonsense, accompanied by poor understanding of speech making and of the difference between the requirements for a speech-giver, the speech-listener (the audience), and for the reader of a printed document. These are three different things. Tufte—and other critics—seem to think they are one and the same thing. Nonsense, I say, once again.

People have been giving bad talks for centuries. Yes, I share the frustration of the critics, but don't blame the technology: blame the speaker. I have also seen truly excellent talks, some without visual aids, some with photographs, and guess what, some using PowerPoint. The critics are so busy blaming the messenger that they have lost track of the point.

WIN WITH POWERPOINT

Slide after slide of three-bullet sentence fragments is an awful thing to watch. If the presenter reads them aloud, it makes a bad spectacle worse. Yet PowerPoint has become the language of business.

PowerPoint is also learning's most popular authoring tool. Many software packages enable you to narrate a PowerPoint and upload it to the Web, compressing the files for download or online viewing. But if live lectures are ineffective, prerecorded lectures on the Web are *very* ineffective.

Being an expert doesn't make one an expert presenter. Sadly, many business experts think the purpose of a PowerPoint presentation is to expose the audience to content, as if emotion played no part in getting a message across. Nevertheless, it makes no more sense to blame PowerPoint for boring presentations than to blame fountain pens for forgery.

Steve Denning (2005), the author of several fine books on storytelling, recalls not being able to get into someone's PowerPoint presentation because the speaker was presenting *his* framework. He recognized that PowerPoint can be too concrete and abandoned it in his own presentations in favor of telling stories. No one missed it. When you hear a powerful story, you make it your own. Your imagination makes it *your* story, and that's something you'll remember.

Cliff Atkinson literally wrote the book on how to prepare dramatic presentations. His *Beyond Bullet Points: Using Microsoft PowerPoint to Create Presentations That Inform, Motivate, and Inspire* (2005) shows how to use Hollywood's techniques to write a script to focus ideas, storyboard the script to clarify ideas, and produce the script to engage the audience.

PowerPoint is not just words. Atkinson recently told me the story of a presentation that made a $253 million difference. Attorney Mark Lanier had pleaded the case against Merck in the first Vioxx trial. Before preparing his presentation, he scanned every book on using PowerPoint he could find. When he read *Beyond Bullet Points*, he invited Atkinson to Houston to lend a hand putting together his presentation. Atkinson says, "We used the three-step approach from the book. Then Mark's flawless delivery took the experience beyond what I imagined possible. He masterfully framed his argument with an even flow of projected images, and blended it with personal stories, physical props, a flip chart, a tablet PC, a document projector and a deeply personal connection with his audience."

> Lanier is considered one of the best trial lawyers in the United States, and he appeared to be in top form throughout his argument, using a fast-moving PowerPoint presentation to back his contention that Merck had denied Vioxx's risks and deceived doctors and consumers [Berensson, 2005].

"The key portion of the trial was the opening statements," Lanier said. "We used a compelling visual montage as part of a PowerPoint opening. The defense basically read behind a podium as if delivering a scientific dissertation" (Tooher, 2006). In his three-hour opening statement, Lanier addressed jurors in simple language and without notes, using projected PowerPoint images—including an ATM machine and a bulldozer—to symbolize the powerful marketing push behind Vioxx. Lanier said his part-time preaching has helped him connect with jurors. "One important aspect of preaching is speaking to people's hearts and minds," Lanier said. "You try to give information, but also try to motivate" (Tooher, 2006).

Fortune magazine said Merck's legal team read much of its presentation and used PowerPoints with "stodgy, corporate headshots" or excerpts from jargon-laden documents (Illinois Trial Practice Weblog, 2005). If you are thinking, "I don't have time to do something elaborate like that," then hold it. Put that in perspective. If you spend months on a project, it's worth a few days to wrap the results in an effective presentation.

If you're using PowerPoint as an authoring system, remember that a presentation and self-directed learning are totally different experiences, and the fact that they both might be in PowerPoint doesn't change that fact. Posting PowerPoint to a Web site does not make for effective eLearning, no matter how rapid the process.

MAKE NOTES

When I was in graduate school, my notes were logical. I boiled topics down to their essence. Once I committed these distillations to paper, they'd take up residence in my head through exams and perhaps a few months more. Figure 7.2 shows a typical example of my notes from that era.

FIGURE 7.2. Taking Notes in Business School

Today I use notes as an active thinking tool. They are experimental. I have stacks of journals filled with unruly scribbles like those shown in Figure 7.3.

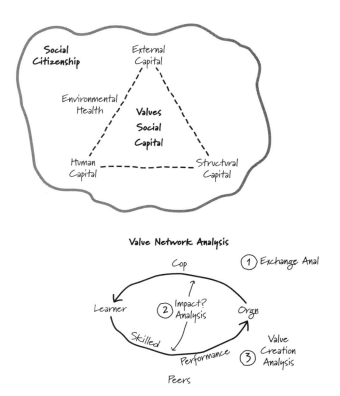

FIGURE 7.3. Making Notes: Thinking About This Book

Mind maps are not maps of the mind. Rather, they are network diagrams that show relationships as well as facts. They're handy for brainstorming, planning a presentation, describing a complex idea, taking notes, or indexing a book or report. You can draw them by hand or let your computer help out. Figure 7.4 shows a small chunk of a mind map I drew while thinking about the structure of this book.

I generally draw mind maps on my computer. I enjoy being able to change things with a simple drag-and-drop. Also, it's a snap to export a computer-generated map to an outline or a graphic.

Mind maps are best learned by drawing a few. Go to the site of MindJet (http://www.mindjet.com), download a trial copy of its software, and play with it. Begin by labeling a spot in the center, say, "Presentation." Pressing the Insert key yields another branch. Give it a short label, say "Introduction." Press

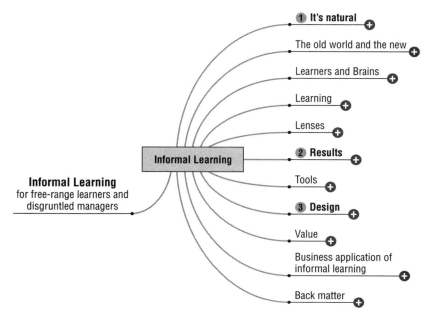

FIGURE 7.4. Early Mind Map for This Book

Insert again and you get subbranches. You might name them "Why this matters," "What's in it for you," and "How to get some." Click the center again and press Insert; you get another primary branch. This may sound complicated, but it's not. In fact, it's so intuitive, you'll be jotting down mind maps for all manner of things. There are several kinds of mind-mapping software on the market. MindJet is my runaway favorite; I've used it for years. In fact, when I'm preparing a white paper or a presentation, firing up MindManager (MindJet's offering) is the first step in the process.

Sometimes my mind maps are for high-order organization to which I add detail later on, as shown in Figure 7.5.

Linear thinking may appear accurate but doesn't convey the experience of seeing a mind map and immediately understanding. Mind maps are also useful in collaboration because participants can literally see what's going on. Relationships are clear. People join one another in making the map work rather than sparring over different viewpoints.

AND DON'T FORGET

Reflection is a vital part of learning. It's like editing is to professional writing. If your writing is going to be the best that it can be, you must revisit your work

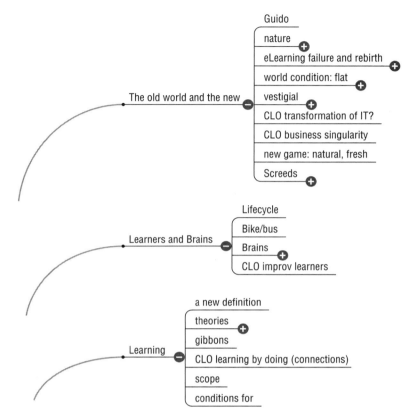

FIGURE 7.5. Expanded Portion of Figure 7.4

to tighten up, squeeze out the awkward parts, fix the grammar, and otherwise polish it. If you want to retain and use what you learn, you must revisit it. If you learn something and don't come back to it in a day or two, at least half of it will have disappeared. If you want to plant something in memory for a good while, revisit it soon after the first exposure and then again a week or two later.

Immediate repetition keeps thoughts from dropping out of your short-term memory, which has quite limited capacity. When you meet someone for the first time, the way to remember the person's name is to repeat it in replying to him or her. For longer-term memory, visiting something again strengthens the mental pathway to that idea. Repetition can be boring but useful for gluing things into place. More effective than that is linking what you've learned to what you already know. As James Burke advised on his television series, *Connections*, "Whenever you encounter a new idea, make a connection."

Sometimes my mind churns new concepts or ideas for days before coming up with productive new connections. Other times they never arrive at all. That's okay. It is a lot more time-consuming to learn stuff over and over (like, right before a test) than it is to never let go, by reflecting on what's new.

HEALTH

It is important to make a distinction between what has been called "neck-up" learning versus "neck-down" learning. What leaders are generally used to is "neck-up" learning, which entails acquiring knowledge, data, and information. It is safe, easy, clean and comfortable. On the other hand, "neck-down" learning occurs at the gut level. It is risky, difficult, messy and uncomfortable. It is also real, deep, transformational and invaluable.
—DEEPAK SETHI

When I was in high school, my biology teacher told us that autonomic functions like heartbeat were controlled by the brain. He was in error. My heart has a mind of its own. It contains its own timers. If a surgeon removes a heart during a transplant procedure, it continues to beat. This background made me receptive to the findings of the Institute of HeartMath, a research group that has been studying "heart intelligence" since 1991, although the roots of its findings are ancient.

Dating back to the ancient Greeks, human thinking and feeling, or intellect and emotion, have been considered separate functions. These contrasting aspects of the soul constantly battled for control of the human psyche. In Plato's view, emotions were like wild horses that had to be reined in by the intellect, while Christian theology has long equated emotions with sins and temptations to be resisted with reason and willpower.

I've watched neurologist Antonio Damasio show pictures of emotions at work; they're quite real. Researcher Daniel Goleman finds that emotional intelligence trumps mere intellect. HeartMath researchers have found that synchronizing the rhythms of emotion and intellect is a pathway to calm and coherence. When heart and mind are out of phase, we become less aware. Incoherence dulls the senses. "The heart," writes the Institute of HeartMath (2004), "is, in fact, a highly complex, self-organized information processing center with its own functional 'brain' that communicates with and influences the cranial brain via the nervous system, hormonal system and other pathways. These influences profoundly affect brain function and most of the body's major organs, and ultimately determine the quality of life."

Stanford brain researcher Robert Sapolsky asks an audience how many have lost a close relation to smallpox. How about scarlet fever? Typhoid? No hands go up, yet these were primary killers of the nineteenth century. Then he asks to see the hands for cancer, then heart attack, stroke, and diabetes. Now, nearly every hand in the room is raised. These are stress-induced illnesses. When the brain is stressed, it shovels hormones into the bloodstream. This is good if you need to outrun a hungry bear, but devastating if left to run rampant for an eight-hour workday. The hormone cortisol shuts down any body function that doesn't channel energy to the immediate task.

In nature, after a while you either escape the bear or get eaten, both of which relieve the stress. In the office, however, the mind conjures up bears that never let up. All-day stress overtaxes the body, shutting down short-term memory, recall, physical growth, sex drive, and more. At the same time, it sets the heart to racing and pumps adrenaline into the bloodstream. The effect is that stress is six times more likely to lead to cancer or heart disease than smoking tobacco, low HDL cholesterol, or high blood pressure (Sapolsky, 2004).

In addition to health problems, stress cuts productivity. Half of American adults report being stressed over the course of a year, and half of them don't find a way to improve their situation. Gloria Mack, a professor at the University of California at Irvine, has studied the workplace:

A picture of 21st-century office work emerged that was, she says, "far worse than I could ever have imagined." Each employee spent only 11 minutes on any given project before being interrupted and whisked off to do something else. What's more, each 11-minute project was itself fragmented into even shorter three-minute tasks, like answering e-mail messages, reading a Web page or working on a spreadsheet. And each time a worker was distracted from a task, it would take, on average, 25 minutes to return to that task. To perform an office job today, it seems, your attention must skip like a stone across water all day long, touching down only periodically [Thompson, 2005].

The Institute of HeartMath (2004) reports:

A recent survey revealed that 75% of Americans describe their jobs as stressful, with more than one in four reporting experiencing high levels of stress "nearly every day." It is currently estimated that 60% of all absenteeism from work is caused by stress, resulting in roughly 1 million persons absent each workday. Moreover, nearly one-fifth of employed adults now acknowledge that workplace stress has caused them to quit a job.

75 to 90% of all visits to healthcare providers result from stress-related disorders. Among the nation's top executives, an estimated $10 to $20 billion is lost each year through absence, hospitalization and early death, much of it a direct result of stress. Multiple long-term studies involving thousands of workers have now demonstrated that people who perceive they have little control over their jobs have significantly increased likelihood of developing heart disease; this association is independent of conventional coronary risk factors, including smoking and high cholesterol levels.

In 1995, Claudia Welss brought HeartMath into the executive program at the University of California at Berkeley. The participating CEOs and business unit heads were expected to return to their organizations with hard solutions to complex global problems, not theories about "soft stuff" like the role of heart intelligence in decision making. When the topic was introduced, there was a stunned silence and the usual signs of withdrawal—heads turning to look out windows, people suddenly realizing they needed to use the restroom. But when the technique was offered and the biofeedback technology was hooked up to a few willing volunteers, seeing was believing. The implications of the internal coherence they observed were obvious. What to do with this new awareness given the prevailing paradigm was not.

Many companies have discovered that the information age requires a new type of intelligence for people to sort through, filter, and effectively process an incredible flow of information:

CalPERS employees effectively transformed an environment of emotional turmoil that had developed in response to the implementation of major organizational change. Key findings after the training indicated significant decreases in anger (20%), distress (21%) depression (26%), sadness (22%), and fatigue (24%), and significant increases in peacefulness (23%) and vitality (10%). There was also a reduction in stress symptoms, including anxiety (21%), sleeplessness (24%) and rapid heartbeats (19%). Organizational quality assessment revealed significant gains in goal clarity (9%) and productivity (4%).

Police officers trained in the HeartMath techniques experienced decreased stress, negative emotions and fatigue, increased calmness and clarity under the acute stress of simulated police calls, and more rapid recalibration following these high-stress scenarios, as compared to an untrained control group. Feelings of depression rose 17% among the untrained officers, while the trained group demonstrated a 13% drop in depression. Fatigue declined among the HeartMath group by 18% and distress by 20%.

At Royal Dutch Shell, rapid heartbeats declined by 38%, tension by 65% and aches and pains by 70%. Participants were 65% less angry, 70% less worried, 87% less fatigued and 68% happier [Institute of HeartMath, 2004].

Time pressure, frustrations with others, unresolved conflicts, and anxiety born of perfectionism stress almost all of us. It doesn't have to be this way. Perceptions lead you into stress, and changing your perceptions can take you away from it.

When you are facing a stressful moment, stop the internal movie that's playing in your mind, and shift your focus to your heart. By shifting your attention to your heart and healthy emotions, you can change your hormonal balance. It educates your perception. By recalibrating your assumptions, you no longer fail to meet expectations.

HeartMath's CEO Bruce Cryer told me that several hospitals have achieved first-year returns of more than $1 million from their participation in HeartMath. Reduced stress translates into lower staff turnover. In one hospital, four hundred nurses and administrative staff practiced HeartMath, and turnover dropped from 27 to 6 percent. Simultaneously, quality of service to patients improved by 20 percent. Another hospital cut turnover from 21 to 5 percent, and a third reduced it from 22 to 9 percent.

HAPPINESS

Happiness may well consist primarily of an attitude toward time. Individuals we consider happy commonly seem complete in the present: we see them constantly in their wholeness, attentive, cheerful, open rather than closed to events, integral in the moment rather than distended across time by regret or anxiety.—ROBERT GRUDIN

Savor the good and de-emphasize the bad. Show gratitude for the good, forgive and neutralize the bad.—MARTY SELIGMAN

My fondest memory is of my son Austin, then three years old, strutting across our living room, saying, "I'm a happy guy."

Are you happy? Happy at work? With life? On a scale of 0 to 10, with 10 being extremely happy, 5 being neutral, and 0 being extremely unhappy, how happy or unhappy do you usually feel? Most Americans rate themselves 7, that is, mildly happy (feeling fairly good and somewhat cheerful). People I've asked usually reply 9 (very happy) or 3 (bummed out).

▷ ▷ *If you're not happy, you should do something about it.*

If you're not happy, you should do something about it. You owe it to yourself. Personally, I've migrated from 3 to 9 on the happiness scale over the past ten years. A major influence was psychologist Marty Seligman (2002). A dozen years back, Marty was pulling weeds in his garden when his five-year-old daughter, Nikki, interrupted with a question. She asked if he remembered what she had been like from ages three to five. She was a whiner, whining every day until her fifth birthday. That day she decided to stop whining. It was the hardest thing she'd ever done.

"Daddy, if I can stop whining, you can stop being a grouch," said Nikki. That precocious observation changed the direction of Seligman's work and sparked the development of the positive psychology movement.

At the behavioral level, Nikki was absolutely right. Her dad had been a hard-charging, no-nonsense sort of guy who sometimes carried the weight of the world on his shoulders. On a deeper level, Seligman realized that a parent's responsibility was not to correct his child's shortcomings or try to make her into something she was not. Rather, the parent should celebrate and reinforce the good things that already exist within the child. Raising children is about amplifying strengths and helping the child find a place in life where they can live them to the fullest (Seligman, 2002).

In January 1998, Seligman and his family were vacationing in a rented house in the Yucatan. He phoned famed psychologist Mihaly Csikszentmihalyi, author of *Flow*, and asked, "I know you and Isabella have plans for New Year's. Would you cancel them and join us in the Yucatan? I want to talk with you about founding a field called positive psychology." Next he invited Ray Fowler, his mentor and CEO of the American Psychological Association. After a week of work, punctuated by hikes in the jungle, the three had come up with the content, method, and infrastructure for directing this shift in the direction of psychology.

A fundamental axiom of Seligman's work is that "you should not devote overly much effort to correcting your weaknesses. Rather, I believe that the highest success in living and the deepest emotional satisfaction comes from building and using your signature strengths" (Seligman, 2002, p. 249). This is a radical departure from psychology as we have known it. Traditional psychology focuses on fixing what's broken. Its goal has been to make deviant people normal. Like medicine, psychology is wedded to the disease model: if you're not sick, we can't help you.

Seligman's direction is to help well people become better. There's no reason to stop improving once you hit acceptable. This is akin to the phrase

Frank Burns devised for U.S. Army recruiting after sampling the zeitgeist of the human potential movement at Esalen: "Be all that you can be."

Authentic happiness tells us that "the good life consists in using your signature strengths as frequently as possible in work, life, and parenting to obtain authentic happiness and abundant gratification. The meaningful life has one additional feature: using your signature strengths in the service of something larger than you are" (Seligman, 2002, p. 249).

You're probably wondering what your signature strengths are. To find out your signature strengths, go to authentichappiness.org and take the VIA Signature Strengths Survey. It's quick and free. When you've finished, you not only learn your top five signature strengths, but also how you compare to everyone who has taken the survey, people of your gender, people your age, people in your line of work, people with your level of education, and people who reside in your and neighboring zip codes.

My results on the survey gave me determination to work and play in ways that grow from my signature values. Since I've been ambivalent about what to do in life since my teens (having been a systems analyst, salesman, manager, marketing director, publicist, trainer, designer, author, entrepreneur, programmer, CEO, Webmaster, army officer, market researcher, sales manager, consultant, direct marketer, speaker, and other things), pinning down my values was a major step for me.

You can think of your work on several levels. You've got a job, which is what you do to pay the bills. You have a career, which is where you advance in pay, position, and prestige. And finally, you have a calling, where you passionately do what you were put on earth to do. Values alone don't tell the story. You are born with a genetic disposition to happiness. That's your point of departure, which is influenced by how you lead your life.

These things can contribute to your happiness: living in a wealthy democracy, getting married, avoiding negative events, building a rich social network, and getting religion. Things that make no difference in your happiness are money, health, more education, changing your race, or moving to a sunnier climate.

Sensual pleasure is fleeting; it won't deliver long-term happiness. I enjoy hiking in the Swiss Alps, a glass of crisp white wine, a bucket of steamed clams, the scent of melted Gruyère cheese, and giving Smokey the Wonderdog a pat on the head. However, these are momentary pleasures. Too much of anything becomes routine, fails to arouse us, and eventually slips out of our awareness. This is why the rich are no happier than you and me.

Seligman (2002) warns that "to the extent that you believe the past dictates the future, you will allow yourself to be a passive vessel and not try to change its course. I think past history in general is overrated" (p. 67).

Choose work that lets you exercise your signature strengths every day. As a manager, select employees whose signature strengths match the work you expect them to do. Lasting, fulfilling activities are what keeps us happy.

AN UNSCHOOLED SUCCESS

Fittingly, Leonard Pitt and I talked while sitting at a café table at Berkeley's French Hotel. I asked him to share his story. After all, he's a self-taught author, historian, lecturer, teacher, and artist.

Leonard hated public school in Detroit. In third grade, the teacher had him stand up and asked for the product of 3 × 3. When Leonard didn't know, she slapped him. The next afternoon, she asked why he'd told his parents she didn't like him. He hadn't. She insisted he was lying.

In high school, one teacher made a difference, and he and Leonard are still friends. The assignment was to make an illustration for this Alexander Pope quotation: "'Tis education forms the common mind; just as the twig is bent the tree's inclined." Looking at Leonard's feeble attempt, the teacher advised him to dramatize. It's like theater, where the action on stage is a separate reality. This triggered a change in perspective. Leonard's mediocre grades turned into A's.

Leonard did not graduate from high school but managed to join a bunch of college graduates at the Art Center School in Los Angeles to study graphic design. During a break, he took a job with an ad agency in Detroit. But it was awful, and he dropped out and moved to Paris.

Leonard moved into a cheap maid's room near the Louvre and remained there for seven years. He soon began studying under Etienne Decroux, a self-educated philosopher and artist who had taught Marcel Marceau the art of mime. He studied grounded movement and came to know the body. He never skipped a class, fearing he might miss one of those "thundering moments" that could cause him to rethink his whole world.

In 1996, Leonard discovered a book of old photos of Paris by Charles Marville (1816–1879), who had been commissioned by the City of Paris to document medieval Paris before its destruction by urban renewal at the hands of Baron Haussmann. He found pictures of his former neighborhood. In the 1960s, he'd thought the buildings ancient, but they had been erected in 1886. Leonard read, read, and read some more. He photocopied photos from the book and went to Paris to find them. Assembling his book of before and after walking tours consumed five years. Unable to interest a publisher in the United States, a French friend said, "Let me introduce you to my publisher." *Paris disparu* (2002) is a best seller in France.

What advice would Leonard offer future free-range learners? "Find out what you're interested in and pursue it." It's like a friend's old dog, he told me. The dog's owner pours the dry pellets of dog food into the dog's bowl. The dog walks over and slams the bowl several times with his muzzle. Pellets scatter across the kitchen floor, and the dog happily laps them up one by one. Leonard prefers messy too.

A mime and photographer, Leonard is a very visual fellow. But aren't we all? The next chapter addresses how we learn through our eyes.

ENVISIONING

8

WE HUMANS ARE sight mammals. We learn almost twice as well from images plus words as from words alone. Visual language engages both hemispheres of the brain. Pictures translate across cultures, education levels, and age groups. Yet the majority of the content of corporate learning is text. Schools spend years on verbal literacy and but hours on visual literacy. It's time for us to open our eyes to the possibilities.

Envisioning is a powerful means of informal learning. *Envisioning* means:

- Seeing from a fresh perspective
- Looking at relationships and nonlinear sequences
- Imagining and prototyping new ideas
- Focusing and documenting the flow of group discussion
- Shortening the time it takes learners to say, "Now I see"
- What visionaries do

Envisioning results in insight, the capacity to gain a clear, deep, and sometimes sudden understanding of a complicated problem or situation. Insight is to informal learning as study is to formal learning. It's how you achieve your learning goal.

Bob Horn's *Visual Language* (1999) quantifies how much visuals improve decision making, make a better impression, shorten meetings, promote group consensus, and persuade audiences (Figure 8.1).

Visual literacy accelerates learning because the richness of the whole picture can be taken in at a glance. Visual metaphors unleash new ideas and

> *No problem can be solved from the same level of thinking that created it.*
> **ALBERT EINSTEIN**

Section C. Design and effectiveness
Visual Language Has a Proven Effectiveness

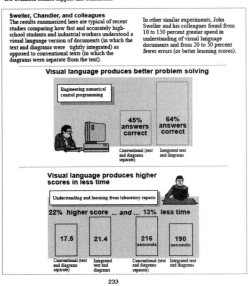

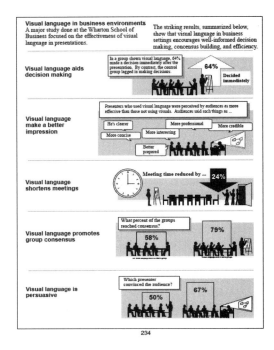

FIGURE 8.1. The Effectiveness of Visual Language

Source: Horn (1998, pp. 233–234). Reprinted with permission.

spark innovation. Visuals accelerate the learning process and make meetings more productive, efficient, and memorable. Having a sharper eye increases the depth of perception and enjoyment of life.

FEED THE EYES

Johannes Gutenberg began printing Bibles in Mainz in the 1450s. These books were massive, not something to carry around. The first truly portable books, paperbacks, were printed by Aldus Manutius in Venice forty years later, about the time Columbus reached America. (You can see pages from both printers' works on the Web at www.informl.com.)

The pages of Aldus's books look strikingly modern. Hold a page of a five-hundred-year-old book next to a page from a book printed recently, and you see why. Both have unbroken blocks of text, similar margins, and page numbers in either the upper or lower outside corner. True, Aldus's books are in italics (Aldus invented italics so he could get more on a page), but aside from the font, books haven't changed much in appearance since the 1490s.

Where are the pictures? Why is the text all one color, the letters all one size? Like book publishers, the business world seems to pride itself on dull presentation techniques, whether mind-numbingly boring financial reports or three-bullet PowerPoint presentations. Although it is an oversimplification, some of us favor our brain's left hemisphere and others favor the right. Many left-brained learners don't need or want business documents that contain graphics as well as words; many right-brained learners can hardly live without them.

Graphics are not fluff. Consider how they can improve informal learning throughout any organization. Graphics work wonders when you need to:

- Bring deeper understanding to complex subject matter.
- Share results of dynamic meetings with others.
- Help the senior team see the big picture and focus attention.
- Improve the decision-making process.
- Integrate a new initiative throughout an organization.
- Speed adoption of major change.
- Help everyone picture their role in organizational transformation.

Graphics are similar to prototypes, for they are an external representation of ideas, a shared space for discussion. Imagine a senior management team discussing a new strategy. A business artist simultaneously translates the thrust of their conversation into large, wall-mounted drawings—paper murals. Periodically the group checks the murals and the relationships they imply. Is that what we meant? Is there a better way? The group tries to make the picture represent the best outcome instead of trying to score political points off one another. When they have concluded, a redrawn map is how they communicate the substance of the meeting throughout the organization.

XPLANE and I developed the poster shown in Figure 8.2 to clarify how graphics clarify meaning and accelerate communication (XPLANE, 2002).

TRANSFORMATION AT NATIONAL SEMICONDUCTOR

Fifteen years ago, the first application of what we now know as group graphics helped National Semiconductor get on the path to the success it enjoys today. In 1967, Charlie Sporck joined National as CEO, moved the company to Silicon Valley, and ruled the highly successful company for the next twenty-seven years.

National was the leader in analog semiconductor chips, the chips that regulate voltage in iPods and television sets and that make radios work. These chips can be found in almost all electronic products. The military consumed them at a record pace throughout the cold war, and the chips made the lunar

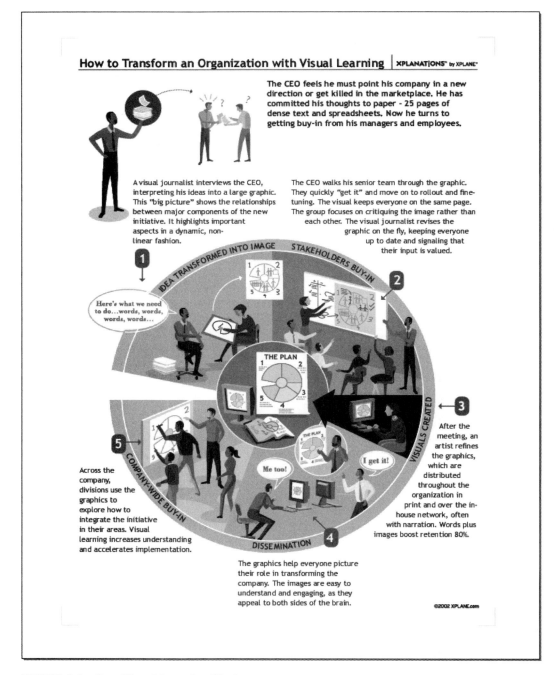

FIGURE 8.2. How Visual Learning Works

Source: XPLANE. Copyright © 2002. Reprinted by permission.

missions possible. With this heritage and reputation, National was for many years one of the three most profitable and well-known semiconductor firms in Silicon Valley, along with Intel and Advanced Micro Devices.

By the late 1980s digital was becoming the dominant technology, and Intel, LSI Logic, and other firms were founded on their ability to design and build digital chips. But National never really embraced the digital age and only dabbled in digital technology. Although it made a number of digital chips, they were not market leaders; the company's expertise still lay in analog design and chip building. Throughout the 1990s, National struggled with whether it should dump analog and embrace only digital or somehow merge the two.

During this time, the threat from Japan became severe, and Charlie Sporck left National to found Sematech (SEmiconductor MAnufacturing TECHnology), a consortium that designed production equipment and processing techniques to compete effectively with Japan. With Sporck away, National was poorly run, and sales and profits fell. Many people thought the company would have to declare bankruptcy and perhaps shut down. Charlie quickly returned to take over again but realized that he was not the right man to take National into the new century. In 1991 he hired Gil Amelio from Rockwell Semiconductor to act as a turnaround CEO to save the company.

Amelio was brilliant technically, a visionary, and business focused. He knew that some tough and unpopular decisions had to be made, and made quickly. Over a holiday period, he wrote up a white paper that set forth his vision for the new National Semi. This document was technical, dense, and virtually unreadable by most of the staff. Few people in Cupertino understood the vision, but Gil wanted the message distributed to five hundred managers around the world. Making things more difficult, he was no Steve Jobs or Jack Welch in the charisma department. He was an introverted engineer and could not communicate effectively or with much excitement. So he asked Kevin Wheeler, who directed National Semiconductor University, to find a way to communicate the vision to the top managers in the company. His initial thought was to simply distribute the document, perhaps by e-mail, and ask them to read it.

Fortunately Amelio had asked Bob Miles, a professor at Emory University and long-time friend, to head up an eight-person change team focused on helping transform National. Kevin and Bob instantly knew that sending this vision out as document would accomplish nothing. Most likely no one would read the white paper.

Kevin had recently attended a workshop on graphic facilitation led by David Sibbet. "Why don't we try visualizing the Leading Change program?" asked Wheeler. He reasoned that visuals might be the prop to help managers understand the vision and think big. It was a huge risk, and no one was confident that technical engineers would respond positively to drawings. The team was also concerned that Gil would find using what many called cartoons to convey this life-or-death vision to five hundred managers would demean the message. But despite many misgivings and a lot of fear, an associate of Sibbet's company, The Grove Consultants was asked to work with Amelio to render the first sketch of the vision, which is shown in Figure 8.3.

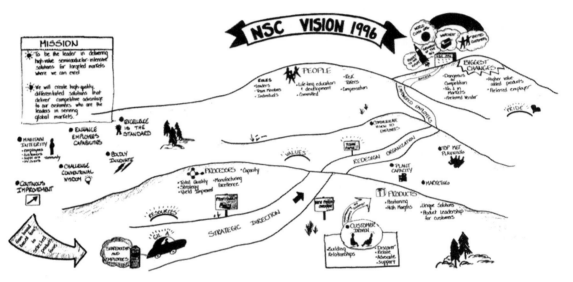

FIGURE 8.3. Initial Sketch of the National Semiconductor Strategic Plan
Source: The Grove Consultants International. Reprinted with permission.

Wheeler and Miles presented this to Amelio early one morning, both pretty certain he would order them to forget all about cartoons. To their amazement, he instantly saw the potential of this kind of presentation and had numerous suggestions about the quality and content of the drawing.

Wheeler had the associate call David Sibbet to develop a more robust presentation. With those assurances, Sibbet joined the planning committee. Over several days of discussion, Wheeler's group gave Sibbet a clearer picture of the business situation: that National Semi was adrift, that Amelio wanted to go where no one had gone before, and that the company needed to focus, dump the junk, and head up-market. Sibbet came back to the change team a few weeks later with another version of the drawing, shown in Figure 8.4, using *Star Trek* as metaphor. The seven-member organizational effectiveness committee loved the metaphor and erupted with suggestions. This was getting closer to something they could use. An additional revision is shown in Figure 8.5.

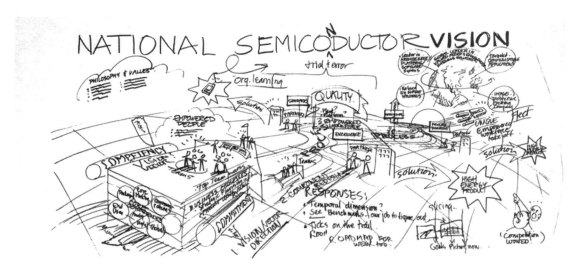

FIGURE 8.4. The First Vision of National Semiconductor as *Star Trek*

Source: The Grove Consultants International. Reprinted with permission.

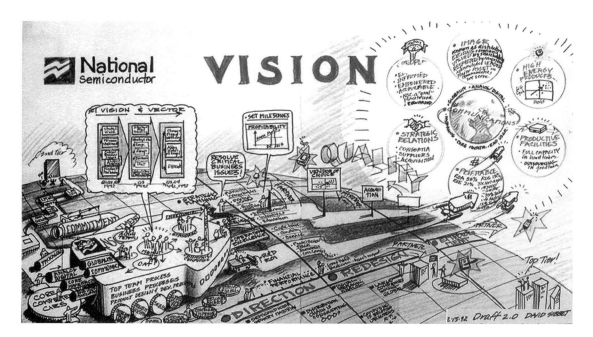

FIGURE 8.5. Refined Vision of National Semiconductor as *Star Trek*

Source: The Grove Consultants International. Reprinted with permission.

The team agreed that the vision elements were effective and that the spaceship metaphor was good, but there needed to be a place where the story of the past and of current progress could be recorded. Bob Miles asked Sibbet to make the mural twice as long, with lots of white space and question marks in the middle to show that the journey to achieve the vision was just beginning (Figure 8.6). No one knew what roads the group would travel. In fact, the organization effectiveness team intended to engage National leaders in answering those questions explicitly through organization redesign and other strategies.

FIGURE 8.6. The Extended Mural
Source: The Grove Consultants International. Reprinted with permission.

The team was so taken with this approach they asked Sibbet to stay and graphically facilitate the design session for the week-long Leading Change workshop that would deliver the new vision, and consult on how to use visuals to support experiential engagement.

The off-site workshop began with two days of PowerPoint presentations in a poorly lit, cavernous room. Then, when senior executives were on a coffee break, Sibbet and Wheeler taped the vision mural to a side wall, since there was no room up front. Because the room was very dark, Sibbet used an overhead projector to spotlight the mural. As the executives began trickling back in, they were immediately attracted to this spotlit cartoon (Figure 8.6) and began congregating around it, discussing some of the words on the mural about the history of National. Sibbet was on the agenda to explain the vision mural, so he stood before the mural and role-played how to use it. He told the vision story as if he were Gil Amelio. The energy level of the room shot up and the group became alive as they began suggesting changes and improvements.

There was general agreement that this was a great way to spread the word about the new vision. Within a few months, that mural became the centerpiece of Leading Change workshops that would cascade down through the organization, each session beginning with an executive telling the story in front of the mural much the way they had seen it done at the off-site meeting.

The team at National charged with communicating the vision and developing the change program knew that focusing around the graphic would be the most powerful and effective way to make the vision real. They developed Leading Change, a week-long workshop featuring lots of interactive discussion around the vision using graphics that the workshop participants were asked to create themselves. It also contained business school–style cases, financial exercises, and deep discussions about change and how to deal with it personally and with employees.

Leading Change was facilitated by the organizational effectiveness team members themselves, without the help of external consultants, but they insisted on being trained in graphic facilitation methods by Sibbet's consultants. As part of the workshop, people were challenged to come up with both feedback on the National Vision and a vision for their own group that aligned with the big vision. Hundreds of Leading Change workshops of thirty-five to forty people were held. Inputs led to two full updates of the overall National Vision and several dozen divisional visions. One divisional vision is shown in Figure 8.7.

FIGURE 8.7. Vision of the Analog Quality Assurance and Reliability Group
Source: The Grove Consultants International. Reprinted with permission.

The Organizational Effectiveness team and consultants from The Grove facilitated many of these subsequent business planning and visions processes. The new visions provided the framework for organizational redesign in major divisions. With a common language and format, people could talk across boundaries.

The pictures enabled everyone to understand where the company was coming from and where it was going. The murals appeared in the company magazine, starred in in-house videos, influenced company conversations, and expanded into quality control. For some employees, graphically facilitated sharing rallies in Singapore were their first professional conference experience.

Annual improvements to the mural were the catalyst for change that rolled through the organization. By year four, 95 percent of National Semi's employee's were familiar with the firm's vision.

In 1994, National Semi was a visually driven company. The company had gone from the brink of bankruptcy in 1991 to profitability in 1994. A variety of factors played a part in the dramatic changes that took place at National: the economy was improving, National was recovering from the heavy costs of acquiring Fairchild Semiconductor, and the electronics industry was booming. But there is no doubt that the work of the internal change team, the global focus on communicating and living change, and the graphically facilitated processes introduced by David Sibbet and The Grove Consultants International, had a big hand in it.

Visualizing went out of style at National when Steve Jobs snatched Gil Amelio to become CEO at Apple. Amelio's successor chose to go his own direction in his own style and did not continue to evolve the vision. Even so, most of what was on the original vision came to be, and National remains a successful company.

Members of the original National organizational effectiveness team spread throughout Silicon Valley and continue to work in creative and visual ways. David Sibbet has discovered that in today's noisy information environment, few other forms are as reinforcing as a poster. Files and books disappear from sight and soon vanish from memory, while posters, or Storymaps as The Grove now calls them, are persistent: always visible, full of life and meaning, and inviting continuing dialogue. Stories are the glue of organizations and Storymaps anchor the memories.

An enormous amount of learning must take place for a large enterprise to catapult from at the brink of death to record profits in less than four years. When five hundred managers can implement a technology firm's complex, global turnaround strategy in a matter of months, that's success. When 95 percent of the employees of a mammoth multinational corporation can describe their employer's vision, that's a lot of learning. Healthy and prosperous, National Semiconductor is today the world's premier analog company. National's technology makes displays clear and vivid, makes sound more robust, and extends battery life in cellphones. As they say in Santa Clara, "National provides the sight and sound of information."

BOB HORN, INFORMAL LEARNER EXTRAORDINAIRE

Bob Horn is the author of *Mapping Hypertext* (1990) and *Visual Language* (1999), the inventor of information mapping and founder of the company of the same name, and a pioneer in the field of informal learning. His apartment in San Francisco's Pacific Heights is decorated in "1950 branch library style," walled with books. We spent hours there engrossed in conversation about informal learning, visual language, and how Bob learns.

Learning theorists say human beings learn 24/7. You go to a meeting, expecting it to be like every other meeting you've been bored by, but a brilliant facilitator runs it entirely differently from what you expected. You're intrigued. You may read a book on facilitation or take a course on facilitation or give it a try next time you're asked to run a meeting.

Another form of informal learning revolves around coaching. Coaching is akin to psychotherapy. It occurs in a space where we're human. People have a deep need for personal relationships, and if the formal structure of a business doesn't support it, things like coaching pop up to meet the need.

Learning is usually a mix of formal and informal, not all of one kind. Bob and I rapidly came up with a list of dimensions that separate the two (Table 8.1).

TABLE 8.1. Dimensions of Formal and Informal Learning

	Most Formal	*Most Informal*
Intentionality	On purpose	Incidental
Timing	Scheduled	Whenever
Location	Fixed	Anywhere
Contract	Written	None
Structure	Highly structured	Unstructured
Control	Strict	Laissez-faire
Outcomes	Specific	Unstated
Content	Certain	Fuzzy

Bob jotted down the dimensions in his ever-present notebook. I drew a little flower in my notebook to remind me to nurture the idea. Alongside Bob's desk are five years of notebooks. Reflection is an important aspect of learning, and for most of us, if you don't write your thoughts down, they will vanish before you get the opportunity to review them. I'm beginning to think that the more creative a person is, the more likely she will carry a notebook.

Bob's affinity for books began early in life. His mother often took him to the library, where one day he checked out a book on judo. As he read about judo, he modeled some of the moves in a sort of air-judo. As it happened, one of Bob's classmates, Daryl, was a bully and chose Bob as a target for intimidation. One afternoon the two boys found themselves in the same aisle of the local five and dime. Daryl lunged to shove Bob. Bob grabbed Daryl's arm, put his other hand under Daryl's armpit, and threw him to the ground. Daryl ran from the store. Bob learned that how-to books work, and since his encounter with Daryl, he has written nearly a dozen of them.

When someone asks Bob what he does for a living, he'll often say visual communications. From the moment he first saw a Macintosh computer, he knew that computer graphics would open an entire new channel for communication. People around the world would be able to share ideas using a combination of written words and pictures; they would communicate in a visual language.

Having glimpsed the future, he set about investigating the properties of visual language—its word-like units and grammar-like structures. To write a book about these things, he needed a structure. He turned to the linking inherent in Apple's HyperCard. Not content to wait for others, Bob wrote *Mapping Hypertext*, describing the concepts of information mapping and structured writing. Written before the World Wide Web debuted, Bob's book describes how a hypertext Web would work in a way that still rings true today.

Visual Language: Global Communication for the Twenty-First Century (1999) should be required reading for anyone whose work relies on outbound communication. I will not try to communicate verbally when a picture from it tells the story better (see Figure 8.8).

Bob has been a television producer, technical writer, conceptual cartographer, educator, systems analyst, training developer, education researcher, instructor at several universities, inventor, information designer, learning theorist, author of five books and editor of another five, consultant, entrepreneur, executive, policy analyst, and other roles I've probably overlooked.

All of us are exposed to learning opportunities, but few of us make as much of them as Bob. Some of the ways he learns:

- Reflection is integral to learning. Bob milks his experiences for lessons. He doesn't just do a lot of stuff; he also looks for its messages. He keeps notebooks of ideas so he can revisit and add to them.

- Bob is mindful, always alert for new developments, asking himself "What's my angle on this?"

- Curiosity leads Bob out of his comfort zone. In fact, he enjoys expanding his intellectual boundaries. He's certainly not averse to trying the new and unfamiliar.

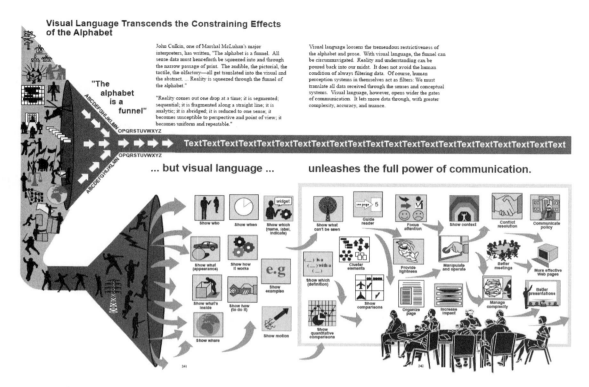

FIGURE 8.8. Visual Language Transcends Words

Source: Horn (1998). Reprinted with permission.

- Experience is the best teacher. Bob loves books. Yet when asked to identify pivotal learning experiences, Bob mentions neither books nor academia.

- Bob knows where things are. He doesn't hide his files in drawers; he keeps them in clearly labeled folders stored vertically so he can scan the topics from where he sits.

- Negativity doesn't get in his way. Bob optimistically takes on new challenges.

Today Bob is working with teams on the biggest global public policy issues of our day, including disposal of nuclear waste, global climate changes, energy security, and health care.

I learned a great deal from talking with Bob. When you think about it, conversation is the main way we learn almost anything. Without it, there would be no knowledge. The next chapter looks at how to nurture meaningful conversations in an organization.

CONVERSATION

9

CONVERSATION HAS MAGIC to it. Dialogue is the most powerful learning technology on earth. Conversations are the stem cells of learning, for they both create and transmit knowledge. Frequent and open conversation increases innovation and learning. Schooling planted a false notion in our heads that real learning is something you do on your own. In fact, we all learn things from other people. People love to talk. Bringing them together brings excitement.

Academically, I made it through tenth grade studying on my own. After that, I couldn't have continued without participating in study groups. When you're taking part in a small group, you spend less time overcoming self-made obstacles and more turning over the concepts of others in your own mind. You give as well as get, and when you teach something to another, you plant it firmly in your own head.

In the Desert Survival Game, a classic organizational development exercise, a small group is told to imagine their small plane has crashed in the Sonora Desert. The task is to prioritize a list of items to help increase the odds of survival. First, each individual ranks the importance of things like the flashlight, the map, matches, and a compass. Then the group comes up with a consensus prioritization. Invariably, the group makes sounder decisions than any individual.

> *Business is a conversation because the defining work of business is conversation—literally. And "knowledge workers" are simply those people whose job consists of having interesting conversations.*
>
> **CHRISTOPHER LOCKE**

Conversation is a meeting of minds with different memories and habits. When minds meet, they don't just exchange facts: they transform them, reshape them, draw different implications from them, engage in new trains of thought. Conversation doesn't just reshuffle the cards: it creates new cards.—THEODORE ZELDIN

Two learners are almost always more effective than one. If two people go through a computer-based learning experience together while sharing one screen, they learn more than if each went at it alone.

What's a manager to do? Often the largest contribution is getting out of people's way, removing barriers, and, in the words of Tom Stewart (2003), "minimizing mindless tasks, meaningless paperwork, unproductive infighting" (p. 87).

STORIES

> This is what human beings are like. There are certain changes here and there, a little movement, but people learn and live through stories and metaphors and connections. That's the sort of animal we are. Dogs sniff each other. Human beings tell stories.—LARRY PRUSAK

> What we are really saying here is that we are constructing knowledge all the time, in conversation, through narrative. We are personalizing it that way, we are constructing it, for ourselves.
> —JOHN SEELY BROWN

Stories are an element of conversation (so long as you don't repeat them word for word). They communicate patterns and give meaning to experience. They are important because we know more than we can tell. They also hold communities together. They are the buzz of the beehive. Steve Denning and Seth Kahan both describe the powerful role of storytelling in reorienting the World Bank to a mission of service rather than simply lending. They sought the highest-leverage change tactics they could implement with zero cost. A story is the ultimate learning object, a self-contained unit of meaning that can be easily distributed.

Steve Denning cautions us that the first step in using a story to change things is to be clear about what change is needed. Positive stories work best. Explicit narratives have more power than abstract principles. To learn to tell stories well, read Denning's recent book, *The Leader's Guide to Storytelling* (2005).

MENTORS, COACHES, AND FACILITATORS

> Live as if you were to die tomorrow. Learn as if you were to live forever.
> —GANDHI

Mentors and coaches initiate conversations. They are a cost-effective way to develop and retain talented people. Some classify the work of mentors and coaches as informal because meetings aren't rigidly scheduled, there's little in the way of curriculum, and often there is no organizational support for them.

It's wise to cultivate a network of experts so you can get answers when you need them. To deal with difficult human situations, good practice is to recruit several colleagues to use as sounding boards and confidential advisers.

Generally a mentor provides career advice and wisdom gleaned from long experience. Often the mentor ventures into the emotional realm, which is off limits in many organizational cultures. Mentorship can be an informal arrangement, or mentors can be assigned. Some mentor relationships last decades.

Coaches usually focus on a particular discipline. The role typically lasts a season or a year or two. Coaches often come from outside the organization and are paid to coach.

You can never see yourself as others see you. Conversation with someone who has already been down the paths you are contemplating is a short-cut to achieving your goals.

A CONVERSATION IN THE UNITED ARAB EMIRATES

People have inhabited the land now known as the United Arab Emirates (UAE) for more than five thousand years. When they arrived, today's arid desert was fertile farmland. As recently as the mid-1960s, most people living in the Emirates raised camels or wandered the desert as nomads. There was not a high school in the land.

In 1970, Dubai began pumping oil. Sheikh Zayed, visionary heir to a three-hundred-year dynasty of Abu Dhabi royalty, brought seven emirates together to form the United Arab Emirates, which sits atop 10 percent of the world's proven oil reserves. Camel paths have become high-speed freeways, dazzling skyscrapers sprout like weeds, the Dubai airport is big enough to get lost in, and green trees and gardens abound (watered from gigantic desalinization plants). Dubai is about as far from Abu Dhabi as San Francisco from San Jose, and the roads through both the UAE and Silicon Valley are bordered with fancy buildings marked Intel, IBM, Oracle, SAP, Microsoft, HP, and other high-tech icons. The late Sheikh Zayed put the UAE in the fast lane, and you can almost see it grow day by day (Figure 9.1).

When you need talent in a hurry, you import it. Four out of five residents of the UAE are expatriates. Europeans, Canadians, and Australians teach school; Americans run businesses; Indians clean houses; Pakistanis pump gas; Nepalese drive taxicabs. The country is currently pushing the UAE private sector to train and employ more locals, a process called Emiratization. Private companies complain that Emirati youngsters lack experience, are disorganized, ask for high salaries, and are not adequately trained.

> The reality today is that we are all interdependent and have to coexist on this small planet. Therefore, the only sensible and intelligent way of resolving differences and clashes of interests, whether between individuals or nations, is through dialogue.
> —DALAI LAMA

FIGURE 9.1. UAE: From Poverty to Ultramodern in Forty Years
Source: Jay Cross.

> There is the possibility for a transformation of the nature of consciousness, both individually and collectively, and that whether this can be solved culturally and socially depends on dialogue.
> —DAVID BOHM

During the Education Without Borders conference for college students from around the world in February 2005, I suggested that the next Emerging Elearning conference could be more pragmatic than in the past and was appointed to chair the international steering committee for the event. The top item on the agenda was the K–12 educational revolution: "How does a country design and implement a world-class, standards-based K–12 educational system? What advice can we offer, especially around issues of technology? What new technologies might enable the UAE to leapfrog current systems? Where do we start? "

It would have been ineffective to simply fly in "experts" to try to shoehorn Western solutions into a Middle Eastern environment. Learning is collaborative. We needed to draw out the best thinking of Ministry of Education officials, local teachers and administrators, students, and our speakers and thought leaders from outside the UAE. A presentation would not suit our needs. Dialogue seemed more on point. We needed to have conversations that matter. The best approach I have seen for creating value from people's collective intelligence and igniting innovation is the World Café.

WORLD CAFÉ

The World Café is a process for fostering conversations that matter. If conversation is the way people create value and innovate in organizations, it is worthwhile to host the best conversations we can.

People spend most of their time at work or at home. Work is a demanding, pressure-packed, rats-in-the-maze race with the clock to get the job done. Home is a comfortable, private space for sharing time with family and individual interests. Neither work nor home, a World Café is a neutral spot where people come together to offer hospitality, enjoy comradeship, welcome diverse perspectives, and have meaningful conversations.

My first experience with the World Café was a meeting of thirty people convened by Brook Manville, McKinsey's first director of knowledge management and later chief learning officer at Saba, to pin down the meaning and utility of the term *human capital*. After a morning of thrashing through whether human capital implied that people were property and other cerebral issues, Eric Vogt, the founder of Communispace Corporation, proposed that instead of the usual call to break into small groups, discuss, and then reconvene to talk what we'd talked about, perhaps we should have a World Café session.

We covered each of four tables with flip chart paper, and someone assigned each table a different aspect of human capital to discuss. People talked among themselves for ten minutes, after which everyone but the table "hosts" switched tables. Each host summarized the discussion thus far, referring to scribbles and diagrams left over from the previous crowd. The groups continued contributing to the conversations, by now searching for patterns and linkages. We rotated once more and then described the fresh insights we had gained.

Since then I have learned from World Café sessions with executives and with close friends. Inevitably, I left with new approaches that I would not have come up with on my own.

> Conversations are the way workers discover what they know, share it with their colleagues, and in the process create new knowledge for the organization. In the new economy, conversations are the most important form of work . . . so much so that the conversation is the organization.
> —ALAN WEBBER

Origins of The World Café

The World Café started in 1995, when organization development consultants Juanita Brown and David Isaacs were getting ready to host the second day of a discussion with two dozen visitors at their house on the slopes of Mt. Tamalpais in Mill Valley, California. Rain was pouring down. While Juanita prepared breakfast and coffee, David arranged TV tables around the living room. A pal said it was beginning to look like a café, but they needed tablecloths; sheets from a flip chart sufficed to cover each table. The friend put a "Café" sign on the front door (Brown & Isaacs, 2005).

> Dialogue is the central aspect of co-intelligence.
> —TOM ATLEE

Conversation began spontaneously, and people began to draw on the café "tablecloths." Excitement built. Someone suggested switching tables to find out what the others were talking about. The energy level rose. After three rounds of conversation, the group shared their drawings and realized they had tapped into their collective intelligence. The World Café was born. It works. But was it appropriate for exploring opportunities to revolutionize education in the UAE?

Brown and Isaacs (2005) recently published a wonderful book, *The World Café: Shaping Our Futures Through Conversations That Matter.* When you decide to host your own cafés, buy the book. For now, I'm going to borrow from it heavily.

The World Café technique is best suited for sharing knowledge and stimulating innovative thinking around real-life issues and questions; the UAE situation filled that bill. The café is good for conducting an in-depth exploration of key challenges and opportunities, also what we wanted to do. The café engages people meeting for the first time in authentic conversation. In the UAE, we had not only strangers, but Emirati, Italians, Americans, Saudis, Austrians, Brits, Chinese, and Norwegians, among them government officials, professors, vendors, consultants, and school teachers. There was a fit.

How to Run a Café

The World Café is one of many ways to foster authentic, purposeful conversations. Others are salons, study circles, Appreciative Inquiry, Open Space, strategic dialogues, and wisdom circles. All of these techniques build on similar design principles (Brown & Isaacs, 2005):

- *Set the context.* Clarify the purpose and broad parameters within which the dialogue will unfold. Remind participants that they are invited to participate in authentic, active conversation rather than be a passive audience.

- *Create hospitable space.* Ensure the welcoming environment and psychological safety that nurtures personal comfort and mutual respect. A little music, some posters, and a few flowers always help.

- *Explore questions that matter.* Focus collective attention on powerful questions that attract collaborative engagement. Be open and non-judgmental, and engage aspirations, not problems. Genuine questions are those we don't have answers for.

- *Encourage everyone's contribution.* Giving—making your contribution— is what brings community alive.

- *Cross-pollinate and connect diverse perspectives.* Use the living-system dynamics of emergence through intentionally increasing the diversity and density of connections among perspectives while retaining a common focus on core questions.

- *Listen together for patterns, insights, and deeper questions.* Share attention in ways that nurture coherence of thought without losing individual contributions. *Intelligence* comes from Latin for "gathering understanding in between." Reflection is the heart of the matter. Leave room between the notes to hear the music of collective wisdom.

- *Harvest and share collective discoveries:* Make collective knowledge and insight visible and actionable. Use visual memory. Tour the tables.

BACK IN THE UAE

The day before the Emerging Elearning conference was to begin in 2005, a group of us met in the library of the college where the event would be held. This is not a typical library. There's lots of open space, plenty of sunlight, many tables to sit at, and computers galore. To convert the library into a café, we pulled together eight tables and put a flip chart "tablecloth" on each. To make things hospitable, we put flowers on each table. I'd hoped to offer coffee, but the library doesn't permit coffee drinking. I'd also hoped for music to create a mood, but students were studying in other parts of the same large room.

The toughest part of designing an effective World Café is figuring out the right question to start things off. You don't want to stifle free thinking or include your own bias. Six of us wrangled over the appropriate conversation for forty-five minutes. Some wanted structure; others wanted free form. Some were concerned with having demonstrable outcomes; others wanted to extract the wisdom of the group, expecting it to be messy. I called for a breather.

We took up the topic of the question again at dinner. Discussion was rich. We were learning about the World Café process itself as we noodled on the best catalyst. "How do they become what they want?" "What does the ideal graduate look like?" "If you had a magic wand, what sort of learning experiences would you create?" "If you could build the nation's K–12 system, starting with a blank slate, what would you do?" "What should a graduate be able to do?" "How would you create a way for today's youth to lead more fulfilling lives?" We had our arms around the issues; I suggested we leave the final wording to two of our party, who would be leading the sessions the next day.

At the Café

After lunch the following day, several dozen people sat down in our café (Figure 9.2). Our moderator explained what we were doing and asked the groups to talk about what questions they would want answers to in creating a better educational structure in the UAE.

FIGURE 9.2. Abu Dhabi World Café
Source: Jay Cross.

My table got off to a roaring start. We wanted to ask about the product—that is, the graduates: What values would they have? What job skills? What life skills? How would they reconcile high hopes and current realities?

After ten or fifteen minutes, we rotated to different tables. The head of a bachelor's degree program said the problem was lack of placements for graduates. Others brought up woefully inadequate classrooms. Tayeb Kamali, vice chancellor of universities, dropped by, and we recruited him into our conversation. He spoke of commitment. I countered that "incrementalism is the worst enemy of innovation" and that real change was going to require more than technology and symbols. He told us of additional billions of dollars being added to the education budget.

FIGURE 9.3. Growing Interest as the "Tablecloths" Filled Up with Ideas
Source: Jay Cross.

Excitement was building (Figure 9.3). Our session in the library began to capture the energy that Juanita Brown and David Isaacs experienced when rain led to the first World Café experience:

> The World Café reintroduces us to a world we have forgotten. This is a world where people naturally congregate because we want to be together. A world where we enjoy the age-old process of good conversation, where we're not afraid to talk about things that matter most to us. A world where we're not separated, classified, or stereotyped. A world of simply greeting, free from technology and artificiality. A world that constantly surprises us with the wisdom that exists not in any one of us but in all of us. And a world where we learn that the wisdom we need to solve our problems is available when we talk together [Brown & Isaacs, 2005, p. viii].

It was my turn to give a presentation downstairs, so I left at this time, rejoining the second café right before closing time. I returned to find people suggesting how we might visualize the discussions.

The Next Afternoon

More people came to a follow-up panel session the next day. Kamali had highlighted the activity in his summary of the day. Conversations at the tables began spontaneously. Our moderator told us what had come the day before and explained that we had put sheets containing graphics picturing the day on three tables: "Today's Challenges," "What We Need to Do," and "Future Goals."

We invited people to take a look and talk about what they'd seen. Then they were to write their own ideas on sticky notes and stick them on the tables. The moderator would call time-out after three minutes. People excitedly flocked to the tables. New ideas were flowing fast and furious. We announced they had another ten minutes.

I later suggested that perhaps nationwide World Cafés could get teachers, parents, students, administrators, business, and government on the same page. We need change management to provide a foundation for honest, heartfelt conversation about the issues. One teacher the day before told one of us in private that she couldn't express her views because there was a National (that is, an Emirati) at the table. Roadblocks like this must be dismantled.

Let me put this in context. The Emirati own the country; they are the undisputed top of the social heap. Think how you might feel if you and your clan were wealthy beyond all measure and had hired and imported your workforce from other countries. Teachers are hired hands. The school principal might well be a National with neither experience nor qualifications for the job.

We received a number of comments, pro and con, about the impact of technology. I had to jump in. I mentioned that technology includes things that don't have keyboards or compute—fixtures, for example. I had just found out that many primary school classrooms are tiny, rigid, wretched places where underpaid teachers struggle to teach under the thumb of inexperienced administrators. Desks are technology too. It's better to address basic issues before complex ones.

Next Day at the Café

Wasta is a local term that means connections, that is, pull or clout. The national minister of education, Sheikh Nahayan Mabarek al Nahayan, exemplifies *wasta*. I was overjoyed when he arrived in his massive chocolate-colored Rolls the following day to join our World Café. I explained that we were borrowing from the traditions of the desert and wanted to figuratively welcome him to our tent for coffee and conversation. He graciously accepted. We showed him the session graphics, by this time dense with sticky notes from café participants with a new viewpoint to add. Dave Gray showed a graphic to demonstrate where we were headed. I handed the sheikh a packet of sticky notes and invited him to share his ideas. "I don't have any ideas," he joked (Figure 9.4).

FIGURE 9.4. Jay Cross Describing the World Café to Sheikh Nahayan
Source: Jay Cross.

People forget most conferences shortly after they are over. We want to keep this conversation going, at least until Emerging Elearning 2006. Today everyone who attended is being invited to join a continuing online discussion. Videos of the sessions are going up on the Emerging Elearning Web site.

XPLANE summarized the process of educational reform arising from the café discussions on a poster; part of it is shown in Figure 9.5.

Technology is putting a sharper, more urgent point on the importance of conversations. Conversations are moving faster, touching more people, and bridging greater distances. These networked conversations are enabling powerful new forms of social organization and knowledge exchange to occur.
—RICH LEVINE

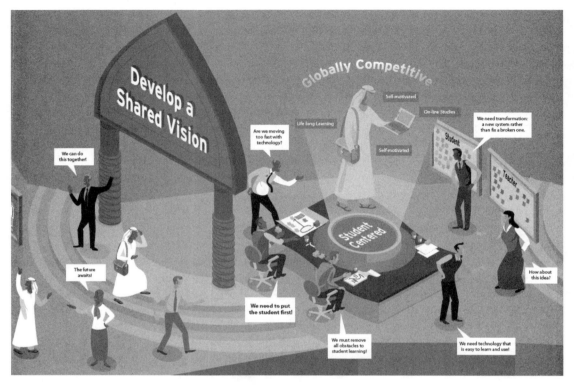

FIGURE 9.5. Excerpt of XPLANE's Visualization of World Café Results

Source: XPLANE. Reprinted with permission.

Note: The entire poster can be viewed at informL.com.

THE WISDOM IS IN THE GROUP

> The key to learning is not the medium nor the message, it is the quality of the dialog with your peers that really matters.—DENHAM GRAY

In 1969, Stanford University began broadcasting graduate school classes to employees of Hewlett Packard, SRI, Sylvania, and GE. Four years later, HP opened a plant in Santa Rosa, fifty miles from campus and therefore outside the broadcast range of the Stanford Instructional Television Network.

Instructor Jim Gibbons hit on the idea of sending videotapes of his master's-level classes in electrical engineering to the group in Santa Rosa. This did not prove effective until Gibbons added a facilitator to the mix. After that, when someone was confused, the facilitator would stop the tape. Generally someone within the group would chime in with, "Here's what you need to know . . ."

The lack of an all-knowing instructor eliminated classroom politics. Learning was purely cooperative, with the engineers helping one another. Staying alert to when to stop the tape put everyone into perpetual self-analysis, checking what they knew and what they didn't. The workaround videotape and facilitator model made better use of resources than the typical classroom.

The engineers in Santa Rosa were technicians, most of them veterans, and they were accustomed to learning by doing. They were savvy, but not of the caliber to be accepted into the on-campus graduate school. Answers to most questions bubbled up from the group itself. When they were stymied, the facilitator would get the solution from Stanford.

Some were skeptical of this distance learning experiment, so when it came time for finals, Jim invited the HP engineers to the campus to take the exams with the students on campus. The Santa Rosa engineers received higher scores than the regular students. John Young, then CEO of Hewlett Packard, was enthralled. HP employees in Albuquerque, Guadalajara, San Diego, Boise, and Bangalore could learn Stanford-level engineering skills.

On retiring from Stanford, Gibbons founded an organization that uses tutored video instruction to help troubled youth make healthy life decisions. Third-party formal evaluations report that the programs are successful for both at-risk youth (in juvenile halls, ranches, and court-appointed alternative schools) and youth in traditional school settings.

> Strategizing depends on creating a rich and complex web of conversations that cuts across previously isolated knowledge interests and creates new and unexpected combinations of insight.
> —GARY HAMEL

CONVERSATIONS AT PFIZER

Twelve hundred managers at Pfizer have learned to have more effective conversations. They've taken part in an instructor-led program called "Courageous Conversations" that varies from two hours to a full day. It's a module in Pfizer First Line, a management development program, but it can be added to an off-site meeting or stand alone as an open enrollment course, offered in response to popular demand.

It sounds like formal learning, and certainly, the workshop portion can be formal. However, reinforcement and the real lessons are learned informally, after the workshop. This is a program with enormous payback; it changes lives.

Why offer a course on conversation? Pfizer believes that it's essential for line leaders to have "the robust ability to engage in highly skillful conversations around challenging issues." Rob Hathaway, a manager at Pfizer Leadership Education and Development, told me the program is really about having more effective dialogue no matter what you're doing.

Conversations are shaped by the ancient defense mechanism known as the fight-or-flight response that's hardwired into every human brain. The fight conversational style is competitive; Pfizer calls this a "win" conversation. The flight style is accommodating, which often involves evading tough issues; this is the "min" style.

Business conversations at Pfizer no longer consist of knee-jerk emotional responses, because people have a means of critiquing the quality of the conversation process. They ask, "Is the information valid? Are we making an informed choice? Are we exercising mutual control over the conversation?"

Pfizer people are inherently polite and avoid overt confrontation. This is curious, given Pfizer's bottom-line orientation and competitiveness. Nonetheless, avoiding confrontation can translate into burying people's true concerns or to decisions that are made behind closed doors to save face.

After the course, both parties to a conversation strive for the exchange of valid information. They watch out for conversational patterns that get in the way. It's not you; it's not me; it's not us. The problem is the process. Let's figure out what's going on and get back to being effective.

> Conversation is the heart of the new inquiry. It is perhaps the core human skill for dealing with the tremendous challenges we face.
> —INSTITUTE FOR THE FUTURE

Overlooking a Star Performer

Consider the situation of a new manager replacing a person promoted out of a group. During their transition, the old manager tells the new manager not to worry about Joe: Joe is a star and needs no coaching.

As time wears on, Joe feels neglected by the new manager, becomes disengaged, and starts looking for a new job. It turns out one of the reasons Joe became a star was due to the mentorship and coaching from the old boss, and he thrived on it.

The new manager becomes frustrated with Joe's mediocre performance and disengagement. Angry at his predecessor for misleading him, he starts to move Joe toward a performance improvement plan threatening possible termination. At just about this time, the new manager finds his way into a Courageous Conversations workshop.

In the session, he confided that he was making a lot of assumptions about Joe and why his performance was sliding. The new manager thought that Joe just didn't like him and his style, and maybe that Joe wanted the manager's job and was disappointed that he didn't get it when the old boss departed.

The Courageous Conversations facilitator encouraged him to test his assumptions with Joe. The manager did and learned his assumptions were unfounded: all Joe wanted was some time, attention, and coaching like the old days.

With his assumptions now shattered, the manager started providing coaching, and just in time. Joe received a job offer from a competitor but decided to pass because he was now having his needs met by his new manager. Joe reengaged and became the productive, valuable employee he was before.

Courageous Conversations had several business impacts: the company retained a valued employee who knew the culture and the organizational networks, customers experienced no disruption in service, and the business saved the direct cost of recruiting, training, and acculturating a Joe's replacement.

Other Examples

- An employee was miffed at being continually passed over for promotion. She felt she was being treated unfairly, and she thought her bosses didn't seem to take her interests seriously. She enrolled in the conversations program.

"What's really going on?" she wondered. She looked in the mirror and realized, "I'm part of the problem." She hadn't been communicating effectively. A self-confessed minimizer, she hadn't articulated her desire to be promoted. She became more expressive and two months later was promoted.

- A manager came into a subordinate's office to inquire about a meeting. He was not enthusiastic. The meeting involved out-of-towners but had been rescheduled four times. The two men played Question and Answer for twenty minutes. Fearing an expensive project was about to be killed off, the subordinate called on the conversation framework: "I just don't understand where you're going with this."

The manager said that he'd been working too hard and hadn't been to the gym in weeks. He was feeling awful. Did he really need to attend the meeting? The subordinate said no—that he would fill in for him and brief him afterward. Next time, these two will be able to save themselves fifteen minutes of frustrating cat-and-mouse games.

- One or the other of a couple who both worked at a Pfizer plant in Michigan was late to work almost every day because they needed to get their son on his school bus. When they started participating in the conversations program, they began exploring what was going on with their son and asked him why he needed them to accompany him to the bus stop. The boy was overcome with relief: now he could be his own person. His mother wrote the instructor a heartfelt thank-you letter for helping her family.

- The day a new product came to market, a companion training program debuted with it. This was fantastic. It had never happened before. "Great job!" said the project manager's colleagues. "Bravo!" But it turned out that the hero of the project, the ace program director, was getting ready to leave the company. He was totally burned out. He'd hardly seen his family while putting the course together. He knew he couldn't keep this up and wouldn't be able to deliver. Celebrating his accomplishment only made things worse. The company is lucky that someone sought a holistic view of what was going on before they lost a dedicated employee.

THE COURAGEOUS CONVERSATIONS WORKSHOP

People at Pfizer attend the Courageous Conversations program because they want to understand what's going on and be more effective. The workshop immerses them in cases. As they role-play various scenarios, tension builds, emotion takes hold, and effectiveness goes out the window. Only then are people ready to look into the mirror and change their behavior.

This course masquerades as a course in effective conversations. In fact, I think this is really a course in candor. The organization has hit on a non-threatening way to call people on their posturing. Is this the best process for us to use?

Consultant Craig Weber developed the Courageous Conversations workshop. Craig described a recent session with a group of executives. "Tell me about your greatest challenges," he asked them. One executive piped up that the firm's top performers were people who were at the top of their game technically and had great social skills. The challenge was that the firm couldn't find enough of them, and once they were found, they were hard to keep.

Craig suggested the executive and his peers use the rules of courageous conversations to reflect, rethink, and reframe the problem. As a result, the executive learned that the sort of people he wanted would not want to work for someone like him. Not only that, he had surrounded himself with managers with similar styles, with the result that the dominant management style of the organization was driving away precisely the sort of people it needed. The executives revamped their style.

The learning here was informal. The group came up with its new understanding of the problem without outside help. Being more open to looking at things from other perspectives was fertile ground for informal learning.

Craig explained to a group of chief engineers at a seminar recently that they had an opportunity for some double-loop learning. At one level, they'd learn about issues, information, challenges, and problems. In tackling these, they'd form mental models and paradigms. If they chose to take things to another level, they would question those models, check with others, and rethink them. The problem may not be some malfunction so much as a misunder-standing of the problem itself.

Craig agreed with my characterization of Pfizer as an organization where being polite got in the way of frank dialogue. The company now has a plat-form for creative problem solving. People know that they make better deci-sions in groups. They deal with stuff that might have been swept under the rug before.

Craig works to make the undiscussable discussable. The typical situation is an issue that has sparked huge concerns. For example, everyone is talking in the hallways about potential problems with the proposed merger. Although emotion runs high, no one brings the issue up with management. They fear being crucified for going against the flow. How can they bring the issues into discussion? Craig advises chatting with a colleague for twenty minutes to think through the situation. You need a "ruthlessly compassionate partner," he says, to engage in this.

In a two-day Courageous Conversations workshop, Craig talks about the importance of good relationships in business. A business, after all, is little more than its patterns of discourse. How much do you think it costs when communication is clogged and issues are allowed to fester? We know the toll at NASA for the *Challenger* and *Columbia* crews, but NASA is hardly alone.

Later in the day, the group looks at a case where the boss says he has an open door policy but in fact hates to be interrupted. How can you deal with this situation productively? Craig plays the role of the boss, and participants try to bring the situation out in the open. Some people try soft-pedaling the issue, but they don't get through to the boss. Others stand up to the boss. They become aggressive and argue.

If things can get this out of hand with two people, imagine what can hap-pen within the group dynamics of an entire organization. Having established the need for it, Craig introduces the courageous conversations framework.

Participants break into groups of three to address real issues they face. Often the undiscussable issue involves a colleague who talks too much, has body odor, or is otherwise unpleasant. How can you give feedback without causing resentment? Or maybe there's a big issue, like an acquisition men-tioned that everyone's keeping quiet about for fear that if they take it up the chain of command, they'll pay for it.

The workshop ends, but the real learning begins. The small groups are en-couraged to use what they've learned. They should call on one another to help assess situations honestly. They may bring in examples from the newspaper.

> Dialogue is the central aspect of co-intelligence.
> —TOM ATLEE

Or they may focus on discussing articles like the classic *Harvard Business Review* article by Chris Argyris (1991) on the difficulty of teaching smart people. At first, it's difficult, but in time, people grow into it.

 An effective community of practice is like a beehive. It organizes itself, buzzes with activity, and produces honey for the markets.

"Human conversation is the most ancient and easiest way to cultivate the conditions for change—personal change, community and organizational change, planetary change. If we can sit together and talk about what's important to us, we begin to come alive. I believe we can change the world if we start listening to one another again. Simple, honest, human conversation. Not mediation, negotiation, problem-solving, debate or public meetings. Simple, truthful conversations where we each have a chance to speak, we each feel heard and we each listen well" (Wheatley, 2002, p. 4).

Conversations take place among people with shared interests, that is, communities. Purposeful communities are the topic of the next chapter.

True learning organizations are a space for generative conversations and concerted action which create a field of alignment that produces tremendous power to invent new realities in conversation and to bring about these new realities in action.—FRED KOFMAN AND PETER SENGE

COMMUNITIES

IN *KITCHEN CONFIDENTIAL* (2001), Anthony Bourdain describes how he became a chef. He learned under the guidance of more experienced workers in the kitchen, moved from dishwashing to salad prep to pastry making to sous chef, and finally joined the ranks of chefs. His knives are a symbol of his profession—the equivalent of a doctor's stethoscope or a carpenter's hammer. He knows hundreds of people in the restaurant business. He hangs out with other chefs, goes to chef bars, and tells chef jokes. His hands bear the scars of cutting fingers instead of meat. Bourdain didn't just learn cooking. It's much more than that: he *became* a chef.

Chefs and the people in the kitchen who aspire to be chefs are a community of practice. Newcomers learn the ropes from working alongside veterans. Respected elders add to the common ground, or store of knowledge, that fuels the evolution of the chef community. All take pride in membership, as one would in a guild. When you become a chef, you play by chef's rules.

An effective community of practice is like a beehive. It organizes itself, buzzes with activity, and produces honey for the markets. Consultant Seth Kahan named his book on the process *Building Beehives* (2004).

Silicon Valley is chock full of communities of practice. Professionals there consider themselves programmers or chip designers or semiconductor engineers first and employees of HP or Intel or Apple second. I know people who have worked for Oracle, Sun, Cisco, HP, and several start-ups, moving on every year or two. In a barroom conversation, an engineer hears about a team forming around an exciting project at another company and submits his resignation the next morning.

There's the rub. Corporations want to run their own show rather than give employees license to do what they feel like. Divided loyalties are at work here. Furthermore, when times are tight, there's not much corporate mindshare to lavish on activities that are not on the immediate agenda like training. When the downsizing axe falls, discretionary items like free-floating communities of practice are always among the first things chopped.

Unless you are a hermit, you are a member of several communities of practice, although you may not have thought of it that way. For example, I just became a member of the WordPress community. (WordPress is a software environment for creating weblogs.) I didn't receive a membership card; no one sent me a plaque to put on the wall. What happened is that I studied the FAQ and the Codex (documentation maintained by users). When I hit a glitch, I searched the WordPress community's knowledge base. I could not find what I was looking for. I was going to post a question about my issue to the WordPress support forums, but first needed to figure out the protocol for asking questions of this group (all of them volunteers).

I read some other people's questions and the answers they received. Then I read some advice on asking questions that appears in the WordPress Codex. This led me to a delightful article by Eric Raymond (2001), "How to Ask Questions the Smart Way." After reading it, I didn't dare ask anything in the forums until I'd documented how I'd made a good-faith effort to find the answer for myself. Following Raymond's suggestions, I began using a search engine for answers and found just the instructions I needed. And at that moment I realized I'd become a member of the WordPress community. I was no longer an outsider; I knew how to play by the rules. Although I am still a novice, I have swapped suggestions with half a dozen others in the community.

Etienne Wenger (2005), who with Jean Lave coined the term *community of practice* in 1987, notes that there "is hardly a Fortune 500 company today that does not have somewhere an initiative to cultivate communities of practice" (CPSquare, 2006). And it is not just business but also nongovernmental organizations and government that are cultivating communities. Nonetheless, Etienne sees the need to continue building learning capacity.

Some of this is so subtle that it's easy to miss. In fact, until I heard him in person and we had a chance to talk briefly, I didn't get Etienne's main messages. At first I took *practice* to mean what novices do over and over again before achieving mastery. But Etienne is referring to *practice* as what professionals do, for example, medical practice or law practice. *Community* smacked of small towns, fellowship, me and the neighbors, backyard barbecues, and Community

Watch; it's wholesome. What Etienne means when he says *community* is a group with shared interests and standards, like the business community, the community of bloggers, or the American Fern Society.

The earliest communities of practice may have been cavemen sitting around a fire talking about the best way to hunt bears. That's the way communities work: practitioners come together to share, nurture, and validate tricks of the trade. Apprentices have always done this. For a while, we mistakenly thought most of the learning was going on between master and apprentice. In fact, apprentices probably learn more from one another.

A friend of Etienne is a wine professional. Describing a wine, the friend said it was "purple in the nose." This meant absolutely nothing to Etienne, because he is not a member of the wine-tasting community. Imagine that the friend is at a wine tasting with his colleagues. He discerns a new element and describes it as a convergence of fire and gravity. If others in the group agree, the fire and gravity meme is legitimized. Here we have the two primary aspects in any community: participation and reification.

Although the word *community* has a warm and fuzzy feel to it, the concept is value neutral. These groups can impede progress, engage in groupthink, or neglect their responsibilities to the larger organization.

In school or workshops, the learning relationship is vertical: there's a provider on top and a recipient. In a community of practice, peers learn from one another. Side-by-side and peer-to-peer replace top-down relationships.

First-generation knowledge management failed because it was top down. Identify the critical knowledge and stuff it in a content management system. Nobody took ownership because no community embodied the knowledge. Now that we appreciate that knowledge lives in communities, we can facilitate knowledge management by nurturing their development. As Louis Pasteur said, "Chance favors those who are prepared."

Etienne Wenger suggests scrapping our industrial model of training and the notions that go with it. Let learning become an integral part of life itself. Teaching will fade in importance; progress along a trajectory of development will replace skills training.

Gustavo Esteva, a former IBM executive, political insider, guerrilla, community organizer, author, and founder of Terra University in Oaxaca, Mexico, takes a commonsense approach to professional education. If you want to become an attorney, you apprentice with a lawyer. If you want to become a plumber, work with a plumber. Students learn not only the tricks of the trade, but the values and standards of the trade. They choose whether this is a community they want to become a member of.

Hewlett Packard no longer has communities of practice. In their place are *communities of purpose*. Communities of purpose, unlike communities of practice, are intentional; they have a job to do. Unlike communities of chefs or WordPress users, a community of purpose begins with specific objectives, and results are measured and documented. An HP community brings people together to do a specific project. In the course of carrying it out, they learn from one another.

CISCO

For a long time, I maintained that communities were organic. Like truffles, they sort of sprouted up on their own, where they wanted, and the most you could do was to nurture them by providing time and space for them to meet. Times have changed. A quarter of the world's truffles are now cultivated on a plantation in Spain. Many companies consciously plant the seeds of community in strategically important areas. If the garden comes up weeds, they rip them out and start anew.

Cisco has fielded teams in a dozen strategically important technical specializations such as security and Internet protocol telephony. You can think of each team as a community of practice. Being selected for a team confers status; team members become the local experts. Twice a year, each team sends one to two hundred members to meet face-to-face for three- to five-day symposia at Cisco headquarters. Their agendas include product presentations, questions and answers with the field, competition, customer interviews, and other business-critical topics the teams deem important. Viewers of the live performance can ask questions in real time. Each symposium generates an average of thirty hours of content. Cisco supplier Altus Learning Systems video-records the sessions in a large meeting room designed specifically for that purpose. The virtual team program produces about 750 hours of streaming content each year.

Every day sales engineers confront too much information and too little time to keep up. Business-critical information is a crucial ingredient in closing deals, but things are moving so fast that salespeople could read 24/7 and still fail to keep up with the latest technology and solutions. The larger the organization and more rapid its rate of change, the more challenging it is to keep people informed. Cisco acquires nine or ten companies a year. On average, it brings out a new product every week.

Cisco's thousands of sales engineers (SEs) access the video online after the symposia for reference and performance support purposes. This is possible because Altus digitizes the content into video on demand (VoD, which rhymes with baud) for later viewing. In addition to video, a VoD includes a synchronized PowerPoint presentation, a downloadable MP3 audio file, and a verbatim transcript, as shown in Figure 10.1. Transcription makes the thousands of hours of content full-text searchable and is delivered over the Cisco Media Network.

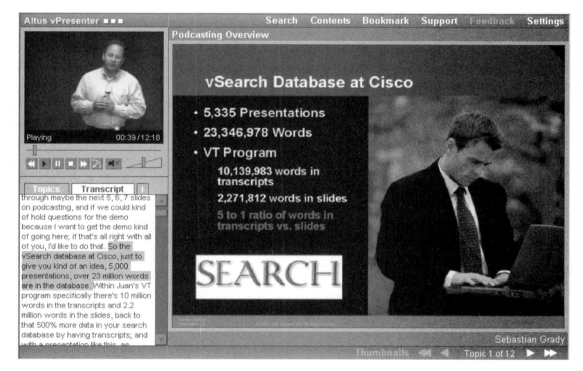

FIGURE 10.1. Altus vSearch, Which Retrieves Video, Transcripts, PowerPoint, and Podcasts in Seconds

Source: Grady & Gamez (2005). Reprinted with permission of Altus Learning Systems.

"We've Googleized our corporate IP," says virtual teams manager Juan Gamez. As fast and easy as it is to search Google, Cisco SEs can pinpoint just the knowledge they're looking for: they query the in-house repository of VoDs, and the system takes them down to the exact sentences or slides of interest. They can stream this information from any Cisco office worldwide in a manner of seconds. Cisco people initiate more than thirty thousand searches for VoDs annually and view more than twenty thousand of them.

Gamez recently noticed an anomaly in his use statistics. SEs accessed 243 percent more VoDs in 2005 than the year before, but MP3 downloads were up a staggering 376 percent. When he investigated, he found that SEs were downloading VoD content onto their iPods. Sensing another means of getting information to the SEs, Gamez investigated what would be involved in podcasting product information and had Altus add RSS (really simple syndication) subscription to the repository of MP3 files.

Just as blogging gave us all a personal printing press, podcasting gives us an inexpensive personal broadcasting studio. Subscribers find short radio shows downloaded to their iPod personal music players. At the 2005 Gnomedex conference in Seattle, Microsoft threw its weight behind the RSS standard that makes all this happen. Podcasting has reached the mainstream.

Future executives will be able to record or telephone in an announcement that can be delivered over the Internet to two subscribers or 2 million in no time at all. People can listen live or listen at any time they choose.

At Cisco, podcasting enables SEs to subscribe to the technical specializations of their choice. These personalized, on-demand radio shows are then automatically downloaded on subscribers' iPods. Altus founder Ted Cocheu told me that podcasting addresses two critical issues in today's learning-on-the-run environment. The first is timely self-service access to the knowledge people really need. The second is mobility—accessing knowledge whenever it's most convenient and wherever they are. Podcasting fits the bill on both counts.

Consider what's happening at Cisco compared to what most other companies do. The old way is to develop product knowledge training in a laborious, expensive, and time-consuming manner:

- Train staff to interview subject matter experts for product information.
- Instructional designers determine the appropriate means of delivery.
- Content is poured into templates, converted into role plays, checked for accuracy, and canned into final form.
- There is a mad rush to finish because customers and prospects are waiting.
- A one-size-fits-all course is rolled out for replay across the company.

What's wrong with this?

- The training department has no credibility with the subject matter.
- The results of interviewing subject matter experts are often garbled.
- "We need it yesterday" demands sacrifice quality for speed.
- Rushing leads to mistakes, insufficient content, and poor design choices.
- Start-to-finish is measured in months.
- It is difficult, if not impossible, to break content into small chunks for selective viewing. It's all or nothing.

- Information is difficult to access after initial session.

And here's what Cisco does differently:

- Respected in-house experts, customers, and product manager meet to swap information, providing content for redistribution almost immediately.
- Start-to-finish ranges from immediate (if viewed live) to a week later (if viewed as searchable recording).
- Content is available as video, PowerPoint, MP3, or transcript. Viewers can download and customize PowerPoint presentations to their needs.
- A powerful search capability enables anyone within Cisco to retrieve content in a matter of seconds.

The typical knowledge worker spends 15 to 30 percent of her time looking for specific information. Fewer than half of those searches are successful. Extrapolated to the Fortune 500, this adds up to direct costs of $60 billion to $85 billion and double that in opportunity cost. Capturing, indexing, and making information readily available enables Cisco people to spend more time with customers and less on fruitless searches.

Salespeople often review VoD content immediately before customer meetings to ensure their facts are up-to-date, and for good reason: human memory is notoriously fickle. An hour after you've learned something, half of it will have disappeared. Wait a month, and 80 percent of the knowledge will have decayed.

A Cisco engineer e-mailed:

```
I just wanted someone to know that I think this (VoD
over vSearch) is one of the most important and useful
sites to a field SE that I have ever encountered. I just
want to thank everyone who assembled this project as I
know it had to be a daunting task. This is incredible.
I now have the capability to train myself better than I
ever have before. I am one happy SE today!!!
```

CIO magazine looked at Cisco's approach and reported (Santosus, 2004):

While the cost of technologies has a definitive price tag, the benefits— more informed employees, streamlined communication with customers, repeatable and consistent processes—often do not. But determining ROI for an e-learning system hasn't been a problem at Cisco Systems. For about eight years, the networking equipment company has been using streaming video to train its sales force. Five years ago, Cisco implemented video search technology from Altus Learning. Available to Cisco's 10,000-strong global sales force, the video search system (called vSearch) saved tens of millions of dollars in fiscal year 2002, according to Tom Kelly, Cisco's vice president of the Internet learning solutions group.

Members of the sales force use the system on average six times each week to find content related to products, pricing, specs, and availability. "The sales force has gotten smarter and is better prepared," Kelly said.

Supporting these and related learning solutions has been Cisco CEO John Chambers, who is a productivity fanatic. He recently told an audience at MIT that Cisco workers must be five times as productive in the United States as elsewhere in the world. Cisco sells $700,000 per employee, a stratospheric productivity statistic. However, to survive global competition in 2010, Cisco must increase productivity to $1 million per employee. With productivity goals like that, Cisco must find the fastest and most effective online learning and knowledge transfer solutions available.

LEGO FANS

Adults who make models with LEGO bricks didn't get much respect when Jake McKee joined LEGO's Community Development Team in 2001. Adult fans accounted for only 5 percent of LEGO sales. Insiders called them the shadow market, as if they were an afterthought.

A refugee from the dot-com world, Jake began his job search by applying to companies he figured he'd enjoy working for. An adult LEGO fan himself, he has become the adult hobbyists' advocate within the company. His goal is to make sure "everybody goes home happy." Inside the company, he explained that the adult fans are far more important than the revenue they generate.

Adult enthusiasts form clubs, much like model railroaders do. Clubs display models in a variety of locations; sometimes malls get crowds of twenty thousand people over a weekend. These displays send a powerful message of realism—showing children and parents that you don't have to work for the LEGO Company or be a professional model builder to make great creations from the little plastic blocks.

Adult enthusiasts take a variety of paths to arrive at the hobby as adults. The typical life cycle of a LEGO fan is as follows. As a child, he makes LEGO models, and LEGO is the favorite toy. Sometime around middle school, his interest in toys wanes as interest in other things (studying, dating, driving) picks up. This time is affectionately known in the LEGO community as the

"Dark Ages." After college graduation and perhaps marriage, a local LEGO show rekindles his interest. He asks one of the modelers at the show for more information and is directed to LEGOfan.org, a Web site that functions as an on-ramp into the community of adult LEGO enthusiasts.

Jake is setting up a certification program to form a deeper relationship between the LEGO Company and model builders who make some or all of their income from building with LEGO bricks.

I hear Jake frantically tapping the keys. He explains that he has to respond to incoming instant messages about choosing the LEGO Ambassadors, community representatives to the company: appointments will be announced tomorrow. In addition to having an ear at the company, ambassadors see and give feedback on secret new developments inside the company. In addition, they work to ensure that communication between the community and the company flows frequently and in two ways.

For the 2003 What Will You Make Roadshow, the LEGO Company set up five tents. It put displays in the first four, and the remaining tent was for local LEGO clubs to bring any type of display to showcase. LEGO management questioned the wisdom of giving the customers so much autonomy, but Jake stood his ground. (He's so tenacious that his wife calls him Bulldog.) The clubs assembled great displays that pleased crowds and convinced colleagues that working together with the fans was a smart and safe idea. The company and the clubs are growing to trust one another.

LEGO hobbyists are a community of practice. Subgroups create their own building standards that allow easy connection of separate components in order to quickly create large displays. The spaceship builders were the catalyst for a new product, a base for modeling space stations analogous to the green squares that serve as ground for terrestrial models. Many clubs and associations maintain their own Web sites, which serve to establish standards and promote practices.

Members of the community respect one another. For the 2005 National Model Railroaders Association convention, fourteen clubs banded together to assemble a twenty-five-hundred-square-foot LEGO layout. Working under time pressure, seventy-five people labored to put the layout together. Everyone was cordial, and no one fought. After all, this was a band of brothers working together, not some bunch of strangers.

Look at the learning that goes on among the fans. There are communities of practice, both in person and virtual, that welcome new recruits, get them up to speed, and set the standards of excellence through example. Thousands of adult hobbyists learn the ropes and become more substantial LEGO customers, all at scant expense to LEGO. And now the liaison with hobby-ist communities of practice creates new product concepts and gives LEGO a listening post in the marketplace. Customer learning thrives despite the lack of customer training.

CULTURE STEW

The United Nations Development Program (UNDP) helps UN offices in 145 countries administer local UN programs effectively. It is a never-ending chal-lenge. I asked my friend Gunnar Brückner, who headed UNDP for many years, to tell me about learning among many cultures, varying skill levels, and Net connections that go from broadband to iffy phone lines.

Turnover at the helm of a UNDP country office is high because of staff ro-tation. Every staff member is required to move on to another duty station every two to six years, depending on the hardship factor at each duty station. The transition from the outgoing UNDP representative to her successor is vital for the smooth functioning of that office.

In the light of the multiple cultures involved, there is no one best ap-proach, and no set of guidelines could describe what to do adequately. It's an ideal situation to use informal learning. Instead of a curriculum, UNDP pro-vides a menu of ideas and suggestions to support the intentional creation of learning opportunities for both outgoing and incoming staff.

The intercultural context represents a complex challenge. It is usually best described by a triangular relationship between the culture of the host coun-try, the culture of the incumbent, and the culture of the incoming staff. All three could be different, and all have an impact on the handover process. Left to chance, problems are guaranteed.

The right approach depends on acknowledging differences and selecting a culturally appropriate induction process. This should be informal, done by the people involved and not prescribed by outsiders. It should be acknowledged that whereas both representatives could (in a best-case scenario if both are cul-turally aware enough) be expected to minimize their differences, it will never be possible to sideline the culture of the host country or, for that matter, the way the handover will be experienced by the staff in the host country. A few dimensions, shown in Table 10.1, show why this is an issue and why an orderly or predetermined handover process might not always be the best solution.

Every country, culture, or person in the world falls somewhere on the con-tinuum of the extremes. The countries in parentheses in the table are more or less clear representatives of the respective preferences, although people do

TABLE 10.1. Cultural Differences Among Countries

Power distance	Equality (Israel, Scandinavian countries, United States)	Hierarchy (Malaysia, Arab countries, many Latin American countries)
Mode of thinking	Task orientation (Japan, Venezuela, Italy)	Relationship orientation (Argentina, France, many African countries)
Communication	Direct (United States, Argentina, Netherlands)	Indirect (Japan, Vietnam, Egypt)
Structure	Order/uncertainty avoidance (Greece, Japan, Argentina)	Flexibility/uncertainty tolerance (India, Jamaica, Scandinavian countries)

not always represent the hallmarks of their overall culture. If the cultures involved in the handover process fall in the middle, we wouldn't expect many problems. When the cultures fall on opposite extremes, it will be necessary to adapt the transition process on the fly.

For example, assume the host country is Argentina. Hierarchies and order are important there, so protocol plays an important role, but there is a good chance that introductions by the incumbent during a social event will take the incoming staff a long way (because of the relationship orientation) and the handover should be structured very transparently to avoid uncertainties among the staff about what's going on. If the incoming staff is Japanese, the value of the social event will be for the office and for the local contacts, whereas the true value for the incoming staff would be derived from a series of one-on-one meetings with the incumbent due to the Japanese preference for indirect communication. The Japanese could benefit from an elaborate handover schedule (due to the task orientation preference), whereas an incoming French staff member does not need that much structure; a series of meetings and get-togethers would probably be more helpful (because of the relationship orientation). If the outgoing person is from the United States, the direct and open communication with the Argentineans will probably shock the incoming Japanese. The combinations are endless, but each triangle combination as it presents itself could be associated with a best-case scenario of things to do.

When people speak different languages and come from countries around the world, the need to leverage those differences is obvious. The UNDP community is alert to culture clash and has developed rules of thumb for effective practice. Corporate communities generally speak a common language, but members may be as far apart as a Cuban and a Sikh. Creating and fostering a learning culture in companies is an indispensable element for continual success in a global knowledge economy.

WORLD JAM

IBM chairman Sam Palmisano wants to overhaul the way IBM does business—tomorrow. He wants to involve a third of a million people in a single conversation. It's sure to give you that real-time buzz. Called a *world jam,* this new platform was designed to give every employee a safe place to ask for and offer practical solutions to everyday challenges over a seventy-two-hour period. IBM has adopted it as a management approach for our open, flat times. Palmisano says he's convinced the firm wouldn't be where it is today without world jams.

I've never jammed with these guys, but I have been party to thirty-minute conference calls with fifty people spread over two continents. As the person trying to harvest wisdom from these IBMers, I didn't find the supersized conference calls a good use of time. However, I understand that the substance of the call is but the tip of the IBM community iceberg. There's a flurry of instant messages back and forth among participants. Some of this was on point; some was along the line of "Sally's baby was born last Friday." This would be frivolous chit-chat if most of these people weren't working from their homes and clients' offices, whetting their appetite for social news of their colleagues.

World Jams and all-hands telephone conferences have become virtual watercoolers where IBMers meet.

In corporate learning circles, the term *blended* is passé. Because we're being informal here, our next chapter is *Unblended*.

UNBLENDED

11

AN INSIDER SEES a lot of tomfoolery, and I've been an eLearning insider since it had an inside to be in. Here are some observations about the learning business I thought you might want to hear.

RETURN ON INVESTMENT?

In 2001, training directors turned their attention to return on investment. If you're going to spend hundreds of thousands of dollars, maybe millions, on learning management systems, courseware, robust networks, and big bills from consultants, your CFO will want to know what's up.

Unfortunately, instead of learning cost-benefit analysis, people who wanted to speak the language of business studied accounting. Accounting looks backward, not ahead. It is a set of rules devised to count merchandise in Renaissance Venice. Created before knowledge work was invented, accounting values intangibles such as human capital at zero and counts training as an expense instead of an investment. Conference speakers, some of whom I know to be otherwise bright people, counseled training managers to go to their finance departments to get an understanding of the returns and the investments. After that it was a simple matter of division. This was spectacularly bad advice.

Has any decision maker anywhere ever bought something on the strength of an ROI number, especially one presented by a staffer? ROI is a hurdle, not a race winner. Convince a decision maker you can deliver the outcome she is looking for at a reasonable price, and you get the budget to give it a whirl.

Cautious corporations that began evaluating eLearning expenditures with business metrics were not amused. Reduced travel and salary expenses were a one-time phenomenon, money that disappeared from subsequent years' budgets. A research study by ASTD and learning impresario and thought leader Elliott Masie found that two-thirds of employees offered voluntary eLearning never bothered to register. One-third didn't register for compulsory eLearning. Many of those who did register dropped out early. You didn't need a very sharp pencil to figure this one out.

eLearning was not out of the woods. Most eLearning was packaged as courses, and few people had time for courses any more.

COURSES ARE DEAD

This meme began in early 2002, when I received an e-mail from renaissance learner Marcia Conner asking a bunch of us about the effectiveness of eLearning, to which I replied:

> i got in from guatemala last night and will use that as
> an excuse for a wimpy answer to your question.
>
> the older i get, the more i trust my gut and the less
> i believe statistics.
>
> my gut tells me that elearning sometimes works well.
> for the successes, i point to my son and his peers learn-
> ing everything from homework assignments to network ad-
> ministration via the Web. that's also where he learned a
> lot more than his dad ever did about meteorology, PERL,
> San Francisco politics, environmental action groups, ob-
> scure singers, and more. in my own case, i've learned
> more professionally from Amazon and Google in the last
> seven years than from a similar span at Princeton & Har-
> vard b-school. at smartforce we accelerated sales devel-
> opment by the better part of a year; it wasn't perfect—it
> wasn't even pretty, but it was at least $10 million more
> cost-effective than the cram sessions it replaced. in the
> informal arena, a lot of what my generation learned on
> the playground is now learned via instant messenger. so
> my gut says elearning works well.
>
> of course, i've seen cases where massive elearning
> projects fell flat. my comparison of elearning to
> napoleon's march to moscow came up with only 10% of cor-

porate elearners achieving their objective. i've attempted courses on communications and negotiations and customer service that were so awful you'd have to be brain-damaged to sit through more than five minutes' worth. i'm not convinced that a two-hour CD on sexual harrassment is going to tame the hormonal urges of preditory beasts. ASTD and Elliott found that a third of the recruits don't even show up for mandatory elearning. a researcher at SRI told me about a $2 million corporate university program that attracted only two participants. both of them dropped out. so my gut says elearning can fail miserably.

sometimes it works; sometimes it doesn't. just like computers. geez. makes me ask "how effective is high school?" i graduated with high honors but damned if i can remember a single formula from trig. speaking french with the owner of my hotel last week, you'd never guess that i finished French IV. looking at the general populace, half of all u.s. high schools grads cannot locate france on a map. more than half of the males attending california state universities and colleges do not possess sufficient skill to read the textbooks in their backpacks. if i'd skipped high school entirely, i wouldn't be able to quote t.s. eliot or tell you the year the magna carta was signed, but i don't know that it would have hurt my career. i learned more about mayans and guatemala in the last ten days than i would have from a three-unit college course. there's a reason that grades in college do not correlate to income, happiness, professional accomplishment, or anything but getting into schools that look at GPAs as an admission requirement. don't get me started on latin.

so i agree with all of you. it's a stupid question. i don't question the effectiveness of my hammer. if the nails go in, it works. if it's the best tool around, i'm not about to try pounding those nails with my shoe or a screwdriver.

god i'm tired.

I e-mailed my words to the group ("Reply All"), and the next day received a reasoned response from author and management consultant Marc Rosenberg:

> Most of the examples Jay points to of elearning working
> are NOT COURSES. If fact, the learning comes from some-
> what intelligent (on the human side) browsing for
> something that actually means something to the browser.
> I understand where courses are the best solution, but
> there is no way courses are the ONLY solution.

Marc's insight sparked further thoughts, which I again recorded in my blog:

> bingo! the course is not the appropriate shell for most
> learning experiences. we all know the story: the fifty-
> minute hour and the two-day workshop were created for
> the convenience of the institution, not the learner. the
> course is a triumph of standardization and it is so in-
> grained in our thinking that we still buy & sell seat-
> time rather than performance improvement. it's the
> industrial model, which puts a higher value on efficiency
> than on effectiveness. you can have learning any color
> you want as long as it's black.

I say, "Courses are dead," for shock value. Courses have a role to play. But I hope courses cease being the knee-jerk solution whenever we think of corporate learning.

WHAT ABOUT THE *E*?

eLearning is learning on internet time, the convergence of learning and networks.

For a brief moment at the end of the twentieth century, eLearning actually meant something. One large technology company delayed projects for six months to quibble over the definition, but before long, there was nothing left to talk about. The net became part of corporate life. Most corporate learning today is at least in part eLearning. It has become trite to point out that the *e* doesn't matter and that it's the learning that counts.

Frankly, I don't think the learning counts for much either. What's important is the doing that results from learning. If workers could do their jobs well by taking smart pills, training departments would have little to do aside from dispensing pills. Executives don't care about learning; they care about execution. I may talk about learning with *you*, but when I'm in the boardroom, I'll substitute "improving performance."

THE BIRTH OF ELEARNING

In 1994, the alchemy of Netscape converted a little-known scientific documentation system in Switzerland into the World Wide Web. I was enthralled by the possibilities. The convergence of learning and the Web would fundamentally change the welfare of the world. I coined the word *eLearning* (although I think a number of us did so simultaneously; it was in the air). I explored the Web-enabled learning with enthusiasm. Naturally, I posted my thoughts about eLearning on the Web.

By 1998, the CEO of CBT Systems envisioned what would follow the PC-based training his company had invented in the mid-1980s. His prototype for the future was a massive project the company had done for UNISYS. UNISYS boosted revenues $100 million a year by accelerating the certification, and hence the billing rates, of its computer services staff. CBT had helped create UNISYS University, which not only delivered content over the Web but also provided personalized learning portals, tracking systems, online newsletters, discussion groups, mentors, and just about every other bell and whistle one could imagine at the time.

CBT assembled a skunkworks to transform the company. It seemed inevitable that everyone would migrate to Net-based learning eventually, just as commerce was morphing into e-business. Investors believed it would be a Web, Web, Web world.

A senior executive entered *eLearning* into Alta Vista, the search engine of choice in pre-Google days, and my name came up nine times, followed by that of Cisco, whose chairman, John Chambers, had just told the audience at Comdex that eLearning was going to be so big that it would "make email look like a rounding error."

I joined the stealth team that led the effort to reposition the former CBT Systems as SmartForce, the eLearning company. For a brief period, SmartForce was the only eLearning game in town.

At a trade show half a year later, you might think every training vendor was in the eLearning business. In reality, most of them had invested in little but new signs. Even the most tenuous connection to the Internet was defined as "eLearning." Some vendors sent e-mail notifications to people taking CD-based training and called it eLearning. Others offered a simple discussion board, called it mentoring, and stuck on the eLearning label. Dot-com delusions filled the air.

How delusional was it? One large vendor put samples of eLearning on its Web site. To those accustomed to wearing a blue suit and white shirt with a red tie, casual Friday had come as a shock to the system. It was little surprise, then, that the company assumed the world needed training about how to dress casually. Why not use eLearning here? The result was (I'm not making this up) an exercise taken from the paper dolls little girls dress up with paper clothes. In the eLearning version, if you outfit the female with a tank top and mini-skirt, you find that this is not appropriate attire for the office. Similarly, the guy in the muscleman T-shirt and sneakers should change before work too.

The same organization put together online exercises on how to act at lunch with a customer. You're supposed to pick the right response from a choice of three. See if you can figure it out:

1. "My fish was great. How was your chicken?"
2. "Boy, nothing like a belt of single malt scotch to conclude a fine meal, eh?"
3. "Mind if I finish up the rest of your chicken?"

When I showed this bit of fluff while delivering the keynote at an eLearning conference in Edinburgh, I noted that the correct response was, of course, 2.

BLENDED LEARNING

In mid-2002, the term *blended learning* began cropping up in conversation. At first, *blended* meant computer learning with classroom learning. Apologists who had shortsightedly defined eLearning as computer-only learning talked of combining eLearning with live workshops. Some people continue to define blended learning as a sandwich made of alternating slices of computer learning and live workshops. More sophisticated practitioners were saying the blend might contain chunks of computer-mediated learning, classroom, lab, collaboration, knowledge management, apprenticeship, case discussion— whatever mix is the best way to accomplish the job.

When Curt Bonk (2005) asked me to contribute a chapter to Charlie Graham's and his book, *The Handbook of Blended Learning* (2005), I refused. Curt is persistent. He asked me again, and again I turned him down, this time with an explanation. I offered to write the introduction to the book, which I'll reproduce here:

> I told him I considered *blended learning* a useless concept. To my way of thinking, *blending* is new only to people who were foolish enough to think that delegating the entire training role to the computer was going to work. I could not imagine *unblended* learning. My first-grade teacher used a blend of storytelling, song, recitation, reading aloud, flash cards, puppetry, and corporal punishment.

Is it not nutty for a learning strategist to ask, "Why blend?" The more appropriate question is, "Why not blend?" Imagine an episode of *This Old House* asking, "Why should we use power tools? Hand tools can get the job done." For both carpenters and learning professionals, the default behavior is using the right tools for the job.

My perspective is corporate, not academic. My bottom line is organizational performance, not individual enlightenment. Not that I am dismissive of research. In nearly thirty years in what we used to call the training business, I have read my share of Dewey, Kolb, Bransford, Gagné, Schank, and John Seely Brown, but as a businessman, I also pay allegiance to Peter Drucker, Stan Davis, and *Harvard Business Review*.

What's a Blend?

First of all, these are not useful blends:

- 40 percent online, 60 percent classroom
- 80 percent online, 20 percent face-to-face
- 80 percent workshop, 20 percent online reinforcement

After reading a few chapters of Curt's book, you see these for what they are: oversimplifications. Four or five years ago, it was commonplace to hear, "We've tried eLearning. People didn't like it. It didn't work very well." This is akin to saying, "I once read a book. It was difficult to understand. I'm not going to do that again." You can no more generalize about eLearning than you can generalize about books.

People do not know what they like; they like what they know. For example, many assume that face-to-face instruction is the one best way to teach and that online learning is inherently inferior. They seek ways for online initiatives to support the high-grade face-to-face experience. Capella University turns this view on its head, asking what face-to-face support is required to supplement online learning. Having found online learning universally effective, Capella uses face-to-face only to further social goals such as building a support network or creating informal affinity groups. From its perspective, a blend may contain no face-to-face element at all.

Blended learning can take place while waiting in line at the grocery store or taking the bus home. Its ingredients may be courses, content chunks, instant messaging pings, blog feedback, Web tours, or many other things. Interaction is the glue that holds all these pieces together.

Interaction comes in many forms—not just learner and instructor but also learner-to-content, learner-to-learner, and learner-to-infrastructure. Interaction can create an experience so compelling that it makes workers hungry to learn and drives otherwise sane people to pay four dollars for a cup of coffee at Starbucks.

What Goes into the Blend?

Great recipes are the product of generations of experimentation, tasting, and refinement. eLearning is at the same embryonic stage as American cuisine when home chefs rarely started a sauce without a can of condensed mushroom soup and garlic was reserved for scaring away vampires.

First-generation eLearning initiated, delivered, and completed online; its consumers lost their appetites. Today's tastier recipes include organizational skills assessments, books, content objects, workshops, clinics, seminars, simulations, collaboration, technical references, learning games, and links to communities of practice.

At the University of Phoenix, I developed a classroom-based business curriculum in 1976. A dozen years later, an online program debuted. More recently, the university introduced blended programs that combine some classroom and some online. Add more classroom, and the result is the local model blend; add more online, and the result is the distance model. Some blends are like "vibration cooking": a pinch of this, a handful of that, and however much wine is left in the bottle.

IBM's four-tier model shows how the ingredients of the blend must be matched to the nature of the outcomes sought. Web pages work fine for performance support. Simulations are good for developing understanding. Groups learn from community interaction and live virtual programs. Higher-order skills require coaching, role play, and perhaps face-to-face sessions. Each dish requires its own recipe.

Blends are more than a learning stew, for blends fall along many dimensions (Table 11.1). The ideal blend is a blend of blends.

Blended is a transitory term. In time it will join *programmed instruction* and *transactional analysis* in the dustbin of has-beens. In the meantime, blended is a stepping-stone on the way to the future. It reminds us to look at learning challenges from many directions. It makes computer-only training look ridiculous. It drives us to pick the right tools to get the job done.

Read Curt and Charlie's book, but don't just read it. Make it a blended learning experience. Discuss its cases with colleagues. Incorporate it into your plans. Reflect on how to apply its wisdom. Blending will help you learn.

Note the last dimension in Table 11.1. There's a place for formal learning and a place for informal. Sophistication comes in concocting the appropriate blend to fit your situation.

TABLE 11.1.   Dimensions of Blended Learning

Fleeting know-how	|--+--+--+--+--|	Lasting knowledge
Individual	|--+--+--+--+--|	Community
Generic	|--+--+--+--+--|	Proprietary
Training	|--+--+--+--+--|	Knowledge sharing
Text	|--+--+--+--+--|	Visual
Self-directed	|--+--+--+--+--|	Guided navigation
Content focus	|--+--+--+--+--|	Experience focus
Exploring	|--+--+--+--+--|	Participating
Push	|--+--+--+--+--|	Pull
Personalized	|--+--+--+--+--|	One-size-fits-all
Skills	|--+--+--+--+--|	Values
Information	|--+--+--+--+--|	Transformation
Formal	|--+--+--+--+--|	Informal

THE UNIVERSITY OF PHOENIX

Marketing executives know the importance of packaging. It's usually all people see before they make a decision to buy. We judge books by their covers. Packaging emphasizes the reputation of the product and its brand. I have not tried what's inside, but I would never buy Pabst Blue Ribbon Beer or Union76 gasoline or a Mounds candy bar. Something about their presentation turns me off.

Every time I go to Costco, I'm reminded that size makes a difference too. Even if it were cheaper than the four-ounce bottle, I would never buy a gallon jug of Tabasco. It just doesn't feel right. The same goes for a case of pickles.

When I enroll in a class that consists of twenty-two meetings of fifty minutes each, I know that package size was probably determined before content or objectives. I expect some classes will consist of five minutes of lesson and forty-five minutes of padding.

In the mid-1970s, a fellow I'd worked with told me he was consulting with some nutty outfit in San Jose that needed some market research. I was recruited for the assignment and went to the major firms in Silicon Valley and the banks in San Francisco to gauge their appetites for an accredited, off-campus degree program in business. Atari, Fairchild, Ford Aerospace, NASA, Bank of America, McKesson, and IBM loved the idea. I spent the next two years developing and marketing the business program what they wanted. In 1978, we became the University of Phoenix.

The University of Phoenix knows packaging. With more than 170 campuses in North America, it is the nation's largest accredited private university, with enrollment of a third of a million students. Asked how they felt about their University of Phoenix education, 90.2 percent of alumni said it met their expectations, 89.3 percent of alumni said it taught them how to learn from others, and 88.6 percent of alumni said it prepared them to be an effective team member. Their University of Phoenix education was cited as a factor by 97 percent of those receiving a salary increase, 90 percent of those who received a promotion, 88 percent of those who obtained a new position, 88 percent of those receiving increased duties, and 89 percent of those starting their own business [www.UniversityOfPheonix.com].

John Sperling founded the University of Phoenix. When I went to work for him in San Jose in 1976, most colleges and universities treated working adults like second-class citizens. Some had night classes, but they didn't have night office hours, bookstores, admissions offices, or administrators. Typically it took eight years to earn a four-year degree. John founded the University of Phoenix to meet these needs.

Thirty years later, John is the same energetic, spunky crusader as before, his energy and interests undiminished by age. You may have read about him in the *Forbes 400* issue or *Wired*. His is quite a character. He has championed the legalization of marijuana, set up a company that clones pets, published and publicized a book lauding the Blue States over the Red in George W. Bush's second run for the presidency, and established a medical facility researching optimal health.

I asked what made the University of Phoenix such a runaway success. He told me:

- Group process
- Small class size
- Clear objectives
- Mandatory attendance
- Faculty as mentor, not instructor
- Catering to an unserved market (working adults)

Except for mandatory attendance, which was dictated by accreditation associations, learning at the University of Phoenix is more informal than on traditional campuses.

I asked John to what he attributed his journey from a cabin in the Ozarks to revolutionizing higher education. "I was stupid until the age of nineteen," he told me. When he went to sea, there was no distracting background noise, and he overcame his learning disability.

After receiving a doctorate in economic history from Cambridge University, he became a professor at San Jose State. Friends thought he was nuts when, in his fifties, he resigned his tenured position to follow his heart and founded the University of Phoenix. (Don't think of Phoenix, Arizona; think of the mythical bird arising from the ashes.) Ever since, John has been doing well by doing good.

THE FUTURE OF LEARNING

"Education often preaches instead of teaches," says author Marcia Conner, former education director at Microsoft and PeopleSoft. "Instead of learning solutions to yesterday's problems, people need to learn how to deal with the unknown. In the real world, the issues we face are ones that no one knows the answers to. Can we afford not to learn how to learn and find more and better ways to learn everything we will need to do in the days and years to come?"

Designers deem a dress a success if people say the woman wearing it is beautiful. Similarly, eLearning will be successful when it is no longer noticed. The monolithic library publishers are dead or dying.

Many learners today are not self-directed; they are waiting for directions. It's time to tell them that the rules have changed. It's in their self-interest to become proactive learning opportunists.

Free-range learners of the world, unite. You have nothing to lose but your pains.

The Web connects us all, and that's the subject of the next chapter.

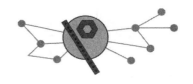

THE WEB

12

THE INTERNET *DID* change everything. The Web connects the people around the world on a scale unprecedented in human history. Ten years ago, there were 16 million Internet users; today they number more than 1 billion. Three years ago, there were half a million blogs; today there are 50 million. No matter where they are, people can use the Web to exchange—or even mutually develop—their most intimate and extensive thoughts or, alternatively, their most casual attitudes and spirits. Emotional experiences, political ideas, cultural customs, musical idioms, business advice, artwork, photographs, and literature can all be shared and disseminated digitally with less individual investment than ever before in human history.

Google is the world's largest learning provider, answering thousands of inquiries every second. The Web is a thesaurus, Latin for treasure house. How else can you describe a medium that gives access to literature, news, history, art, lessons, maps, magazines, weather conditions, and access to and from other people with e-mail, conferencing, and free telephone calls? Most people learn more from the Web than from school, and it's almost all informal learning.

NEW TECH AND OLD

A dozen years ago, most business executives saw no value in the Internet beyond possibly cheaper communications. *CIO* magazine's December 1994 issue sheepishly proposed "not to laud the future of electronic commerce nor to cheerlead the creation of a great national network that, like Godot, may never materialize" (Buchanan, 1994).

A representative skeptic said, "So far, I haven't seen anybody use the Internet for anything that was all that worthwhile." Another chief information officer chimed in, saying, "There's so much nonbusiness stuff on the Internet that you have to wonder if people are getting their jobs done."

The Internet is such a powerful metaphor that it has shaped our expectations of response time, around-the-clock access, self-directed action, adaptive infrastructure, and more. These attitudes and beliefs are derivatives of what I call *Internet culture*:

- *Time trumps perfection.* In the old days, training wasn't released until it passed through a gauntlet of editors, proofreaders, packagers, double-checkers, and worrywarts. (Lots of training was obsolete before it hit the street.) The Internet has taught us to value timeliness over relentless typo searching.

- *Everything is a work in progress.* If it's not finished, label it "draft" or "beta," but don't hold it up. Think of a blog: part of its charm is its informality, the idiosyncrasies of its author, and its status as an opinion, not a law. People learn more when presented with material that is controversial because uncertainty engages the mind. (This book is a beta; you're getting an early peek; expect errors.)

- *The user chooses the package.* Few learners are totally ignorant of the area they seek to learn more about. "Testing out" is absurdly time-consuming compared to simply learning the little bit one needs to know. The Net enables the learner to get just enough and no more. Why take a course if you can get things done with a nugget gleaned from a single book?

- *Online networks facilitate personal connections.* The Net enables one to rely on the kindness of strangers. Hundreds of people I didn't know before have helped me learn; I keep my karma account in balance by helping others learn. The Net even enables you to talk with your heroes if you're daring enough.

- *To learn something, teach it.* The Net empowers each of us to express ourselves publicly. Sharing ideas is both selfish and generous. Explaining something online clarifies your thinking and reinforces your own learning.

- *It's a small world after all.* With Skype, you can talk with people all over the globe through Voice over IP (VoIP) and for free. The world is my oyster. Why not? Fewer than one in five Internet users is based in the United States.

- *Me-learning*. Google and amazon.com have taught me a lot more than four years of honors studies at an Ivy League college. Why? For one thing, I've forgotten more calculus, Wittgenstein, physics, Nietzsche, and French than I'll ever know again because I was driven by someone else's agenda rather than my own.

- *Outboard brain*. You don't need to memorize something if you know where to find it. For the past thirty years, I've been collecting tidbits of knowledge, frameworks for thinking, and useful algorithms, at first on paper and now in bits. Most of this is on the Net. It helps me avoid reinventing the wheel. Haven't you started building your self-help portfolio? Never mind; soon we'll have the Library of Congress on our personal digital assistants.

- *Self-organization*. The Internet is magical. It takes care of itself. From a few standards and protocols, the Net has woven itself without a weaver. It's a tribute to the wisdom of gaining control by giving control. The lesson? Let it be. Some things are destined to happen on their own. Let them.

BLOGS

A blog is little more than an easily updated personal Web site with dated entries. A researcher at University of California at Berkeley named his blog "A Place to Write." Some bloggers show photos, some tell jokes, and some highlight discoveries.

You can set up your own blog for free in five minutes. The details will have changed by the time you read this, and creating a blog will be even easier. Go to the Informal Learning Web site at informL.com for current information.

Unlike tangible things, the more an idea is shared, the more valuable it becomes. It's as if every time I give you something, I get two back in return. The irony is that I often learn more than my readers. The personal payback is astronomical.

I use my blogs to learn and to share ideas (Figure 12.1). My blog has evolved into a personal newspaper for which I write a daily column. My paper is 90 percent Op/Ed. It's whatever comes to mind when I sit down to write. I am the prime subscriber, for the blog helps convert fuzzy thoughts into a form I can share with others; if other people find it interesting, that's an added benefit. Sometimes my writing just seems to come out of nowhere; it's automatic.

Old blog entries never die. The archives of Internet Time Blog contain one layer atop another, like an archaeological site. The layers go back six or seven years, but some material dates from when I bought my first IBM PC in 1984.

FIGURE 12.1. A Blog for Sharing News and Ideas: Internettime.com

Source: http://internettime.com/.

Why Blogs Matter

The military has been justly accused of always fighting the last war. The American revolutionaries waged guerrilla warfare from behind fences against superior British forces who marched in formation wearing bright red jackets. Yankee and Rebel generals studied Napoleonic strategy and sent their men to face devastating fire from greatly improved rifled muskets. The Allies and the Germans in World War I didn't understand the supremacy of the machine gun until tens of thousands perished trying to rush trenches. Not wanting to fall prey again, the French built the Maginot Line, only to have German tanks go right around it. In Vietnam, guerrilla fighters won out over the mightiest military power the earth had ever seen.

The war in Iraq is unlike any other. Car bombs and booby traps are the enemy's weapons of choice. It's nearly impossible to tell the good guys from the bad. Few American soldiers knew any Arabic, and most were unfamiliar with Muslim culture. American forces trained to fight in the countryside found themselves skirmishing in city streets.

In spite of the potential for chaos, American junior officers are coming up with ingenious solutions to daily challenges. Today's lieutenants and captains are Gen-Xers. They don't respect authority. The army is responding by pushing decision making to lower levels in the organization. What's more, today's young officers are savvy about the Internet. They blog.

In every war since World War II, the army has assessed lessons learned and passed that information down to the troops. Central command would print its findings in pamphlets and distribute them to the field. Today, specialists go into combat to document and distribute lessons learned. Most of the information flow remains top-down. Officers in Iraq e-mail questions to CALL, the Center for Army Lessons Learned, and generally receive replies within twenty-four hours. Unfortunately, many replies are off the mark, and most are written in Army-speak: the folks at headquarters have yet to learn to speak like human beings.

Enter two company commanders who knew one another from West Point. On assignment, they lived next door to one another. In the evenings, they'd talk over lessons learned on the front porch of their quarters. Their conversation addressed topics not found in any official publication. Realizing that they were learning from one another, they decided to expand their circle. With money out of their own pockets and no official support, they set up a Web site called Company Command. The first page of the site begins:

CompanyCommand.com is company commanders—present, future, and past.
    We are in an ongoing professional conversation about leading soldiers and building combat-ready units. The conversation is taking place on front porches, around HMMWV hoods, in CPs, mess halls, and FOBs around the world. By engaging in this ongoing conversation centered around leading soldiers, we are becoming more effective leaders, and we are growing units that are more effective. Amazing things happen when committed leaders in a profession connect, share what they are learning, and spur each other on to become better and better.

Every day, company commanders across Iraq tap into Company Command.com to see what's new. The advice is extremely practical, it rings with authenticity, and it's up to the minute. The site is protected, to keep the enemy from finding out what we're learning. A *New Yorker* piece in early 2005 included a sample of topics on the Company Command blog (Baum, 2005):

> Never travel in a convoy of less than four vehicles. Do not let a casualty take your focus away from a combat engagement. Give your driver your 9mm, and carry their M16/M4. Tootsie Rolls are quite nice; Jolly Ranchers will get all nasty and sticky though. If a person is responsible for the death of an individual, they do not attend during the three days of mourning; that is why if we kill an individual in sector, we are not welcome during the mourning period. Soldiers need reflexive and quick-fire training, using burst fire. If they're shooting five to seven mortar rounds into your forward operating base, whatever you're doing needs to be readjusted. The more aggressive you look and the faster you are, the less likely the enemy will mess with you. It is okay to tell your soldiers what the regulation is; but as a commander, you should make the effort to get the soldier home for the birth. A single wall of sandbags will not stop any significant munitions. Take pictures of everything and even, maybe more importantly, everyone. The right photo in the right hands can absolutely make the difference. It's not always easy to reach the pistol when in the thigh holster, especially in an up-armored humvee. If they accept you into the tent, by custom they are accepting responsibility for your safety and by keeping on the body armor, you are sending a signal that you do not trust them. If tea or coffee are offered, be sure to accept the items with the right hand. Do not look at your watch when in the tent.

This informal, spontaneous, vernacular knowledge sharing is not just for the war zone. Imagine that your organization is installing an enterprise software system. One of the first things you might want to do is to set up a Plog, that is, a project Weblog, a place to share stories about how things really work.

WE'VE GOT TO START MEETING LIKE THIS

Every community needs a clubhouse where members can discuss things and draw conclusions. It's painless and free to set up a space online for conversation.

I have an Italian-English phrasebook with an attitude. The English in one entry reads, "Please do not bother me." The Italian words actually say, "Let's talk about your life insurance needs." Experience has taught me I can achieve the same effect by saying, "Let's talk about wikis."

A wiki is nothing more than a Web site where people can write what they want, including revisions to one another's work. Unfortunately, wikis began

life ten years ago as a collaboration tool for geeks. Some features felt need-
lessly obscure. The name itself (*wiki-wiki* is Hawaiian for fast) communicates
nothing.

Not long ago, David Weekly was documenting software instructions for
his employer on a wiki. It worked so well that before long, his entire company
was using wikis for documentation.

On a wiki, if you see a glitch, you fix it. David became convinced that every
organization needs a wiki. He named his company Peanut Butter Wiki because
he felt setting up a wiki should be as easy as making a peanut butter sandwich.
Six months after opening the doors, 21,000 people had created 200,000 pages
of content. (Go to the Web site, pbwiki.com, to see some examples.)

Among the wikis I recently set up was for the steering committee and
speakers for the e-Merging e-Learning Conference in Abu Dhabi, which used
it to share ideas and coordinate schedules (Figure 12.2).

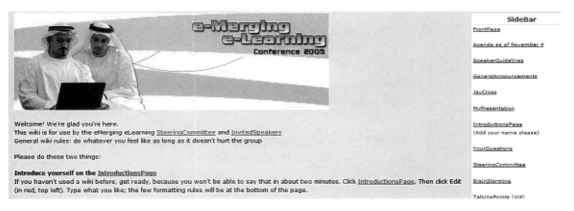

FIGURE 12.2. A Wiki for Organizing an Event
Source: http://pbwiki.com. Reprinted with permission.

I chaired the steering committee for the conference and invited the
brightest people I know. We came into this with different ideas about what
was going on. I set up a wiki for planning purposes.

Participation on the wiki was spotty, but in retrospect, I realize that it
made a major contribution in setting some of the themes of the conference.
Two of us argued in favor of bringing problems out in the open. We wanted
Q&A on stage with the minister of education. Another person pushed for
graphic artifacts to keep the spirit of the event alive. Yet another chimed in to
add a bit of logic to our chaos. Someone else stressed the importance of the
Web, social networking, wikis, and more to ensure that learning does not become a one-shot deal, forgotten when one graduates.

During a one-day workshop in Taipei the week before I arrived in Abu Dhabi, we set up a wiki to record links to references, photos, and post-workshop dialogue (see Figure 12.3). Setting this up took all of five minutes.

FIGURE 12.3. A Wiki for Keeping Track of Members of a Class
Source: http://taipei.pbwiki.com. Reprinted with permission.

For all of their benefits, wikis have a downside that can be fatal: they are odd, and people don't have anything to compare them to. A wiki gives everyone the ability to write (and erase) in a shared notebook. I could not recommend using a wiki unless participants have a fervent interest in working with one another, for example, in a crash project where close coordination is required.

WEB 2.0

Some people evangelize Web 2.0, also known as "the Web as platform" or the "writable web," as the next big thing. Others argue that it doesn't exist. A few say it doesn't make any difference. *Web 2.0* is one of those terms, like *eLearning* or *broadband,* that describes the future in fuzzy terms. It's just far enough out of sight for rumor and speculation to rule the day.

The World Wide Web began life as a network for displaying technical content. Companies and individuals designed Web sites that resembled on-line brochures. They were hard-coded and rarely changed. Web 1.0 was static, like a book. Then Flash made sites flashy; bloggers spewed forth personal news and gossip; style sheets and content management systems made it possible to create Web pages on the fly.

Change is always more interesting than stasis. Several years ago, people thought I was radical when I made my blog my home page. Now that's com-monplace. Google empowered and simplified the Web by doing the heavy lifting of locating things with massive server farms out of the public's eye. The open source movement (a philosophy, a set of rules, or a political belief, de-pending on where you stand) created more and more interoperable widgets. Users could now subscribe to Web feeds that brought news and gossip to them without searching.

Programmers assembled new applications from open source code fragments glued together with JavaScript and XML. The "open" of open source began to mean transparency as well as availability of code. Every laudable application came with an interface that let other applications interact with the data inside. This interoperability gave software developers the power to do "mash-ups," combinations of full-fledged applications, for example, combining Google maps and Craigs List to create a street map of apartments for rent. "Folksonomies," tags any user can assign to a Web page or photo, gave entries the meaning that cumbersome semantic approaches couldn't pull off. The tags are indexed by a number of systems, so you can call up, for example, photos of gray cats or Web sites dedicated to researching informal learning. The plummeting cost of mass storage propels services like FlickR, which not only stores photos but connects thousands of amateur photographers in elaborate sharing schemes.

The Internet is becoming a computing platform on its own. You can call up a word processor, a spreadsheet, a calendar, contacts, graphics programs, project management tools, a customer relationship management system, e-mail, free telephone calls, live conferencing, and other applications on the Web. I've used all of these, and for free. Some people expect the Web to re-place desktop software, although I suspect them of being relatives of the peo-ple who forecast the paperless office.

Six months will pass from the time I finish the manuscript for this book until the book hits the bookstores. By that time, the vocabulary will have changed. Time will have judged whether Google became king of the moun-tain, Sun fell over the edge, service-oriented architecture saved the day, or Larry Ellison gobbled up more of his enemies. That being the case, I'll describe some trends that are in the air, many of which will have an impact on how we learn and do business. Come to the Informal Learning Website for my take on today's situation.

THE UNWORKSHOPS

Recently I hosted a series of unworkshops on learning with blogs, wikis, and Web 2.0 tools. Why the *un?* I wanted to crush the old paradigm of workshop leader spoon-feeding participants. We would replace the virtual lecture hall with a virtual water cooler (Figure 12.4).

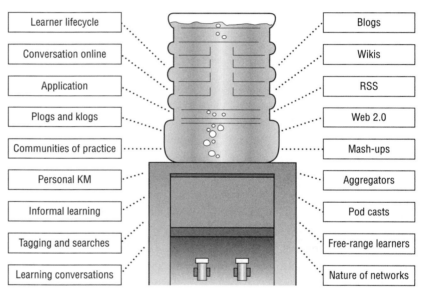

Learner lifecycle		Blogs
Conversation online		Wikis
Application		RSS
Plogs and klogs		Web 2.0
Communities of practice		Mash-ups
Personal KM		Aggregators
Informal learning		Pod casts
Tagging and searches		Free-range learners
Learning conversations		Nature of networks

FIGURE 12.4. Application of the Latest Web Technology to Learning in Unworkshops

The unworkshop covered the topics surrounding the watercooler. Table 12.1 is an abbreviated synopsis of some of the applications of Web technology in informal learning that we discussed.

INTERNET INSIDE

Imagine having an in-house learning and information environment as rich as the Internet. You'd have blogs and search and syndication and podcasts and mash-ups and more. You'd also have a platform just about everyone already knows how to use. CGI, a large Canadian services company is doing precisely that.

TABLE 12.1. Learning Applications for Web Technologies

Web Application	Description	Business Value
Blogs	Everyone can create learning objects and find information online instead of in a file cabinet	Capture ongoing knowledge; give voice to workers
Tags	Informal descriptions added to blogs and other digital data	Recall by topic; hassle-free knowledge management
Team blogs	Shared space online	Coordinate projects; share rules of thumb
Wikis	Collaborate over time; share ideas; co-create practices; share insights	Cooperative decision making and documentation
FAQ	Answers to the most common questions people ask	Don't reinvent the wheel; single-source reference
Screencasts	Electronic show and tell, "look over the shoulder" demonstrations	Explain "how to" by showing the real deal
Communities of practice (wiki, RSS, blogs)	Create and share professional knowledge	Real-time subscriptions, knowledge retrieval
Guided tours	Simple tours of Web sites with narration	Great discovery learning tool
Collaborative software	Converse; create and share knowledge	Circuitry for learning, innovation, and change
Simple Web tool set	Frequent, no-risk prototypes	Innovation
"Internet inside"	Internet software behind the corporate firewall	Interoperability; lower total cost of ownership
Instant messenger	Immediate connection to selected colleagues and customers	Text or voice; can tell when someone's available
Wizards and support	Provides just the information needed	In lieu of reading the manual
Jams	Mass rally without the travel cost	Creates team spirit, rapid roll-out
Podcasts	Download in-house news, expertise to iPod	Use commute or treadmill time productively
Storytelling	Memorable, natural way to spread values and goals	More sophisticated than text; oral tradition reinforces meaning

CGI

At a technical conference in Seattle, I was polling individuals about whether they thought Microsoft's embrace of RSS technology was for real or for show. (Most thought Microsoft was for real.) I talked with a fellow named Ross Button about informal learning, and he told me about a self-maintaining, nearly instantaneous knowledge infrastructure he was implementing at his firm, CGI. It relied on RSS, commercial, and open source software from the Internet. As he described what he was assembling, I flashed on the term "Internet Inside."

Ross and CGI were taking some of the most flexible, freely available systems from the Web and creating an Internet of their own behind the firewall.

CGI operates on a massive scale: twenty-five thousand professionals working from over a hundred offices in nineteen countries. Founded in 1976, CGI is the eighth largest independent information technology and business process services firm in the world. Ross is corporate vice president of technology leadership.

The technology and services CGI offers are constantly changing. CGI provides consulting, systems integration and the management of business, and IT functions as well as industry-specific solutions. It employs a compelling and unique global delivery model—a flexible, scalable, and cost-effective solution to its client's IT needs. Clients choose from a palette of offerings to create the on-site, off-site, near-shore, and offshore combination that gives them the savings, efficiencies, and control that they want.

Keeping Up

Reporting directly to the chief technology officer (who reports to CGI's president), Ross's mission is to help CGI excel in technology leadership. His team has crafted the Technology Leadership Program, a dynamic environment of programs, people, process, and technology to keep CGI professionals at the forefront of IT technology (Figure 12.5).

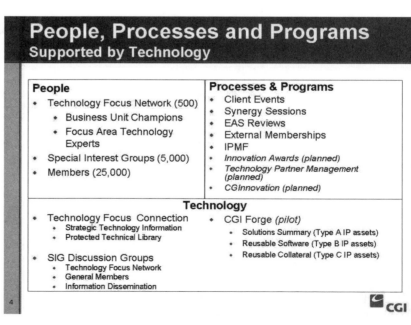

FIGURE 12.5. The CGI Technology Leadership Program
Source: CGI internal presentation. Reprinted with permission.

The Technology Focus Connection (TFC) is a tool, Web site, aggregator, communications vehicle, technical library, and repository of items of strategic interest, all rolled up into a single portal. CGI put the TFC in place to:

- Help its technical community understand strategic and emerging technological advances
- Improve the ability of CGI members (employees) to communicate, leverage, and share technical knowledge, experience, and components
- Provide optimum solutions for customers

Putting the Technology Focus Network in Place

CGI identified eight strategic topics, among them data center, emerging network, enterprise Unix, enterprise Java, security, and virtualization. Each topic is assigned to a small number of people who are responsible for soliciting, reviewing, managing, and publishing the content related to that strategic topic. The concept is to have a few people tracking and reporting on each area instead of hundreds of senior architects doing it in parallel. The TFN is the place for information. Each topic has a lead who is the ultimate expert.

Overall, about 350 professionals are members of the network. Membership is by invitation only. It is considered an honor to be selected as a technology leader, akin to being named a fellow in other corporations. These technology leaders keep up with the latest research, inform fellow members what's going on, and build vibrant user communities. They scan RSS feeds, Web sites, and trade sites; post information to the TFC; filter material submitted by members; and support online discussion areas. The average topic is supplemented with ten fresh entries per week. The TFN is central to the Technology Leadership Program (see Figure 12.6) and entirely virtual.

Components of the TFC

Information flows into people's mailboxes daily, weekly, or monthly. The companion Technical Library is inside the firewall and password-protected, so internal documents, presentations, and materials that were once e-mailed back and forth are easily located and shared from a central source (Figure 12.7).

TFC's special interest groups (SIGs) provide e-mail subscriptions on more than a hundred topics. People can set up SIGs for business units or product areas. Past messages are stored in a repository, which becomes an ongoing corporate knowledge reference.

CGI Forge serves for sharing Internet protocol in-house, along the lines of SourceForge with its million members working on ninety thousand open source projects (Figure 12.8).

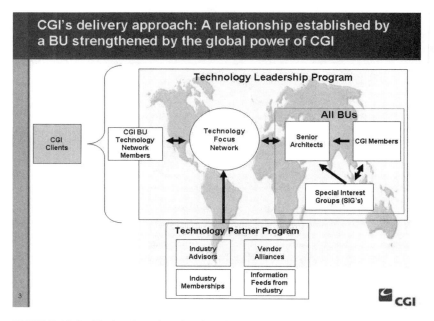

FIGURE 12.6. Technology Leadership Program

Source: CGI internal presentation. Reprinted with permission.

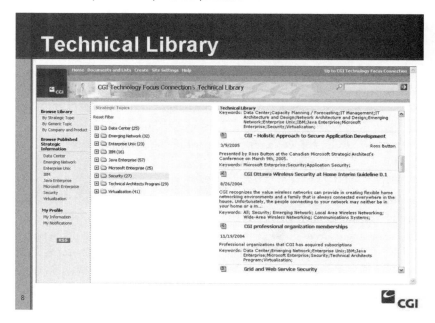

FIGURE 12.7. Technical Library

Source: CGI internal presentation. Reprinted with permission.

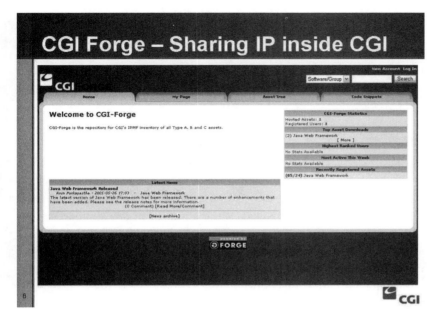

FIGURE 12.8. CGI Forge: Sharing IP Inside CGI
Source: CGI internal presentation. Reprinted with permission.

Ross calls the technology RSS Everywhere, to reflect the use of RSS as the glue to tie together the engine and information sources as well as internal blogs and wikis. This design concept is evolving as a knowledge integration and delivery platform and is serving as the foundation for CGI's second-generation intranet.

Building Support for the TFN

Step one was recruiting subscribers to a strategic intelligence feed or SIG announcement stream. Members participate as observers, as contributors to the TCF, as members of SIGs, and by nominating members from their teams.

I caught up with Ross in Geneva, part of a whirlwind tour of CGI offices to meet the tech teams and explain the TFN program. Members tell him they feel more connected to the company than ever before. When a member needs information, others in the network help her find it. CGI's culture and the visibility of the TFN drive contributions to the network; no additional incentives are necessary.

From a business standpoint, the TFN leverages the size of the company to serve its customers. Hundreds of people are increasing the expertise of twenty-five thousand members. CGI's commitment to technology leadership is becoming visible to members and customers alike, a hallmark of the way it does business. By the time you read these words, Ross expects to have rolled out a parallel structure that focuses on lines of industry, not technology.

What do you call an effort like this? It's not training. It provides flows of information, direct channels to experts, and a library of resources. It's similar to knowledge management but it's bottom-up; knowledge management is usually top-down. Fifteen years ago, we might have called this office automation. Ross tells it like it is: this is CGI's Technology Leadership.

The Thought Leadership project took about a year of working on the people network and the technology network in parallel. The prime task for the people was recruiting. The project was not to introduce technology; rather, it was to introduce a collaborative network. This is about people.

Recently a member in Canada had a question on telecommunications data warehousing; the answer came from the telco group in Portugal. A configuration management question from Germany was answered by a member in Canada. Small centers are talking with large centers. People who previously had no way to contact one another are now free to help one another absent the boundaries of time and geography.

By-product statistics on conversations, duration of conversations, and document transfers enable Ross to perform social network analysis. If one office has gone dark, Ross calls them to find out what's going on.

By starting small within CGI, Ross was able to install a lightweight system, largely from open sources parts, for a tenth the cost of a commercial enterprise system. It's assembly, not invention, and not a lot of training is required. Everyone already knows how browsers and e-mail work. There's no learning curve. Members may swap code and other IP via an in-house version of SourceForge.

Membership is growing. The number of countries and digital contributions and conversations are growing fast. Ross sees this as planting a seed. It's to be encouraged, nurtured, and tweaked as feedback rolls in.

SMALL PIECES

The Internet was made for informal learning. It's always on. It connects to people and information. It's a network environment. It's available almost everywhere. It makes things available in real time. It's user driven. You can pick what you want and take a little or a lot. It's the learning platform of the present and the future.

Acquiring knowledge and making major changes need not require training at all. The next chapter discusses a major transformation at BP.

GROKKING

13

TO *GROK* IS TO UNDERSTAND profoundly through intuition or empathy. The word *grok* was coined by science-fiction writer Robert A. Heinlein in his *Stranger in a Strange Land* (1961). Heinlein invented *grok* because English lacks a word that captures *grok*'s connotation of instantaneous, holistic recognition.

A picture is said to be worth a thousand words, but sometimes it is worth much more. Images take a direct path to the right hemisphere of the brain. An appropriate visual can simplify the complex by providing a snapshot of an entire system.

> The real voyage of discovery consists of not in seeking new landscapes but in having new eyes.
> **MARCEL PROUST**

BP

BP, formerly British Petroleum, is one of the largest integrated oil companies in the world, with nearly a hundred thousand workers in one hundred countries. BP's nineteen refineries process 2.6 million barrels of crude oil a day. It sells through 28,500 service stations, 15,000 of them in the United States.

BP is in a complex business, and that complexity is exacerbated by the firm's growth by acquiring Amoco, ARCO, Burmah Castrol, and Veba Oil. Several years ago, BP initiated a massive corporate change program to optimize internal operations. The program included aspects of business process reengineering and Six Sigma in more than a hundred categories.

One of these initiatives was launched with the objective of improving the interface between the Refining division and the Integrated Supply and Trading (IST) group. This could not be done totally within either of the two business units, for success depended on how well IST and Refining worked with

> See things as you would have them be instead of as they are.
> **ROBERT COLLIER**

To succeed in business
it is necessary to make
others see things as
you see them.

JOHN H. PATTERSON

one another. The goal was to achieve "a seamless and efficient interface between Refining and IST based on partnership, common processes, and common organization that will enable sustained commercial performance growth."

Initially, it was tough to define the problem the team was trying to solve. People on the Refining side of the house had one understanding of relationships with their counterparts in IST, and the IST people had another. The change team made several attempts to map the interface between Refining and IST using available tools, but none of them fully captured its essence. The change committee realized that without a visual representation of the situation that everyone could understand and agree with, the change project would not be able to achieve its full potential benefit.

BP called in XPLANE to assist the change project. XPLANE is an information design firm that develops visual maps and stories to make complex business issues easier to understand. Its first iteration developed a process map that resembled the famous map of the London Underground. The stations on the Tube map were decision points, the color of the routes signified which division was involved, and notation along the routes specified the action required to advance from one station to the next. The map gave the change team a clear, common vision of what they were talking about and highlighted the points where smooth functioning was required (Figure 13.1). However, it didn't portray the role individuals needed to play to achieve the best over-

FIGURE 13.1. Examining the Big Picture Using the Tube Map at a Refinery in Germany

Source: XPLANE. Reprinted with permission.

all result for BP. The map showed interrelationships but stopped short of showing what to do about them.

Implementing a change process to improve the quality of the Refining-IST interface was tough because things were already working reasonably well. To gain traction with business leaders, the implementation coordinators would need to overcome the prevailing attitude of "if it ain't broke, don't fix it."

Unlike the situation we saw at National Semiconductor, which focused on communicating and getting commitment to an overall corporate strategy, BP sought to have a small group of high-potential workers reconfigure their jobs. The workers were challenged to come up with the optimal mix of individual accountabilities and competencies.

XPLANE developed another poster, this one showing the roles of workers involved at each decision point (Figure 13.2). The IST-Refining Interface

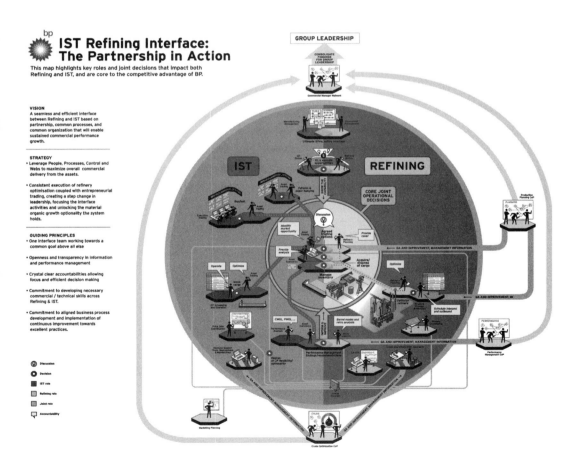

FIGURE 13.2. The Cartoon Map: An Overview of the Critical Interface

Source: XPLANE. Reprinted with permission.

map provided sufficient detail for individuals to identify their accountabilities, decisions, roles, and authority. The "cartoon map," as it came to be known, became the centerpiece of one-on-one meetings and group sessions. Some BP divisions framed the map and hung it for all to see. XPLANE's cartoon map became a frequently used platform for conversation.

The map made it possible to explain and sell the change to key leaders within the organization. The change initiative was approved, and as a next step, BP leaders set up an implementation support team led by Brad McCracken.

After the team met initial resistance from several sites, Brad assigned one of his team members, Ann LeBeau, to develop a communication program to support leaders in explaining the initiative and help get the sites more engaged so they would take ownership of the change. Roger Peterson joined Ann to help implement the program.

Extensive analysis uncovered succession planning, clear accountabilities, and competencies as the fulcrum for developing effective managers and knowledge workers.

The first issue was how to engage people in different locations consistently on sensitive topics. Ann and Roger, two of the five implementation coordinators, would kick things off, but in time their roles would change and others would need to carry on in their place. XPLANE was asked to develop methods to help implementers and managers get their arms around the situation in such a manner that the process would live on following Ann and Roger's inevitable departure for other projects.

Management had identified sixty-five foundations, that is, areas ripe for specific improvements. Ann and Roger sought a way to get staff to seek opportunities rather than voice complaints. XPLANE developed a set of twenty-five cards addressing friction points (see Figure 13.3). Instead of the customary pre-

FIGURE 13.3. Examples of Decision Cards

Source: XPLANE. Copyright © 2005. Reprinted with permission.

sentation of needs from the organization's point of view, the cards described situations from the workers' perspective, for example, "We lack leader support."

The cards were a novelty that sparked discovery and expression. Workshop participants literally played cards. Handling the cards got people involved and made them pay attention. They joked about them and propped them up on their desks. The cards provided the structure that facilitated unstructured but productive interaction.

Roger was originally a skeptic. Then the cards proved extremely effective in one-on-one sessions. The XPLANE cards raised the level of the conversation. Breaking complex issues into their component parts enabled people to isolate and rearrange issues. Roger has become a true believer. He has seen people use the accountability cards when handing the reins to a successor. As frequently happens with informal learning, what started as an educational tool morphed into a work process tool. Not long ago, Ann started a workshop she deemed too simple to warrant using the cards. "Where are my cards?" demanded participants who had talked with colleagues in advance.

XPLANE developed two sets of cards at BP. The pain pack gets people engaged, gets issues on the table, and gains buy-in. A second deck aims at knowledge transfer. These cards break down a job description into its component accountability sets. Managers can swap them back and forth and discuss them until they are clear about who owns what accountability.

Roger has spent three years with the project. Recently, the cards have led to deeper conversations than he achieved in the first two and a half years, a three- to fourfold improvement in the quality of conversations. In addition, several hundred managers and professionals have used the cards to improve the quality of conversations around organizational change. Ann and Roger are experimenting with using the XPLANE cards and tool kit in online sessions to spread the XPLANE technology throughout BP.

REFLECTION

With over $100 billion worth of oil sloshing back and forth between IST and Refining each year, even minuscule improvements are significant, but there are other lessons to be gained from this example.

BP sought changes in the way business was done, but senior management realized that training was not going to change anything. Among other things, the people who best understood the details of the functions involved were the very people who needed to change. The posters and cards provided a foundation for meaningful conversation about how things should work.

Senior project director Brad McCracken told me, "The project has been very successful in improving the effectiveness of the partnership between

Refining and IST. The major factors behind this success were simple: articulating how to put competent people into roles and keep them there, then defining exactly what you expect them to do and who has what decision authority. All of the material produced by the project, including the XPLANE materials, helps people understand the concepts and promote increased conversation around the hurdles that had held us back in the past."

Training courses often end up in binders that are never opened again. BP's posters and cards are artifacts that continue to reinforce understanding of how the business works.

Again and again, we have encountered informal learning situations where the best solution was to clarify what was going on, remove obstacles to shared understanding, and get people on the same page. If you have experience with the traditional methods of reengineering, realigning job competencies, and developing common practices after large mergers, you can appreciate the rare lack of memos, bureaucracy, and wasted effort in BP's approach. It's much more effective for people to simply grok the situation rather than being taught.

COMMUNICATIONS DESIGN

XPLANE, the visual thinking company, is a global design firm that enables companies to master the art and science of communication. Visual thinking helps XPLANE's customers deliver faster, more consistent understanding, leading to action and results. Figure 13.4 shows how XPLANE's graphics ("XPLANATIONS") work.

FIGURE 13.4. Examples of XPLANATIONS

Source: XPLANE. Copyright © 2003. Reprinted with permission.

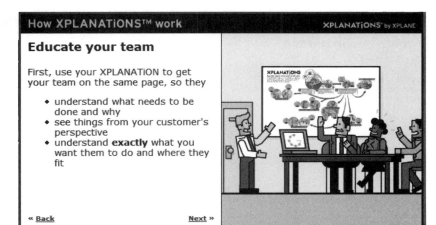

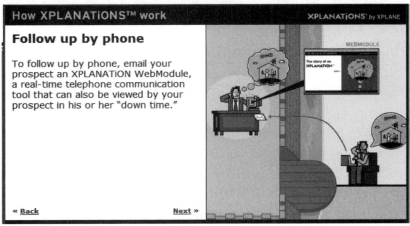

FIGURE 13.4. Examples of XPLANATIONS, Cont'd.

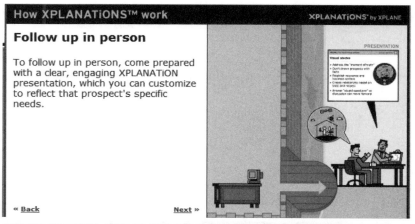

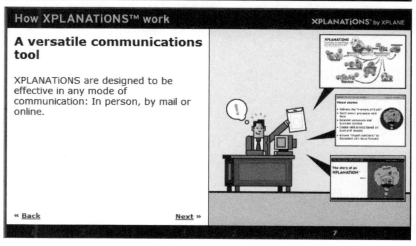

FIGURE 13.4. Examples of XPLANATIONS, Cont'd.

FIGURE 13.4. Examples of XPLANATIONS, Cont'd.

Effective communication is the most important competency for informal learning. Nothing is accomplished without it. In the next chapter, we examine how to make communication in meetings more effective by replacing the authority-to-audience model with collaborative peer-to-peer learning.

UNCONFERENCES

I'm sitting here at a conference that I flew all the way
to Paris for. for two days, and damned if it isn't full
of panels, broadcast mode all the way, telling the audience how it is. And well. it's so freaking undynamic.
Because it's not a discussion. These are bloggers. They
know a lot. They know what it is. These 300 people make
media every day on their blogs and yet, panels are here
giving us time to email the office, our cats or the mail-
man about a critical lost postcard.

This audience is creative, bright, thoughtful and our
brains are being numbed to death by one-way talk about
how blogs are about losing legacy control and we're all
taking it back. Somewhere there is a tragi-comedy in
here. It's time for a revolt. Please, please, please can
we do all conferences from now on differently? For the
love of transparency, aliveness, I hope we can.
Mary Hodder, Napsterization

BUSINESS MEETINGS USED to come in one flavor: dull. New approaches
are creating meetings that people enjoy, often organized in scant time and at
minimal cost. These meetings are not events; there's typically activity before
and after. If something is working well, why not share it with everyone, and
why not keep it alive as long as you can? Successful gatherings are those where
everyone participates.

Unconferences generally share these characteristics:

- No keynote speaker or designated expert
- High learning—breakthrough thinking born of diversity
- High play—having fun dealing with serious subjects
- Appropriate structure and control—emergent self-organization
- Genuine community—intimacy and respect

GEEK GATHERINGS

Geek used to refer a carnival performer who bit the heads off chickens. Now it's the proud moniker of techies. The Jargon File, the online compendium of hacker slang, says a geek is:

A person who has chosen concentration rather than conformity; one who pursues skill (especially technical skill) and imagination, not mainstream social acceptance. Geeks usually have a strong case of neophilia. Most geeks are adept with computers and treat hacker as a term of respect, but not all are hackers themselves—and some who *are* in fact hackers normally call themselves geeks anyway, because they (quite properly) regard "hacker" as a label that should be bestowed by others rather than self-assumed.

See also propeller head, clustergeeking, geek out, wannabee, terminal junkie, spod, weenie, geek code, alpha geek.

Geeks are dedicated learners who go to great lengths to stay ahead of the curve. Not content to merely implement the ideas of others, they are driven to invent the future. The way they meet, share information, and conduct their meetings holds many ideas for corporate meetings, starting with the fact that the geeks love to go to meetings like these:

- Gnomedex. Four hundred techies and developers find the zeitgeist to change the world.
- FOO Camp. Originally designed as a party, this notoriously self-organizing camp is an opportunity for people to meet and come up with cool ideas about how to change the world.
- BAR Camp. Perhaps the first "flash conference," from conception to execution in less than a week.
- Learning 2005. Fourteen hundred early adopters flock to Elliott Masie's informal learning event.

GNOMEDEX 5

Four hundred of us convened in the Bell Harbor Conference Center in Seattle in 2005 to take part in Gnomedex 5, an exhilarating conference focused on developments that are propelling the next wave of innovation from the Internet. In the closing keynote, former MTV host Adam Curry compared Gnomedex to Woodstock. Spirits were high, geek culture ruled, everyone was friendly, and networking was intense. Gnomedex lives on through wikis, photos, recordings, news groups, podcasts, and more on the Web.

Gnomedex is an extension of the most energetic guy I have ever met, Chris Pirillo. A perpetual clown, Chris is always laughing, joking, smiling, and enthusiastic, the sort of fellow who lights up a room. Somehow he still finds time to be a geek's geek, one of those guys who seems to know every arcane detail of the latest Microsoft patch and at the same time able to envision the technology space many moves ahead. In his spare time, he writes newsletters and books, appears on radio and television, and consults to tech companies.

FIGURE 14.1. Chris Pirillo: How He Sees Himself

Source: Chris Pirillo. Reprinted with permission.

The Gnomedex show began as a conference that treated its audience as well as its speakers. Chris held the first three Gnomedexes in his home town, Des Moines, which made it the cheapest PC conference around. A conference in Tahoe came next, leading up to the big event in Seattle.

The evening reception the night before things opened up featured endless hors d'oeuvres and an open bar, but it wasn't just the alcohol that created this schmooze fest. It was instant community and shared interest—the sense that we're all in this together. Alpha developers and top tech pundits were fully accessible. Throughout the conference, the meals, breaks, and events left plenty of time for schmoozing.

A new technique for creating and subscribing to newsletters and homemade radio shows (RSS) was the nominal reason for the gathering. By the time we departed, numerous people were saying Gnomedex would go down in history as the tipping point where people took back control of the media from Hollywood and the *Fortune* 500.

Imagine, if you will, four hundred hard-core geeks, each with a laptop and with on again, off again wireless Net connections, and countless phone cams, video cams, heavy-duty digital SLRs, microphones, DAT recorders, and more, all documenting what was going on, many in real time.

Ninety minutes after the close of the conference, participants had posted fifteen hundred photographs on the Web. Have a question about a particular session? You could watch one or more video recordings and read the opinions of dozens of people on what you just watched, among them some of the most astute in the business.

In what will soon be commonplace, the conference had a spot on the Web where anyone could post announcements or check the attendance list, including the Web sites of most attendees. The wiki will live on until next year's Gnomedex.

The conference was streamed over the Net. A fellow in Florida wrote in the real-time chat that the quality was awesome, and a number of people in the audience were swapping ideas on the Net during the presentations.

The first keynote speaker, software entrepreneur and pundit Dave Winer, told us this was not a speaker and audience. Clearly there was more intelligence in the room than on the stage. The audience brings more to the party than the speaker. So this is an *unconference*. The audience talks, but a runner holds the microphone for them. Nobody gets to monopolize the conversation. It's not you and me; this is for us.

Several sessions were recorded for replay as podcasts. The popular Gillmor Gang audio program hosted a lively session with the brothers Gillmor

(Steve and Dan), Doug Kaye, Dave Winer, and Adam Curry. Doug, who invented and runs IT Conversations, which distributes technical conference sessions and interviews for free, pointed out that at least 100,000 people would hear this session in recorded form.

FOO CAMP

Every year, O'Reilly and Associates, the boutique publisher of avant-garde computer books, invites several hundred people "who're doing interesting work in fields such as Web services, data visualization and search, open source programming, computer security, hardware hacking, GPS, and all manner of emerging technologies to share their work-in-progress, show off the latest tech toys and hardware hacks, and tackle challenging problems together." Here's Tim O'Reilly's introduction from the event wiki:

> FOO Camp started out as a lark. We had a lot of extra space in our new building as the result of the dotcom meltdown, and we wanted to do something fun to make use of the space. Internally, we tended to use the term FOO for "Friends Of O'Reilly," and we'd occasionally do "FOO parties" at our conferences for the conference committee, speakers, and authors in attendance. Sara Winge, our VP of Corporate Communications, used to joke about having a "FOO Bar" at these parties.
>
> So we invited a bunch of people up for a big party at our new campus, and decided to run it as a self-organizing conference.
>
> It was such a success that we decided to do it again. And we realized that it actually had a great business purpose: to make us smarter as a company, by introducing our employees to our extended family of people who collectively comprise "the O'Reilly Radar," and by introducing these people to each other. Each of us had great contacts who we wanted to introduce to other folks at O'Reilly and to each other, and we also had people we wanted to meet that an occasion like this gave us a great excuse for reaching out to.
>
> So now, the way we think of FOO is this: it's our chance to get to know new people who are doing interesting work in fields that we are trying to learn about.
>
> Here's the problem: the first FOO camps were so successful that all the original people want to come back. We had to choose between just throwing a party every year, with the same people coming each time, or mixing it up, inviting a mix of people we already know and love, and people we think we'd like to know and think we're going to love. We only have room

for about 200 people, so we have to make some hard choices about who to invite.

FOO camp is *notoriously* self-organizing. O'Reilly provides food, showers, facilities, and a wi-fi network. Participants make up the agenda when they arrive.

You bring your ideas, enthusiasms, and projects. We all get to know each other better, and hopefully come up with some cool ideas about how to change the world.

Last year, Business 2.0's John Batelle wrote, "Talking with attendees, I couldn't help thinking that FOO was more than fun—it was important, and not just to the characteristically self-involved lot who proudly wear the geek label."

O'Reilly is located an hour north of San Francisco in Sebastopol, once the world's largest producer of apples and now famous for its Zinfandel wines. FOO campers are encouraged to sleep over, either outside in the former orchard or in someone's work space inside. And there's the problem: there's not enough space for every A-list geek. One influential Google employee posted this to his blog:

```
Why I'm not going to Foo Camp
I wasn't invited.
    If you are the type of person who reads this blog and
might be prone to drop one of those 'so . . . going to
Foo Camp' lines to see what brand of smart kid I am—well,
I didn't make the cut. I don't know what to tell you.
```

The following day, another person blogged:

```
I just read your post about not going to Camp Foo, and
wanted to chime that I'm wasn't invited back this year
either. Unlike you, however, I'm quite upset about it.
I personally know enough people who are going to make
it somewhat embarrassing—like I didn't make some sort
of intellectual or professional cut or something.
```

BAR CAMP

Less than a week before FOO Camp 2005 was set to open, this post appeared on Andy Smith's blog:

```
FOO Camp happens every year, it is an invite-only event
for tech luminaries hosted in Sebastopol, CA at the
```

O'Reilly headquarters. People camp out, have sessions, and work with other great tech minds to come up with awesome ideas. The problem is the exclusivity: everybody isn't invited.

Meet BAR (meaning "beyond all recognition") Camp, an open, welcoming, once-a-year event for geeks to camp out for a couple days with wifi and smash their brains together. It's about love and geekery and having a focal point for great ideas, like FOO but open.

BAR Camp came together in under a week. Chris Messina and Andy Smith started the BAR Camp ball rolling. This is from Chris Messina's blog:

When we embarked on this strange and fantastic journey, we knew that we had a week. We had no money, no sponsors, no venue and no idea if just the five of us or 50 random folks would show. But we knew that we had to stage BAR Camp and that, among other things, it would serve as a demonstration of the decentralized organizing potential of the *Web2.0 Generation*. We set out to prove that what the good folks at O'Reilly could pull off in a year with a couple years' experience and tens of thousands of dollars, could be cobbled together in a week by a crazy gaggle of savvy geeks, leveraging only the Web and our reach into our social networks.

So here we are, five days later and two days from the event. We've had a venue donated to us. [Three days before things were to start, Ross Mayfield volunteered SocialText's new offices in Palo Alto as an urban campsite.] We've got a fabulous logo (*thanks* Eris!). We've got some sponsors lining up and a bunch of great advisors. And we've got buzz.

This is turning out to be the exact kind of unprecedented success we were hoping for—and from here it can only get better as we lead up to the kick-off.

Remember flash mobs? People coordinate on their cell phones to all show up at a given location at the same time. Two hundred people cram into, say, the lobby of the St. Francis Hotel or Harvard Square and before management can figure out what is going on, the crowd vanishes. BAR Camp strikes me as a "flash conference." Lots of people, technology, logistics, and experts create a successful conference in six days flat.

Ross Mayfield, CEO of SocialText and our host, blogged that

```
you need to remember what has changed—the cost of group
forming has fallen—so anyone can create one of their
own, almost instantly. This will not lead to more com-
petition between groups, but understanding across them.
```

On Tuesday, Dave Winer's blog pointed to Andy's page about BAR Camp, quoting "an open, welcoming, once-a-year event for geeks to camp out for a couple days with wifi and smash their brains together."

I commented on Andy's blog: "Where's the BAR Camp wiki?" He replied "barcamp.org" and added, "And yes, we'll be documenting the whole thing—one thing we want more than anything is for BAR Camp to live beyond this one weekend. Think: BAR Camp in a Box. That's basically what we want coming out of this year's event."

Around seven o'clock on Friday evening, Chris stands atop a concrete pedestal in the courtyard outside SocialText's new offices to kick things off. People are asked to introduce themselves to the group using no more than name, location, company affiliation, and three words. Some of the words of three that I remember: *geek, entrepreneur, save world, ninja, real-time, fanatic, blogger, society.* I say "author, informal, learning" and later will explain that I'm at BAR Camp both as a geek and as an anthropologist studying how techies learn about new stuff from one another.

A dozen large pizzas arrived, beer bottles were opened, and three or four discussions among five to a dozen participants got going. Eugene Kim, president of collaboration consultants Blue Oxen Associates, and a handful of us hunkered down outside to discuss extreme usability. We passed the talking stick, speaking the argot of software design and programming to relate extreme usability to agile software development, extreme programming, rapid prototyping, constructive friction, pair programming, Homer Simpson, and Ruby on Rails. The Homer episode and Ruby were new to me, so that part of the discussion would have meant about as much to me in Greek. I drew analogies to developing business processes that John Seely Brown and John Hagel describe in *The Only Sustainable Edge* (2005). Eugene facilitated the session, encouraging everyone to contribute. He was also recorder, tapping notes into his PowerBook to be posted to the wiki later on.

In one room, five people were hunched over their laptops, tapping away. I asked if this were a session. No, they replied, not a session. What were they doing then? "Just hacking," came the response. This seems to be a standard behavior at geek events: dropping out of the live event and hooking into the virtual reality of the Net to check mail, tweak code, or surf blogs to see what's going on in the next room. These are all as legitimate an activity as conversing face-to-face. I sense that just being among their own kind gives off sort of a contact high.

I spied a fellow I'd met at lunch during Gnomedex: Scott Beale, proprietor of Laughing Squid, the Web hosting service for artists. He's managing publicity for BAR Camp. I wanted to tell him how much I enjoyed his photographs of Gnomedex and also to show him the purple Laughing Squid sticker on my ThinkPad. Geeks put stickers on their computers just as Harley riders get tattoos. Geeks have introduced themselves to me in airports because they assume someone whose computer sports stickers for Laughing Squid, FireFox, Creative Commons, and the Michelin Man must be a member of the tribe.

This camaraderie is a major shift from the dot-com era of the late 1990s. Then geeks talked about getting rich, the value of their stock options, and which model Ferrari they should buy. People found it tough to live in their own skins. Everybody wanted to be a Steve Jobs. Then came the dot-com meltdown. It was like nuclear winter. Companies went down the tubes. Money vanished. Everyone disappeared. Traffic jams in Silicon Valley became rare. People are coming out of that now, but they are coming back as themselves, with no more play acting. They're out to change the world.

Geeks are passionate. That's the rule in many communities, from owners of Mini Coopers to collectors of guitar picks. There are people who lay in bed at night thinking about their particular cause. Employers look for this level of enthusiasm in prospective employees; it's more important than technical chops.

Shared norms make geeks a community of practice, and that makes it possible to host instant meetings like BAR Camp. Most traditional employers I've talked with do not encourage membership in communities outside the corporate firewall. They are unwittingly taking themselves out of the grapevine that announces new ideas and sparks innovation.

A woman comes by with a tray of BAR Camp buttons. She says that in the old days, this would have taken weeks. Now "the Asian sweatshop button factory" (she and a volunteer) is operating in the front room. As if by magic, BAR Camp T-shirts appear. Event T-shirts are yet another badge of belonging to the geek community.

On the ride home, I reflected on how BAR Camp differed from corporate sessions. A corporation would have tried to cram everything you needed to know into the two-day session. Content would have oversaturated people's brains after two hours, and excess information would be pouring out of their ears. They'd be learning more and more about less and less.

BAR Camp, in contrast, provided exposure and teasers for dozens of contents. We focused on breadth, not depth. If something grabbed your attention, you could follow up with the speaker afterward or check a recording or see what was listed on the wiki or go to the relevant Web site. This format treats learning as an ongoing process; the meeting is but the first step.

BAR Camp also created a social structure that may or may not persist. If I want to check something out with someone I spoke with, I can locate them through the wiki.

At most corporate events, presenters parade to the podium, facetiously saying they want to share their thoughts, while their body language, tone, and PowerPoints tell another story. Most of them want to tell you how it is and how it's going to be. This is like your boss "sharing" his thoughts on what you're going to do next. Questions come after the presenters have finished.

There were no presentations at BAR Camp. No PowerPoints. No better-than-thou. No podium. No positions carved in stone. Instead of presentations, campers had conversations. We were equals, codiscovering new ways to look at things. We sat in circles. No one was in charge because we were all in charge.

Doc Searles, a highly influential blogger, wants to "reboot the whole conference system." In *Linux Journal*, Doc writes:

> The problem is mass habituation. We're so used to the whole routine: picking up badges, grabbing coffee and cookies, sitting in rows behind tables with laptops flopped open, surfing the Web or answering e-mail while keynoting CEOs from sponsoring companies drone PR while the PowerPoint deck shuffles by, complaining about the absent power strips and bad Wi-Fi connection. The list goes on. And on.

What's the alternative? Give control to the audience. Respect what they bring to the table. Here's Doc again:

> A guy I was talking with had a cool idea for conferences like this one. Set it up like any other conference—with speakers, panels and so on—and then announce at the beginning that all the speakers were bait, that the whole conference is completely open. Anybody can learn anything from anybody. Bring up the house lights, arrange the chairs in circles, roll out the hors d'oeuvres.
>
> With no speakers, every attendee's expertise is a "source" for every other attendee. Conversation becomes

the most efficient and effective means for moving and growing knowledge throughout the whole crowd. The idea here is a profound corollary to Bill Joy's observation that "most of the smartest people work for somebody else." The balance of smartness in any conference session heavily favors the audience. So, what's the most efficient and effective way for everybody to share what they know?

We've been lecturing at conferences for the last umpty years. Audiences have been opting out through schmoozing in hallways, hanging out on IRC channels, blogging, IMing and e-mailing each other. In other words, they're going to other sources of knowledge.

Doc has many suggestions.

- Hold collegial meetings, not sessions. Some of the best sessions at conferences are the BoFs, or birds-of-a-feather sessions, held after hours.
- Record all sessions, and make them available online in open audio formats. This also helps sell attendees on coming to the next conference.
- Make the Web a living and permanent resource and document archive. Provide Wi-Fi.

LEARNING 2005

Elliott Masie is a larger-than-life figure in the learning business. He has great stage presence, a big heart, an incredible record of accomplishment psyching out trends in learning, brilliant intuitive marketing skills, an impeccable sense of timing, and a large following.

He got on the computer training bandwagon before it was popular. He sold his conference to a technology publisher, which promptly ran it into the ground. As soon as his noncompete agreement with the publisher expired, Elliott began producing the popular TechLearn conferences. He sold the TechLearn franchise for millions a month before 9–11 put the kibosh on travel and conferences. When *that* noncompete agreement expired, Elliott announced Learning 2005, an unconference breaking all of the rules, to the delight of his fans and forward-looking learning professionals.

Learning 2005 set out to be an informal learning event. Believing that discussions in the hall are more important than formal sessions in the breakout rooms, Elliott set out to made breakouts more like hallway discussions: "One of my pet peeves is the way in which one-hour sessions at events overpromise the content to be addressed. And when leaders roll out a two-dozen-slide presentation, there goes the interaction. So we are changing the model by dousing the overhead projector, placing the one-pagers on interactive wikis for pre- and post-viewing/expansion and limiting the session leaders to a one-pager."

Elliott told us that everything at Learning 2005 was about extreme learning. That's experimentation that is one standard deviation away from your comfort zone. You can't experiment unless you're willing to fail. Elliott encouraged us all to push the envelope, to become comfortable with the unpredictable.

Among the experiments at Learning 2005 were these:

- Building a learning lab and training marketplace in a virtual reality environment.
- Hosting the conference program, announcements, and session feedback on an openly accessed wiki.
- An online social networking system to enable participants to hook up with like-minded souls and set up times for personal meetings.
- "LearningLand," an immense open space with ten or so "pods," chairs grouped around giant flip chart boards, with each pod intended to seed a community or special interest group. Visual journalist Eileen Clegg had drawn starter graphics to get people thinking. Chairs and tables are spread about to foster conversation.
- In one corner of LearningLand, you could take a break by learning to throw pots (as a potter does) on a wheel.
- Wireless response devices to gather instantaneous audience feedback.

On opening night in Orlando, more than a thousand participants filed into a big ballroom to the beat of a country/zydeco band. Elliott took the stage and told us Learning 2005 was going to be different from past events. We were going to have lots of conversations, discussions, arguments, a variety of folks, citizen journalism, voting, liquid learning. We were going to mix it up.

Times are way faster, more challenging, and more confusing than ever before. That's why we're embracing extreme learning, which deals in high velocity; we can no longer afford to take eighteen weeks to develop a program. We'll talk about personalization. Google is responsive; PowerPoint is not. We want scalability. We've been training the competent and available; the incompetents never make it to the session. We're going through different generations of learners.

At one point, Elliott said, "I've lost control," missing the point that the future entails getting control by giving control. I began to classify what I was experiencing here as old school or new school (Table 14.1).

TABLE 14.1. Old School Versus New School

Old School	*New School*
Talking at us	Talking among ourselves
Control	Connection
Keynotes	Interviews
Audience	Participants
Follow the rules	Push the boundaries

My session on informal learning the following day was packed with enthusiastic people. It was fun. This was my first presentation in longer than I can remember that used no PowerPoint. It improved the flow. Things felt more spontaneous—because they were. Many sessions were more dialogue than presentation, and audience involvement came naturally. The exception were the vendors, who almost universally presented PowerPoint sales presentations to people lined up in rows (which doesn't promote informality). If the vendor community doesn't change with the times, the times will break them.

FIGURE 14.2. A Layout That Discourages Interaction
Source: Jay Cross.

The day after I flew back to Berkeley, my mind was on fire with ideas. Snippets and flashes of Orlando were still in turmoil in my head, seeking connections with my life's stored patterns. The mind's postprocessing is one reason that evaluation sheets completed immediately at the close of a session are meaningless. You don't know what will last until patterns have started to sink in and connect to your worldview, and experience has settled on which ones are keepers.

Throughout Learning 2005, people struggled to force-fit new ideas into old frameworks. How can I add some informal learning to our formal learning? How can I measure informal learning with my learning management system? How can I ensure that they learn what they need to? Can't our competency management system run things?

I'm of two minds on these issues. Organizations can profit immediately from applying the techniques described in this book. Many of the techniques can increase revenue and innovation while diminishing cost and bureaucracy. But a piecemeal approach will never spark organizational transformation. Getting the most out of a broader definition of learning requires unlearning the vestiges of the way we're accustomed to interpreting the world.

"Incrementalism is the enemy of innovation," said Nicholas Negroponte, founder of MIT's Media Lab. You can't retrofit all the new innovations to last year's model. Is your organization ready for extreme innovation?

In spite of forewarning, some people thought they had signed up for just another conference. Their three-day experience bore little resemblance to mine. Many were uncomfortable with the flexibility, the alternatives, and the margin for confusion compared to their expectations. Some griped about anything unconventional, but I sense many of these poor folks always drink from a half-empty glass.

Beauty is in the eye of the beholder, as are effectiveness, value, enthusiasm, brilliance, opportunity, and the softness of the pillows. I became a different person at Learning 2005, and I hope to continue waking up as a new person every day. To learn is to be. Change requires a new way of being in the world. Be all that you can be. Think of it as extreme makeover.

JUST DO IT

IT'S TIME FOR less push and more pull, less top down and more bottom up, and less going through the motions and more creating.

How was God able to create the universe in six days? He didn't have an installed base. You, however, are not starting from scratch. Your organization has routines, sacred cows, information hoarders, in-house politicians, rules of thumb, and paradigm drag. Of necessity, you will right the balance of formal and informal incrementally. Let's begin by examining roadway engineering in the Netherlands.

> *If a man thinks he can do a thing, or that he can't, he's right.*
> **HENRY FORD**

TRAFFIC IN THE NETHERLANDS

Hans Monderman is a Dutch traffic engineer gaining fame for what he doesn't do. Monderman does not like traffic signs. Overengineering drains things of context: civic responsibility fades away, reckless driving ensues, and people get hurt.

Monderman was asked to design a bike path for a village. Twenty-five hundred children a day would ride on the path. Following his standard routine, he invited the village elders for a walk in another village. There they saw a road with no speed bumps and no chicanes. The lack of signs and obstacles made drivers take responsibility for their actions. Drivers immediately reduced their speed by 10 percent when alongside the bike path. Eventually their speed dropped to 50 percent of what it had been originally, and there it stayed.

> *What humans can't engineer, evolution can.*
> **KEVIN KELLY**

Monderman has worked his magic in more than a hundred Dutch communities. He uproots signs and clears barriers so drivers can easily see pedestrians. Traffic accidents in Holland are 30 percent of what they were when he began.

When you remove the center line from a country lane, people drive more safely. Clutter a road with signs and barriers, and people feel sufficiently protected to drive as fast as they like. Traffic signs indicate a failure of a road's architecture to communicate context naturally. Hand a traffic engineer a village lane, and he'll make it a speedway.

Imagine a jazz band making its way across a modern city. Are they strolling along calmly, talking about their next gig? No. They look more like a military platoon making an escape through enemy territory. Cars, buses, and trucks are the enemy. The city was engineered for vehicles, not pedestrians. Is this any way to live?

Monderman says that if you treat people like fools, they act like fools. Take off the training wheels, and they drive like grownups.

Being told to take a training course is like driving on a road with signs, stripes, and bumps. If a worker takes a training course but doesn't learn, what's her reaction? "The training wasn't any good." Instead of training, what if you tell the worker what she needs to know to accomplish the job? Offer a variety of ways to get up to speed, from treasure hunts to finding information on the company intranet. This makes the learner take responsibility. There's no longer an excuse for not learning.

Open up a training course at your company. How many useless signs do you see? Some of them are equivalent to saying, "Here, let me connect the dots for you." But people want to connect the dots for themselves. That's the point.

To make someone a trusted, loyal employee, you treat that person with trust and respect. If you want workers to be self-motivated and exercise good judgment, you give them a challenge and the authority to carry it out. Failing to do these things is why most workers give at best 20 percent of their energy to their work.

> *Focus on opportunities rather than problems. Problem solving prevents damage, but exploiting opportunities produces results. Exploit change as an opportunity, and don't view it as a threat.*
>
> **PETER DRUCKER**

NO MORE TRAINING

An astute vice president at LSI Logic was concerned with the meager results of the company's classroom training. He wanted LSI to focus more on building competencies and less on training events. Employees had been happy to pick and choose traditional training from a buffet of offerings. Taking away their choices would require extreme measures.

So LSI shut down its training department, and focus shifted from training to talent management. A talent management steering committee representing the vice presidents from each major function was formed and backed the plan. In place of training, LSI put online development plans in place. Employees work with their managers to determine what competencies they must master. They agree on a path to get there: on-the-job learning, coaching, books, and other means.

Nearly four years later, LSI is letting some training creep back in. Compliance and certification had never really gone away. A new CEO favors management development workshops. Training is allowed, but other development options are encouraged first.

I am not advocating the dissolution of training departments. Withdrawal is not pleasant. I am in favor of dumping the term *trainee*. In a knowledge society, learning is the work, and the work is learning. There is no separate reality in a classroom outside the workplace.

CREATING THE LEARNSCAPE

Developing a platform to support informal learning is analogous to landscaping a garden. A major component of informal learning is natural learning, the notion of treating people as organisms in nature. The people are free-range learners. Our role is to protect their environment, provide nutrients for growth, and let nature take its course. Self-service learners are connected to one another, to ongoing flows of information and work, to their teams and organizations, to their customers and markets, not to mention their families and friends. We can improve their connections and nurture their growth, but we cannot control them or force them to live.

A landscape designer's goal is to conceptualize a harmonious, unified, pleasing garden that makes the most of the site at hand. A learnscape designer's goal is to create a learning environment that increases the organization's longevity and health and the individual's happiness and well-being.

Gardeners don't control plants; managers don't control people. Gardeners and managers have influence but not absolute authority. They can't make a plant fit into the landscape or a person fit into a team.

The late Peter Henschel (2001), former head of the Institute for Research on Learning, wrote, "The manager's core work in this new economy is to create and support a work environment that nurtures continuous learning. Doing this well moves us closer to having an advantage in the never-ending search for talent." How else could it be? Neither nature nor the workplace will cooperate by going into suspended animation so we can tweak the details without things changing all the time. Everything flows. You go with the flow, or you are out of it. Every learnscape has a history and a future, but the present is a moving target.

> *When I examine myself and my methods of thought, I come to the conclusion that the gift of fantasy has meant more to me than my talent for absorbing positive knowledge.*
>
> **ALBERT EINSTEIN**

LEARNING OVERSIGHT

Talent is scarce, and competency is a competitive weapon. Corporate learning is now on the executive agenda. Informal learning will be soon. The focus of the learning function is moving from training and certification to all facets of learning, including collaboration, knowledge management, and support of communities.

Governance, assigning enterprise-level accountability for learning, is vital. Unless you are blessed with a rare, sensitive executive management team, you must address governance or scrap plans of getting the benefits you've been reading about. Informal learning is too important to leave to chance or the training department.

A superlative training department is not enough to manage learning strategically. Learning warrants a long-term approach, multiyear investment, and strategic management. Effective governance requires senior-level buy-in, support, and participation. Major firms are chartering learning governance bodies, sometimes called learning councils, to:

- Drive organizational and cultural transformation
- Build knowledge to support innovation and growth
- Sponsor nontraining aspects of informal learning
- Nurture the leadership to create a learning culture

Best practice is to establish a governance structure to define the rules, processes, metrics, and organizational constructs needed for effective planning, decision making, steering, and control of learning to achieve business goals. Ideally, a senior executive will establish and empower a learning council to:

- Put an enterprise learning strategy in place
- Ensure that the learning strategy supports the business strategy
- Cascade strategy and goals down into the enterprise
- Provide organizational structures that facilitate implementation

The evolution of learning governance is accompanied by concurrent changes in budget, time horizon, focus, tactics, and other dimensions. Just as some children walk before others but learn to read behind the pack, these dimensions of change don't move together in lockstep. The organization's strategy, current situation, recent history, internal rhythm, degree of collegiality, and management flexibility accelerate or retard the rate of change.

Some organizations create governing bodies at the enterprise level, mini-boards if you will, to coordinate investments in support of enterprise objectives. Centralized organizations envy the freedom and flexibility of their decentralized cousins; decentralized organizations covet the efficiency and calm of a group that has things under control. In time, most organizations reach a state of equilibrium.

Governance organizations accommodate the tension through federation. Important business units represent their constituencies in the learning council. The chief learning officer promotes what's good for the whole organization, backed up by the senior management member of the council. Services are shared to realize enterprise efficiencies and lessen the risk that each line of business will reinvent the wheel. Equally important is what's not shared. Business units continue to manage local issues. They know what their customers and people need, and the learning council must not usurp their responsibilities in these areas.

No two learning councils look alike. Some are tightly centralized; others are loose federations. How the council operates and makes decisions is heavily influenced by the parent organization's culture, values, and history: its DNA. The maturity of existing training, knowledge management, communications structures, and technical infrastructure will determine whether council members act as missionaries, pioneers, or nurturers. Tackling major changes requires a resilient, tightly knit learning council.

FREEDOM!

Western cultural views of how best to organize and lead (now the methods most used in the world) are contrary to what life teaches. Leaders use control and imposition rather than participative, self-organizing processes. They react to uncertainty and chaos by tightening already feeble controls, rather than engaging people's best capacities to learn and adapt.
—MARGARET WHEATLEY

Civilization evolves. Early peoples believed they were controlled by gods and had no voice in what happened to them. Eons later, people felt they were born to their station in life. Once a serf, always a serf. If your father was a blacksmith, most likely his father was a blacksmith, and you were going to be a blacksmith too. (Your name was probably Smith.) God could change things, but God was accessible only through a layer of priests. Throughout most of human history, a person has been only a pawn in someone else's game. Royalty, nobles, gods, and priests made the rules.

Some people refused to play the game. Buddhists strived to escape to a higher game by looking at this lifetime as but one move in a larger game where each of us lives many lives. Gurus drop out of the game during their lifetime by reaching nirvana, which involves an entirely new set of rules. Artists, criminals, revolutionaries, and other free spirits rebel against the game or simply didn't understand the rules.

These are game-changing times. In the new game that began to evolve when the printing press accelerated the sharing of ideas, individuals decide for themselves the degree to which they play the game or let themselves be played. Opportunity abounds as more and more people become players.

Play is what Harvard psychologist Ellen Langer (1990) calls *mindfulness*. To be mindful is to be aware, look at the world through multiple perspectives, and take responsibility for one's decisions, that is, to be a player. We all know people who haven't made this leap; they see themselves as victims and pawns. Langer calls these people *mindless*.

You're going to spend your entire life learning, so you might as well get good at it. Embracing mindfulness is your first step. You'll need to be flexible, look at things through different lenses, reflect on what you see, try new things, run thought experiments, and pay attention. A mindful person often cuts off the mindless autopilot of aimless living to follow Nietzsche's advice to "become who you are."

This morning, there's nothing on my calendar. Busybody that I am, I can use the time to mindlessly work items off my to-do list. Or I can mindfully start by reflecting on how I'd like to feel at the end of the day. The mindful approach leaves room for new ideas, but the to-do list confines me to old stuff. Naturally I'm going to try to face the day mindfully.

One Fortune 100 company counsels its executives to meditate for fifteen minutes before entering an important meeting. Of course. Why would anyone risk wasting hours in a suboptimal meeting by failing to get their act together before facing the situation?

Almost everyone I know well has a learning disorder; that's what drew them to helping people learn. The enlightened among them see their disorders as an advantage. If society lacked deviants and rabble-rousers, progress would come to a standstill.

WORK = LEARNING; LEARNING = WORK

As work and learning become one, good learning and good work become synonymous. I didn't want to say this early on because you might not have decided to buy the book, but many workers will never be good informal learners because they do not enjoy their jobs.

Half of all American workers lack the motivation to improve their work. Four in ten cannot work collaboratively with fellow employees (Goleman,

2001). Polls tell us that 17 percent of the American workforce is actively disengaged from work; they are there physically but left their minds behind. Stress
at work is commonplace. What's worse, many people don't enjoy their lives.
Unhappy people are more likely to miss work, get sick, annoy coworkers, cause
accidents, botch deals, and get into fights than their happy counterparts.

Motivational speaker Lance Secretan says we don't need to be motivated
to work; we need to be inspired to do so. After hearing Lance speak recently,
I wrote down my calling. It makes my work more personally rewarding: "I am
dedicated to helping people become more effective in their work and happy in
their lives. I try to change the world by helping people learn. My calling is to
spread the adoption of practical ideas through writing, speaking, teaching,
and selling ideas."

Mihaly Csikszentmihalyi's first book, *Flow* (1991), describes the routine
of an elderly woman in the remote mountains of northwest Italy. From dawn
until dusk, she does her daily chores, things like carrying water and firewood
for miles, that many people today would consider cruel and unusual punishment. Was she complaining? Quite the opposite. Living up to her potential
and expectations was utterly fulfilling.

You can't have good informal learning without good working conditions.
You won't have good working conditions without good learning. Neither of
these things happens on its own. Both take leaders who care.

LESSONS OF EXPERIENCE

Keep it simple. Simplicity is the ultimate sophistication.

Guess what server software dominates the Internet. Microsoft? IBM? Sun?
No: more than 70 percent of the Web servers in the world run Apache.
Apache is bundled with IBM WebSphere, Oracle, Novell NetWare, and Mac
OSX. Apache supports 24 million real-time Web sites.

Want to buy stock in this software goldmine? You can't. There is no
Apache Corporation. There are no employees, and never have been. The entire operation sprouted ten years ago from the work of eight volunteers.

In a Berkeley coffee shop, I asked Brian Behlendorf, the original leader of
this pack, the secrets of mounting and maintaining a project of this scope. He
told me:

- Be humble. When the Java community of Apache became toxic, it
  was disbanded.
- Be transparent. Make decisions in the group. Keep the decision-making process open to all. (You can still read every original Apache
  e-mail on the Web.)

- Think of the user community. Set up self-correcting mechanisms to address any potential tragedy of the common situations. (Spam has ruined e-mail. IM and VoIP are next in line for Spam attacks.)
- Look for passionate people. IBM software architect Fred Brooks says a top programmer outperforms a mediocre one by two orders of magnitude.
- Communications skills are vital. These should be taught in school.

Training? Everyone on the Apache team was self-taught. They read the online documentation and explored. Linguistics majors are natural programmers. People learn Apache through observation and osmosis. They lurk, watching how others respond to challenges. They incorporate other people's ideas in their work with grace.

It is amazing what people can accomplish once you clear the organizational barriers and bureaucratic claptrap from their lives.

Do the Possible

The serenity prayer repeated at meetings of Alcoholics Anonymous offers great advice: "Grant me the courage to change the things I can, to accept the things I can't, and the wisdom to know the difference."

You cannot boil the ocean. You cannot change tomorrow's weather. You can't force people to learn. You can't accomplish anything single-handedly. You can't slow the pace of progress. You can't avoid surprise.

Thirty years ago, San Francisco doctors Meyer Friedman and Ray Rosenman wrote a best-seller called *Type A Behavior and Your Heart* (1974) that theorized that stress was the result of unmet expectations. The first evening's assignment for people attending their workshop was to try to cross the San Francisco–Oakland Bay Bridge at the height of rush hour without losing their cool. Anyone who swore or honked at other drivers or became angry had to do it over.

In time, people realized they do not control the traffic or their organizations. Frustration when reality is not what you'd like it to be saps the strength you need to deal with things you can change. It burns you out. I chuckle to myself when I get on the Bay Bridge in heavy traffic. I expect it. I've learned the lesson.

Here are a few other things I've learned: Everything flows. All things are relative. People are good. The old ways are dying. Nothing is certain. Nature knows best. Control is an illusion. Don't sweat the small stuff. Not everything goes right; live with it. Enjoy the ride.

Envision Opportunity

I've written a lot about letting things happen, getting out of the way, and taking control by giving control. That doesn't mean I lack for purpose. The reason I talk of landscape architecture or cultivating crops is that they are not accidental. The gardener or farmer begins with a concept of where his or her efforts are intended to lead.

"Increasing sales" or "achieving ISO 9000 certification" is not visionary. There's no "there" there. Rarely is a vision the laudatory paragraphs from the CEO at the front of the company's annual report to shareholders.

Remember National Semiconductor's vision? It played on its strengths. Its leaders talked it through. They cascaded the message throughout the organization, with each layer exploring its individual part. When they finished the first cycle, everyone knew what the company was trying to achieve and understood their part in it. The next year, they did the entire cycle again, factoring in the previous year's experience. And the year after, National Semi did it once more. Now, that's a vision.

David Cooperrider and his associates at Bowling Green University have been achieving great results with a visioning process called Appreciative Inquiry (Cooperrider & Whitney, 2004). There's plenty of information on the Web about it, so I'll just highlight a few aspects here:

• Don't start with problems. Beginning with problems starts you off on the wrong path. You may solve the problem but miss a fantastic opportunity that was yours for the taking. I used to think of myself as a problem solver. David has convinced me it's better to be an opportunity seeker.

• Involve the entire organization. The goal is not to come out with a jazzy-sounding statement for the venture capitalists and the public relations department. This vision is important to people's lives. It must be co-created. All must take ownership. This is the direct opposite of the strategic planning departments of yesteryear, where a small cadre of inexperienced whiz-kids would play word games until they had a "strategy."

• Start at the bottom. Use paired interviews to warm to conversation. Encourage people to tell stories that show us in our best light. Identify successes. Then, swapping partners as if this were a square dance, explore the topic, "What is the world asking us to do?"

• Build on what we discover and what gives us joy. Groups intermingle. If there are our dreams, how do we shape our organization to fulfill them? We're still half in dreamland, so it's okay to explore stretch goals and off-the-wall proposals.

- What would our organization look like if it were designed in every way possible to maximize the qualities of the positive core and enable the accelerated realization of our dreams?

This may sound like the latest incarnation of EST or some cult. Appreciative Inquiry *is* a little too touchy-feely and revealing for some people. However, the U.S. Navy, not known for being a bunch of softies, sings its praises. An administrator at the Monterey Institute told me amazing tales of admirals having honest dialogue with ordinary seamen. And lately, Soren Kaplan's Icohere Group, a pioneering collaboration software firm, has been facilitating the Appreciative Inquiry process remotely, which not only saves on travel costs but also opens the door to rapid turnaround of results.

Culture Matters

Wait a second, we can't just keep throwing boxes over this wall, without going over the wall and helping our clients implement and make it all work.—LOU GERSTNER

Lou Gerstner took over a thoroughly demoralized IBM that was weeks from bankruptcy and turned it around. Gerstner, a star consultant at McKinsey and a successful leader of American Express, knew every trick in the bag: finance, marketing, product development, and many more. He attributes IBM's amazing turnaround to one element: culture.

A creative knowledge society is built on different foundations than a corporate bulwark of the past era. An adaptive, creative culture runs on:

- Trust
- Challenge
- Self-direction
- Relevance
- Immersion
- Passion
- Talents

The theme of trust runs through all of the literature of collaboration, community building, Appreciative Inquiry, and e-relationships. When a network is vital, you need to have confidence in what's coming at you through the inbound pipe. Otherwise garbage obscures what's meaningful; noise drives out signal; evil triumphs over good.

The most exciting and revolutionary business book of the late twentieth century is *The Cluetrain Manifesto* (Locke, Weinberger, Levine, & Searles,

2000). The clue is that the Internet enables person-to-person conversation, and everyone is the wiser for it:

> Markets are conversations. Their members communicate in language that is natural, open, honest, direct, funny and often shocking. Whether explaining or complaining, joking or serious, the human voice is unmistakably genuine. It can't be faked.
>
> There are no secrets. The networked market knows more than companies do about their own products. And whether the news is good or bad, they tell everyone.
>
> Companies need to lighten up and take themselves less seriously. They need to get a sense of humor. Getting a sense of humor does not mean putting some jokes on the corporate web site. Rather, it requires big values, a little humility, straight talk, and a genuine point of view [pp. xi–xii].

Remember how Pfizer's Courageous Conversations program empowered people to get through the emotional smokescreen to the heart of the issue?

Recently I met with a group where every party seemed to have a hidden agenda. Someone would say something in public, only to laugh it off in private. All decisions were made behind closed doors. People in one sector considered people in another sector sneaky and double-dealing. It was as if no one was presenting his or her authentic self.

Don Tosti, one of the pioneers of instructional design, told me of one organization where employees didn't feel their managers were being open with them. He gave the managers cards to hand to employees. Each card read, "In the spirit of openness . . . I feel free to raise any issue or concern, and expect a considered response from you." When an employee felt misled, she would "play her card." Simple means of making things explicit like this puts them behind you.

A Look in the Mirror

How well do the following statements describe your organization? How do you think your managers would respond? Your workers?

- Most of us are clear about our company's strategic direction for the year.
- My team often talks about the trends and forces that drive our business.
- People in our company are not learning and growing fast enough to keep up with the needs of our business.
- People understand how their work is linked to the overall performance of the organization.

- People here are encouraged to experiment with new ways of doing things.
- Relationships between departments here are cooperative and effective.
- People here are more likely to hoard information than share it.
- I have a mentor at work—someone I can go to for advice in gray areas.
- People here are encouraged to network outside the company in order to grow professionally.
- Our partners and distributors are well informed.

Fifty companies answered these questions as part of the research for this book, but how a small, nonrandom sample of companies saw themselves is unimportant. (I'll post their responses at informL.com.) What matters is where you feel *your* organization stands.

Your Turn

This book has told the stories of how more than a dozen firms are applying informal learning to:

- Increase sales by making product knowledge a snap to find with a search engine.
- Improve knowledge worker productivity.
- Transform an organization from near-bankruptcy to record profits.
- Generate fresh ideas and increase innovation.
- Help workers learn to learn for sustainable competitive advantage.
- Improve your own learning and communications skills.
- Reduce stress, absenteeism, and health care costs.
- Unlock worker potential to be all that they can be.
- Invest development resources where they will have the most impact.
- Increase professionalism and professional growth.
- Cut costs and improve responsiveness with self-service learning.
- Improve morale and reduce turnover.
- Keep pace with rapid technological change.
- Replace training programs with learning platforms.

Do you want to join them? If not now, when?

ONE MORE THING

In the 1920s, Russian psychology student Bluma Zeigarnik watched a waiter taking orders in a coffeehouse across the street from the University of Berlin. The waiter could remember elaborate orders in his head, but when the bill was paid, the orders vanished from memory. Zeigarnik hypothesized that people remember things that are unfinished because their minds are tense while awaiting closure. Ultimately Zeigarnik proved that people remember unfinished tasks about twice as well as completed ones.

Thus, an instructor who wants students to remember a presentation will end the class in midsentence, before drawing a final conclusion. When you put a book down, take a break in midchapter, not at a more natural stopping point. If you want to keep something actively in mind, don't close it out. Let it hang.

I don't want to deny you the pleasure of making it to the end of the book, so I'll stop here, but this is not the end of the story of informal learning.

A vitally important aspect of rocke

(The sentence, and the tale, continues on the Web. Find out what's new. Rejoin me at http://informL.com.)

APPENDIX A: INFORMAL LEARNING IN A NUTSHELL

WORKERS LEARN MORE in the coffee room than in the classroom. They discover how to do their jobs through informal learning: talking, observing others, trial-and-error, and simply working with people in the know. Formal learning—classes and workshops—is the source of only 10 to 20 percent of what people learn at work. Corporations overinvest in formal training programs while neglecting natural, simpler informal processes.

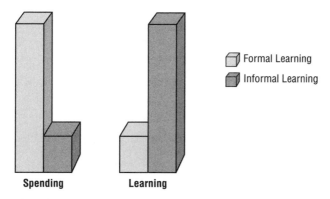

Formal Learning

Informal Learning

Spending   Learning

The Spending/Outcomes Paradox

OUT OF TIME

More happens in a minute today than in one of your great grandmother's minutes. Not only is more and more activity packed into every minute, the rate of change itself is increasing. Measured by the atomic clock, the twenty-first century will contain a hundred years. Measured by how much will happen in the twenty-first century, we will experience twenty thousand current years (Kurzweil, 2005).

Change itself is accelerating. People are anxious. The future is unpredictable. Companies are run by sound bites. People plan; God laughs. The traditional mode of training employees is obsolete.

INFORMAL LEARNING

Learning is that which enables you to participate successfully in life, at work, and in the groups that matter to you. Informal learning is the unofficial, unscheduled, impromptu way people learn to do their jobs.

Formal learning is like riding a bus: the driver decides where the bus is going; the passengers are along for the ride. Informal learning is like riding a bike: the rider chooses the destination, the speed, and the route. The rider can take a detour at a moment's notice to admire the scenery or go to the bathroom.

Learning is adaptation. Taking advantage of the double meaning of the word *network*, to learn is to optimize the quality of one's networks.

SHOW ME THE MONEY

Executives don't want learning; they want execution. They want the job done. They want performance. Informal learning is a profit strategy. Companies are applying it to:

- Increase sales by making product knowledge instantly searchable
- Improve knowledge worker productivity
- Transform an organization from near-bankruptcy to record profits
- Generate fresh ideas and increase innovation
- Reduce stress, absenteeism, and health care costs
- Invest development resources where they will have the most impact
- Increase professionalism and professional growth
- Cut costs and improve responsiveness with self-service learning

Knowledge workers demand respect and expect to be treated fairly. They thrive when given the freedom to decide how they will do what they're asked to do. They rise or fall to meet expectations.

Training managers have complained for years that senior managers don't understand the value of training. Lots of formal learning programs do not work. Maybe the executives *do* understand the value of formal training. They've determined that in its present form, it's not worth much.

Tragically, many firms have mistaken measuring activity for measuring re-sults. Training directors measure participant satisfaction, the ability to pass tests, and demonstrations. They don't measure business results because they don't own the yardstick by which business results are measured.

EMERGENCE

Training is something that's pushed on you; someone else is in charge. Learn-ing is something you choose to do, whether you're being trained or not. You're in charge. Many knowledge workers will tell you, "I love to learn but I hate to be trained."

Formal learning takes place in classrooms; informal learning happens in learnscapes, that is, a learning ecology. It's learning without borders.

Critics say that it's impossible to formalize informal learning and there-fore informal learning is unmanageable. In fact, I don't want an executive managing learning; that's the worker's responsibility. What I want to do is op-timize learning outcomes. Optimization means removing obstacles, seeding communities, increasing bandwidth, encouraging conversation, and so forth.

CONNECTING

Reinventing the wheel, looking for information in the wrong places, and an-swering questions from peers consume two-thirds of the average knowledge worker's day. Slashing this waste provides a lot more time to devote to im-proving the business, reducing payroll, or, more likely, a bit of both.

Knowledge management is no longer the intellectual high ground it once was, by and large because it didn't work. Knowledge lives in people's heads, not in mere words. You can no more capture true knowledge in a repository than you can trap lightning in a box.

The informal organization is how most business gets done, yet executives miss it because they can't see it. Mapping social networks make the pattern clear.

It's not who you know that's important; it's who those others know.

META-LEARNING

Learning is a skill, like playing golf. The more you practice, the better your performance is, but if golfers followed the pattern of businesspeople learning, they would arrive for a match without ever having thought about the game or touched a club.

Many traditional training departments concentrate almost all of their energy on providing training to novices. That's like providing kindergarten classes to high school students to save money. In truth, the more mature learners, typically the top performers, are simply going to skip it entirely or become disgruntled.

Intuition is often more effective than logic because it calls on whole-body intelligence. It is born of relationships and patterns. It draws on the power of the unconscious mind to sort through meaningful experience as well as the immediate situation.

LEARNERS

If something improves the overall value of the ecosystem and the welfare of the individual worker, I'm in favor of it. This includes helping workers build personal strengths and overcome personal obstacles.

If your basic mental systems are out of whack, you may be working extra hard just to cope.

It should come as no surprise that workers don't like training. Most training is built atop the pessimistic assumption that trainees are deficient, and training is the cure for what's broken. Everybody wins if the starting point is, "Be all that you can be."

You may have the best thoughts in the world, but if you don't communicate them effectively, they won't help you or anyone else. I'm thinking about how you converse, tell stories, speak in public, and write.

If you're not happy, you should do something about it.

ENVISIONING

We humans are sight mammals. We learn almost twice as well from images and words as from words alone. Visual language engages both hemispheres of the brain. Pictures translate across cultures, education levels, and age groups. Yet the majority of the content of corporate learning is text. Schools spend years on verbal literacy but only hours on visual literacy. It's high time for us to open our eyes to the possibilities.

Graphics are not fluff. Consider how they can improve informal learning throughout your organization. Graphics work wonders when you need to:

- Bring deeper understanding to complex subject matter.
- Share results of dynamic meetings with others.
- Help the team see the big picture and focus attention.
- Improve the decision-making process.

CONVERSATION

Conversations both create and transmit knowledge. Frequent and open conversation increases innovation and learning. Schooling planted a false notion in our heads that real learning is something you do on your own. In fact, we learn things from other people. People love to talk. Bringing them together brings excitement.

People spend most of their time at work or at home. Work is a demanding, pressure-packed, rats-in-the-maze race with the clock to get the job done. Home is a comfortable, private space for sharing time with family and individual interests. Neither work nor home, a World Café is a neutral spot where people come together to offer hospitality, enjoy comradeship, welcome diverse perspectives, and have meaningful conversations.

Business conversations at Pfizer no longer consist of knee-jerk emotional responses, because people have a means of critiquing the quality of their conversations. They ask, "Is the information valid? Are we making an informed choice? Are we exercising mutual control over the conversation?"

COMMUNITIES

Unless you are a hermit, you are a member of several communities of practice, although you may not have thought of it that way.

For a long time, I maintained that communities were organic. Like truffles, they sort of sprouted up on their own, where they wanted, and the most you could do was to nurture them by providing time and space for them to meet. Times have changed. A quarter of the world's truffles are cultivated on a plantation in Spain.

As fast and easy as it is to search Google, Cisco sales engineers can pinpoint just the knowledge they're looking for. They query the in-house repository of VoDs, and the system takes them down to the exact sentences or slides of interest.

LEGO hobbyists are a community of practice. Subgroups create building standards that enable them to create large displays quickly.

UNBLENDED

It has become trite to point out that the *e* of eLearning doesn't matter and that it's the learning that counts. I don't think the learning counts for much either. What's important is the doing that results from learning. Executives don't care about learning; they care about execution.

In 2001, training directors turned their attention to return on investment. Unfortunately, instead of learning cost-benefit analysis, people who wanted to speak the language of business studied accounting. Created long before knowledge work was invented, accounting values intangibles such as human capital at zero and counts training as an expense instead of an investment.

Consider how we managed to end up with a VCR in every classroom. Was it because teachers wanted to show nature documentaries? Hardly. Massive demand by America's seemingly endless thirst for pornography drove the unit price to $100. Smart phones, voice recognition, and virtual reality are learning tools, but learning won't drive their development. Courses are dead.

THE WEB

The Internet changed everything. In 1996, there were 16 million Internet users; in 2006 they number more than 1 billion. Google is the largest learning provider, answering thousands of inquiries every second.

Recently, I hosted a series of unworkshops on learning with blogs, wikis, and Web 2.0 tools. Why the *un*? To crush the old paradigm of workshop leader spoon-feeding participants.

Imagine having an in-house learning and information environment as rich as the Internet. You'd have blogs, search, syndication, podcasts, mash-ups, and more. You'd also have a platform just about everyone already knows how to use. CGI, a large Canadian services company is doing precisely that.

GROKKING

To *grok* is to understand profoundly through intuition or empathy.

Learning without training is alive and well. BP employees in vital positions grok their roles in an extremely complex organization digesting several mega-mergers.

UNCONFERENCES

Business meetings used to come in one flavor: dull. New approaches are creating meetings that people enjoy, often organized in scant time, and at minimal cost. These meetings are not events; there's typically activity before and after. If something is working well, why not share it with everyone? And why not keep it alive as long as you can? Successful gatherings are those where everyone participates.

There were no presentations at BAR Camp, no PowerPoints, no better-than-thou, no podium, and no positions carved in stone. Instead of presentations, campers had conversations. We were equals, codiscovering new ways to look at things. We sat in circles. No one was in charge because we were all in charge.

JUST DO IT

Management must assign enterprise-level accountability for learning. Unless you are blessed with a rare, sensitive executive management team, you must address governance or scrap plans of getting the benefits you've been reading about.

Natural learning requires an attitude of surrender and acceptance. Informal learning is unbounded. It enables us to find a voice to take its place alongside other parts of who we are as humans. We need all of who we are to be fully engaged, outside and with inner realms to meld with larger wisdom in the world.

As work and learning become one, good learning and good work become synonymous.

Don't start with problems. Beginning with problems starts you off on the wrong path. You may solve the problem but miss a fantastic opportunity that was yours for the taking.

APPENDIX B: WHERE DID THE 80 PERCENT COME FROM?

THE FIRST TIME I heard the meme that 80 percent of corporate learning is informal was in a presentation by the late Peter Henschel, then executive director of the Institute for Research on Learning (IRL). IRL used an anthropological approach to research that enabled it to see things others were missing.

Other studies, as noted below, confirm IRL's basic finding. A word of caution is in order here. Some studies say 70 percent, others 80 percent, and some even 90 percent. Why? For one thing, *informal learning* has many definitions. Furthermore, the ratio of informal to formal learning varies with context. Learning to ride a bicycle involves a higher proportion of informal learning than learning to fly a plane. Most of us learned to use chopsticks informally but learned algebra formally.

- Marcia Conner (2005) writes that "most learning doesn't occur in formal training programs. It happens through processes not structured or sponsored by an employer or a school. Informal learning accounts for over 75 percent of the learning taking place in organizations today." She also notes, "In 1996, the Bureau of Labor Statistics reported that people learn 70 percent of what they know about their jobs informally."

- Many organizations report that 85 to 90 percent of a person's job knowledge is learned on the job and only 10 to 15 percent is learned in formal training events (Raybould, 2000).

- In 1997, the Education Development Center, a research organization in Newton, Massachusetts, released findings from a two-year study of corporate cultures involving Boeing, Ford Electronics, Siemens, and Motorola. One of the most noteworthy findings of the study is support for estimates from previous studies that "attempted to quantify formal training's contribution to overall job knowledge: 70 percent of what people know about their jobs, they learn informally from the people they work with" (Dobbs, 2000, pp. 52).

- "Not only do employee learning programs based on informal methods and self-study increase employee knowledge and productivity far more than more formalized methods, they also cost less, according to preliminary research by CapitalWorks LLC, a human capital management service in Williamstown, Mass. Approximately 75 percent of the skills employees use on the job were learned informally, the study found, through discussions with coworkers, asynchronous self-study (such as e-mail-based coursework), mentoring by managers and supervisors and similar methods. Only 25 percent were gained from formal training methods such as workshops, seminars and synchronous classes" (Lloyd, 2000).

- Approximately 70 percent of Canadians say that their most important job-related knowledge comes from other workers or learning on their own rather than employment-related courses. The National Research Network on New Approaches to Lifelong Learning (NALL) at the Ontario Institute for Studies in Education of the University of Toronto surveyed fifteen hundred Canadian adults on informal learning. Approximately 70 percent of Canadians say that their most important job-related knowledge comes from other workers or learning on their own rather than employment-related courses. Principal investigator David Livingstone summarized the results as follows: "The major conclusion from this survey is that our organized systems of schooling and continuing education and training are like big ships floating in a sea of informal learning. If these education and training ships do not pay increasing attention to the massive amount of outside informal learning, many of them are likely to sink into Titanic irrelevancy" (Vader, 1998).

- In January 2005, an eLearning Guild survey of its members found that "over 70 percent of respondents found or sought information on their own initiative. . . . These results truly put more shape and depth to the 80/20 rule. Not only does it confirm the significant frequency of informal learning, it demonstrates that informal learning shows up in many ways: e-Learning, traditional book study, social learning, and experience" (www.elearningguild.com).

APPENDIX C: INSTITUTE FOR RESEARCH ON LEARNING

THE INSTITUTE FOR RESEARCH ON LEARNING (IRL) was founded in 1987 as a response to the escalating learning crisis in the United States. IRL's mandate, to "rethink learning," addressed the root cause of this crisis: a limited understanding of successful everyday learning. IRL did pioneering work in informal learning and communities of practice. In March 2000, the institute closed its doors, its employees joining WestEd or a consulting spinout.

IRL's Seven Principles of Learning

1. Learning is fundamentally social. While learning is about the process of acquiring knowledge, it actually encompasses a lot more. Successful learning is often socially constructed and can require slight changes in one's identity, which make the process both challenging and powerful.

2. Knowledge is integrated in the life of communities. When we develop and share values, perspectives, and ways of doing things, we create a community of practice.

3. Learning is an act of participation. The motivation to learn is the desire to participate in a community of practice, to become and remain a member. This is a key dynamic that helps explain the power of apprenticeship and the attendant tools of mentoring and peer coaching.

4. Knowing depends on engagement in practice. We often glean knowledge from observation of, and participation in, many different situations and activities. The depth of our knowing depends, in turn, on the depth of our engagement.

5. Engagement is inseparable from empowerment. We perceive our identities in terms of our ability to contribute and to affect the life of communities in which we are or want to be a part.

6. Failure to learn is often the result of exclusion from participation. Learning requires access and the opportunity to contribute.

7. We are all natural lifelong learners. All of us, no exceptions. Learning is a natural part of being human. We all learn what enables us to participate in the communities of practice of which we wish to be a part [Institute for Research on Learning, 1999, p. x].

GLOSSARY

Andragogy Word coined by Malcolm Knowles to describe how adults learn, which is different from how children learn ("pedagogy"). I'm beginning to suspect *pedagogy* denigrates children and that andra is the gogy to go with for all. Main points are: What's in it for me? Let me decide how I'll learn it. Where does this fit in relation to the other stuff I know? Sell me on learning this. Remove the obstacles from my path, please.

Appreciation A process of discovering and freeing the spirit, the essence, the strengths, and the genius in self and others. Appreciative processes can fan the life-giving sparks that exist in every individual, initiative, organization, or situation if you look for them. Appreciative processes are distinct from and complementary to problem-solving processes in that they focus on appreciating and building on what already exists.

Bandwidth A description of how much information can squeeze through a data pipe. An intranet has high bandwidth; a dial-up connection has low bandwidth. Also used anthropomorphically: "He has low bandwidth" is equivalent to "He is a taco short of a combo plate" or "Her elevator doesn't go all the way to the top."

Bipolar thinking The tendency to see everything in black and white when faced with shades of gray.

Blended Using more than one learning medium—generally adding an instructor component to Web-based training. Blended is a revelation only for people who had been trying to do everything with just one tool: the computer. Classroom teachers having been blending various means of learning (lecture, discussion, practice, reading, projects, and writing, for example) for eons.

Blink Rapid cognition (also known as "gut feel). Making snap judgments, often valid, on the basis of a few data points. A subconscious process. Popularized by Malcolm Gladwell (2004) in a book of the same name.

Blog Shortened form of *web-log*. An easily updated personal Web site, generally updated daily.

Blogosphere Originally a joke term, this has become the standard word for the ecosystem of blogs, wikis, and related communications on the Web.

Boiling the ocean Trying to cure all problems at once, often with a single tool.

Broadband Unscientific term for sufficient bandwidth to receive streaming video and sound. Usually refers to bandwidth equal to or greater than DSL or cable modem speed.

Capacity-building Capacity refers to an organization's capacity to develop those new capacities or improve whichever existing capacities it finds to be important to its effectiveness and sustainability. The greater an organization's capacity-building capacity is, the more resilient it will be to external and internal change challenges. Adopting generative approaches to developing an organization's capacity-building capacity could be one of the more effective strategies for ensuring long-term organizational sustainability.

Certification Awarded on passing the test. This started with technical subjects, such as Certified Novell Engineer and Microsoft Certified Professionals. Since there's no credentialing authority legitimizing, expect a continuing proliferation of these things. Certifications simplify hiring decisions; on the downside, they encourage studying to the test.

Chat Real-time communication—text or voice. Generally messages disappear when the session's over. Popular with those who do not want to leave a paper trail.

Co-creative dialogue The intentional act of being together in an open and trusting commitment to pushing the envelope of relationship and ideas; exploring being in the world as uniquely whole persons; creating a context where synergistic breakthrough experiences occur. This process is central to developing co-creative relationships.

Collaborative filtering Presenting the choices of people with similar tastes. Example: Amazon tells me that other people who like the books I like are buying a particular book.

Collective intelligence The capacity of a social organism, such as a corporation, to sense its needs and those of its environment (stakeholders), generate choices that will satisfy those collective needs, anticipate the consequences of those choices, make choices that best serve the well-being of those affected by those choices, and learn from the consequences of those choices.

Community A group of people united by a common purpose who share information and knowledge with one another.

Community of practice A group that shares values, perspectives, and ways of doing things.

Complexity It's a nonlinear, interconnected world, and you will never figure it out. Self-organization holds it together.

Conceptual box An individual's collection of myths, beliefs, and other mental models implicit in my patterns of acting, thinking, feeling and being. Everyone has his or her unique conceptual box. For most, that box will vary to some degree with the situation and evolve through time. More complex social organisms such as families and corporations have their unique conceptual boxes.

Connectionism Coined by George Siemens to describe learning based on actionable knowledge and knowledge foraging in a real-time, networked world.

Content What's being learned, information. If it doesn't cause change, it's not information. The challenge is how to get the right content to the right person at the right time. This involves media choice (for example, paper versus on-screen), speed, delivery cost, relevance, learner motivation, and other factors. Content management system (CMS) A CMS supports the creation, management, distribution, publishing, and discovery of content. It helps users find what they're looking for. It also separates content from presentation.

Context The environment of content. Who's talking? When? Why? Content and context are like inside and outside: you can't have one without the other. The interrelated conditions in which something exists; the consciously or unconsciously chosen set of beliefs, distinctions, frameworks, lenses and mental models that shape how we perceive reality.

Core group The core group, as defined by Art Kleiner (2003), contains the people "who really matter." Often the most senior people in the hierarchy are members—but not always. Sometimes the people who matter can extend far down the corporate ladder or even reach outside the company to include key customers, labor union leaders, and stockholders.

Course A rigid unit of learning, generally expressed in hours or days and led by an instructor.

Dead-tree media Paper-based publications.

DIY Do it yourself. With roots in hacker culture, tinkering, remix, Home Depot, and repurposing, this movement is gaining momentum. Guys who can no longer work on car motors hack into the car's onboard computers instead.

Doggie treats Incentives, targets, measurements, and other numerical signals of direction. These tend to trump all other core group signals as drivers of organizational behavior (Kleiner, 2003). *See also* core group.

Double-loop learning The ability to critically reflect on one's own behavior and identify the ways that this behavior contributes to the organization's problems (Argyris, 1991).

Dynamic information In real time; current, up to the second. Instead of reading pages prepared in advance, the pages are assembled on the fly, incorporating current information and taking into account current needs.

Ecosystem Any dynamic and interdependent community of living things such as a forest, a human family, a business, or a city. All of these are ecosystems, as natural in their own way as anything we find in what we usually mean by nature (Kiuchi & Shireman, 2002).

eLearning Best practices for learning in the new economy, implying but not requiring benefits of networking and computers such as anywhere-anytime delivery, learning objects, and personalization. Learning on Internet time. Coined by Jay Cross (and probably others simultaneously).

Emergence The idea that new properties are created when simple entities combine to form more complex ones. The property of wetness, for example, does not exist in either hydrogen or oxygen. It emerges when the two combine to form water.

Explicit knowledge Knowledge that's easy to communicate. The opposite of tacit knowledge.

Facilitate Supporting communication among people to improve creativity, decision making, and productivity.

Folksonomies Unstructured taxonomies created by users. Anyone can invent and pin tags on objects. An object may have an infinite number of tags. Metadata for the masses.

Framework A basic structure of distinctions that facilitates seeing and acting on a larger whole.

Free-range learner Someone who learns as he or she chooses; often discovery learning.

Frog boiling Apocryphal science experiment. Drop a frog in a pot of boiling water; he jumps right out. Put a frog in a pan of cool water and slowly heat it on the stove; the frog never senses a big change in temperature and stays in the water until poached. The Greek version of this has a farmer lifting a calf over the fence until one day he's lifting a two-thousand-pound bull.

Gap analysis Figure out what to do by assessing the gap between where you are and where you want to be. Most people then begin building from the present into the future. Some people favor looking at the step right before the ultimate one and backing toward the present one step at a time.

ILT Instructor-led training; generally a workshop.

IMS A standards body developing and promoting open specifications for facilitating online distributed learning. Its traditional emphasis surrounded meta-tagging specifications.

Informal and formal learning Formal learning is a class, a seminar, a self-study course. Everyone recognizes it as learning. Informal learning is over the watercooler, at the poker game, asking the person in the next cubicle to help out, collaborative problem solving, watching an expert, or sharing a terminal for eLearning. Most learning is the informal kind.

Infrastructure The underlying social and technical processes, systems, and structures that constitute the basic framework of an organization and are intended to define its patterns of performance.

Instructional design A systems approach to designing a learning experience. Heavily promoted by U.S. Department of Defense investment following World War II, formal instructional design is currently under attack for fostering slow development, a printed-paper mind-set, and insufficient attention to informal learning.

Intangible Something that cannot be perceived by the senses. Accountants and financial types only grudgingly concede that some intangibles have value, and they find it in things like brand names and patents. Because you can't immediately sense a person's capability, a customer's loyalty, or a relationship with a supplier, accountants say these things have no value. Investors see what accountants overlook.

Intellectual capital (IC) Includes much more than knowledge, skills, and information assets that can be formalized, captured, and accessed in ways that are value adding—for example, patents and technological databases. Also includes the intelligence and wisdom that is developed within the members of a social organism (such as a corporation), where its accessibility and value-adding capacity are dependent on the quality of the web of relationships that make it the social organism it is.

International Society for Performance Improvement (ISPI) The instructional designers' community of practice. Originally the National Society for Programmed Instruction.

Internet If you don't know what the Internet is, none of the rest of this will make any sense to you.

Internet time The accelerated time frame of the new economy brought on by eBusiness and the Internet. A year of Internet time may equal seven years of calendar time (or more or less). The seven-year figure came from Netscape's accomplishing in one year what would have taken a traditional company at least seven years.

Intuition The power, ability, or facility of attaining direct knowledge or cognition without rational thought or inference. We all possess this ability. In a rationality-centric culture, this ability may atrophy.

Job Increasingly obsolete way of packaging work.

Job aid Generally a piece of paper or prompt that helps you do your job, such as a cheat sheet, checklist, or process map.

Just-in-case learning Learning in advance of the need to know. Much just-in-case learning is forgotten in the interval between learning and application.

Just-in-time learning Getting the right knowledge to the right person at the right time.

K Log Knowledge blog. A euphemism used by corporate types who don't want to be typecast as mere bloggers.

Koan Zen. A riddle without an answer: "What is the sound of one hand clapping?" This demonstrates the inadequacy of logic to explain things.

Knowledge management (KM) Whatever you want it to mean.

LAMP Open-source software: Linux-Apache-MySQL-Perl, Python, or PHP.

Learner-centric Organized for the benefit of the learner, not the instructor or the institution. A core tenet of eLearning.

Learning Traditional definition: To gain knowledge or information of; to ascertain by inquiry, study, or investigation; to acquire understanding of or skill; to learn the way; to learn a lesson; to learn dancing; to learn to skate; to learn the violin; to learn the truth about something. Practical definition: Improving one's connections with networks and communities that matter. Adapting to relevant ecosystems.

Learning content management system (LCMS) A multiuser environment where learning developers can create, store, reuse, manage, and deliver digital learning content from a central object repository.

Learning management system (LMS) eLearning infrastructure. At the simplest level, a tracking system. These systems range from simple course-by-course registration systems to immense real-time databases that deal with personalization, learning prescriptions, job competencies, and parsing learning objects.

Learning object A machine-addressable chunk of learning. When labeled with metadata, an eLearning system can mix and match learning objects to create individualized learning experiences. Controversy swirls around how large a chunk is. A course is too large—that's yesterday's object. A couple of sentences is too small—you would lose the context that provides meaning. The accent is on the second syllable of the second word: ob ject'.

Learning service provider (LSP) Delivers eLearning—including learning management—over the Internet. A learning application service provider. Focus in-house information technology on core processes; outsource eLearning to an LSP.

Lecture The dominant form of instruction at major universities. *The New York Times* of August 14, 2002, in an article entitled *The College Lecture, Long Derided, May Be Fading,* reported "One day in 1931, Hamilton Holt, president of Rollins College in Winter Park, Fla., startled his colleagues at an academic conference when he declared that Yale and Columbia, which he had attended in his youth, 'taught me virtually nothing.' The reason, Mr. Holt explained, was that the lectures delivered by his teachers, as with those delivered by professors almost everywhere, were examples of 'probably the worst scheme ever devised for imparting knowledge.'"

Lens In the realm of generative change, used as a metaphor for any distinction or mental model that helps us make the invisible essentials visible that helps us focus on that which is essential to see through the otherwise opaque walls of our conceptual boxes.

Low-hanging fruit In an apple orchard, the apples on the low branches; in business, the easy sales. The problem is that you run out of low-hanging fruit long before you become profitable.

Mashup A Web site or Web application that combines content from more than one source (Wikipedia).

Meatspace The physical world. Atoms, not bits. The opposite of cyberspace.

Megasite On the Web, a destination site that links to other worthy sources of information.

Meme A self-replicating idea that propagates through people and networks, much like computer viruses. A thought gene. Coined by Richard Dawkins.

Metacognition A theory that learners benefit by thoughtfully and reflectively considering the things they are learning and the ways in which they are learning them. A common phrase used by its advocates is "thinking about thinking." In classroom situations, metacognition could well involve thinking aloud with a partner, so that each participant gains insight into the processes that lead to intellectual conclusions. Carried to further levels, metacognition might involve reflective thinking by students about the value or the applicability of the things they are learning.

Metadata Information about information; often metatags describe what's inside a chunk of learning. Generally machine-readable. Analogous to a bar code on an incoming shipment. Informal metadata is called a folksonomy.

Meta-learning The process of learning. Learning to learn is a major component of meta-learning.

Metatags Descriptive labels applied to media assets, pages, information objects, and learning objects that describe the object so it can be managed more effectively. Machine-readable.

Moblog A combination of "mobile" with "blog." Web sites where people post pictures taken with mobile phones in real time.

Neophilia Being excited and pleased by novelty (*The Jargon File*).

Net Short for *Internet*.

Nurnburg funnel The metaphor of training being akin to pouring knowledge into a person's head.

Opportunity cost The cost of not doing something, for example, the sales the rep didn't make because she was away at a seminar. Often the largest cost associated with training programs.

Organizational nervous system Made up of knowledge infrastructure and people. Knowledge infrastructure includes both social and technical infrastructure, specifically those information-based processes, systems, and structures that augment knowledge work.

Paradigm drag When old thinking holds back new (from Gelernter, 1998).

Peer to peer When the PC is both client and server, able to swap resources (for example, files, songs, videos, processor cycles, disk space) directly with other PCs.

Performance The goal of learning. Also referred to as productivity and results.

Performance support Learning embedded in work. Often a better alternative than training.

Permalink A permanent marker or reference point to a certain document on the Web. Most commonly used for blogs, news sites, and newspapers.

Personalization Learning opportunities tailored to the learner's background, style, previous knowledge, and other characteristics. Mass customization and one-to-one marketing applied to learning. Results are saved time, accelerated learning, more wheat and less chaff, and phenomenal performance gains.

Plog Project weblog, a low-risk/high-reward knowledge sharing tool. Coined by Michael Schrage.

Podcasting The distribution of audio or video files, such as radio programs or music videos, over the Net using either RSS or atom syndication for listening on mobile devices and personal computers. Podcasting's essence is creating content for those who want to listen when they want, where they want, and how they want (Wikipedia).

Portal (1) A synonym for entry screen. Widely hyped in 1998–1999 because anyone could imagine the utility of an in-house Yahoo. (2) Transactional portal. A front end that lets you do as well as see things.

Positive psychology Posits that we should stop relying on what we've learned from the mentally ill when advising people who are mentally healthy. It is better to look at what makes happy people happy. Take this approach organizationally and you get Cooperrider's Appreciative Inquiry.

Prairie-dogging Popping up from a cubicle to ask a question. Usually entails asking for help from someone available rather than someone who is likely to have the answer.

Presence awareness Network software that knows a person's physical location. If the urinal in the airport bathroom knows when I'm there and when I'm not, should we expect anything less from our computer networks?

Pro Am An amateur who does something to professional standards, such as writing Linux routines for Linus. *See also* DIY.

Pronoia The belief that the world is conspiring to make you happy and successful.

RDF Resource description framework. A dictionary and thesaurus for XML tags that sits between XML and an ontology.

RLO Reusable learning object. A discrete chunk of reusable learning that teaches to one or more terminal objectives.

ROI Return on investment or benefit-cost ratio. Dated term of art from the industrial age.

RSS Real simple syndication, among other definitions. A format for subscribing to blogs. Important symbolically because the content can come to the user rather than the user going after the content.

SCORM Sharable content object reference model. The U.S. government's standard that seeks to track and manage courseware developed by various authoring tools using a single system. The objective is to bring together diverse and disparate learning content and products to ensure reusability, accessibility, durability, and interoperability. Built on the work of AICC (Aviation Industry CBT Committee), IMS, the IEEE (Institute of Electrical Engineers), and others. Coming under fire for narrow focus on self-directed learning as well as for military backing.

Search learning When you learn from perusing Amazon, looking up topics on a search engine, or paging through business magazines on the airplane.

Self-service learning Pump your own gas. Use the ATM. Be a free-range learner. The self-serve customer does the work once done by others.

Semantic Web Web founder Tim Berners-Lee's vision of the next evolution of the Web, where computers will understand meaning and be able to talk with one another.

Serendipity A "happy accident." People can develop a state of mind that makes serendipity more likely, more frequent, and far more consequential. Fortune favors those who have a cause or mission and pursue it with sagacity, sensitivity, and wisdom. Applying this approach throughout an organization's culture prepares it to expect the unexpected, notice what others miss, and be receptive to impressions and intuitions.

Shelf-life of knowledge Knowledge is perishable. Some suggest it be labeled with pull-dates, like cartons of milk.

SOAP Simple object access protocol. Describes how one application talks to a Web service and asks it to perform a task and return an answer. SOAP makes it possible to use Web services for transactions—say, credit card authorization or checking inventory in real-time and placing an order.

Soft numbers Term of derision used by people who don't understand that intangibles are more important in our economy than hard assets. Soft numbers include the value of training, customer relationships, brand, prestige, organizational knowledge, and all forms of intellectual capital.

Stakeholders All who are involved in or are affected by the activities of a given organization; those who have a stake in the choices that an organization makes and the consequences of those choices. The immediate stakeholder family includes stockholders, suppliers, customers, members (employees), strategic partners, community, government regulators, nature, and even competitors. An extended family of stakeholders ripples out from this first group and includes families, society, and future generations.

Stories A compelling way to share knowledge and learn informally. Stories are natural, entertaining, and engaging. When fully engaged, readers' minds work in concert with the storyteller to focus entirely on generating the virtual world of the story. The power comes from propelling listeners to invent their own stories. Then they own the outcomes.

Synchronous Live event.

Tacit knowledge Tacit knowledge is knowing how; it's impossible to transfer it to you with words alone.

Tag Descriptors that individuals assign to objects, in the practice of collaborative categorization known as folksonomy.

Technophilia The belief that technology will solve all ills. Especially prevalent during the dot-com era and encouraged by *Wired* magazine.

Training An effort to impose learning, often more at the convenience of the provider than the recipient.

UDDI Universal description, discovery, and integration. A virtual Yellow Pages for Web services that lets software discover what Web services are available and how to hook up to them.

VOIP Voice over Internet protocol. Phone calls over the Internet. Use Skype or GoogleTalk or Gizmo to call computer-to-computer for free.

Web Short for World Wide Web (WWW). A global information space that people can read and write using computers connected to the Internet. The term is often mistakenly used as a synonym for the Internet itself, but the Web is a service that operates over the Internet, just like e-mail. Invented by Tim Berners-Lee at CERN, the Web came online in August 1991 (Wikipedia).

Web 2.0 The next evolution of the Web. The Web as platform. Two-way; anyone can create content and syndicate it.

Web log A blog. A personal Web page, frequently updated, with the freshest material at the top.

Web services Standards that enable interoperability of applications on the Net, for example, XML, SOAP, UDDI, and WSDL.

Wikipedia Begun in 2001, Wikipedia has rapidly grown into the largest reference Web site on the Internet. The content of Wikipedia is free, written collaboratively by people from around the world. Wikipedia contains more than 1 million articles in English; every day hundreds of thousands of visitors from around the world make tens of thousands of edits and create thousands of new articles to enhance the amount of knowledge held by the Wikipedia encyclopedia.

Work flow learning The merger of work and learning.

WSDL Web services description language. If UDDI is a virtual Yellow Pages, WSDL is the little blurb associated with each entry that describes what kind of work the Web service can do—say, give access to a database of postal codes.

XML eXtensible markup language. Like HTML but more flexible because users can redefine tags to say whatever they want. This enables computers to talk with one another without human intervention.

YMMV "Your mileage may vary." Recognition that your results may not be the same as mine.

RESOURCES

FURTHER READING

The books in this list influenced my thinking but aren't directly referenced in the text. When I was in school, we combined this with References and called it *bibliography*.

Adams, J. (1999). *Thinking today as if tomorrow mattered*. San Francisco: Eartheart Enterprises.

Aldrich, C. (2003). *Simulations and the future of learning*. San Francisco: Jossey-Bass/Pfeiffer.

Aldrich, C. (2005). *Learning by doing*. Hoboken, NJ: Wiley.

Alexander, C. (1977). *A pattern language: Towns, buildings, construction*. New York: Oxford University Press.

Alexander, C. (1979). *The timeless way of building*. New York: Oxford University Press.

Allee, V. (2002). *The future of knowledge: Increasing prosperity through value networks*. Burlington, MA: Butterworth-Heinemann.

Allen, D. (2001). *Getting things done*. New York: Penguin Putnam.

Allen, M. (2001). *Michael Allen's guide to eLearning*. Hoboken, NJ: Wiley.

Ayre, R. (1999). *Spiritual serendipity*. New York: Fireside.

Barabasi, A.-L. (2003). *Linked: How everything is connected to everything else and what it means*. New York: Plume.

Bing, S. (2005, December 12). All I want for Christmas. *Fortune*. Available at http://money.cnn.com/magazines/fortune/fortune_archive/2005/12/12/8363134/index.htm.

Bronson, P. (2001). *What should I do with my life?* New York: Random House.

Brown, J. S., Denning, S., Groh, K., & Prusak, L. (2004). *Storytelling in organizations*. Burlington, MA: Butterworth-Heineman.

Brown, J. S., & Duguid, P. (2000). *The social life of information*. Boston: Harvard Business School Press.

Brown, M. (2005, July–August). Learning spaces design. *Educause Review*. Available at http://www.educause.edu/apps/er/erm05/erm054.asp.

Carliner, S., & Driscoll, M. (2005). *Advanced Web-based training strategies*. San Francisco: Jossey-Bass/Pfeiffer.

Coffield, F., Moseley, D., Hall, E., & Ecclestone, K. (2004). *Learning styles and pedagogy post-16 learning: A systematic and critical review*. London: Learning Skills and Research Centre.

Collins, J. (2001). *Good to great: Why some companies make the leap and others don't*. New York: HarperCollins.

Conner, M. (2004). *Learn more now*. Hoboken, NJ: Wiley.

Conner, M., & Clawson, J. (2004). *Creating a learning culture*. Cambridge: Cambridge University Press.

Cooperider, D. (1998). *The appreciative inquiry thin book*. Bend, OR: Thin Book Publishing Company.

Cross, J., & Dublin, L. (2002). *Implementing eLearning*. Alexandria, VA: ASTD Press.

Cross, J., & Quinn, C. (2002). The value of learning about learning. In *Transforming culture: An executive briefing on the power of learning*. Charlottesville: University of Virginia, Darden Graduate School of Business Administration.

Crowe, S. (1994). *Garden design*. Woodbridge, Suffolk, UK: Antique Collectors Club.

Csikszentmihalyi, M. (2004). *Good business*. New York: Penguin.

Dalai Lama. (2003). *The art of happiness at work*. New York: Riverhead.

Davis, S., & Meyer, C. (1998). *Blur*. Norwood, MA: Capstone Publishing.

Davis, S., & Meyer, C. (2003). *It's alive: The coming convergence of information, biology, and business*. New York: Crown.

Dawson, R. (2001). *Living networks*. Upper Saddle River, NJ: Financial Times Prentice Hall.

De Bono, E. (1986). *De Bono's thinking course*. New York: Facts on File.

Dewey, T. (1934). *Art as experience*. New York: Milton, Balch & Company.

Drucker, P. (2001). *Managing in the next society*. New York: Truman Talley Books.

Edelman, G. (2004). *Wider than the sky*. New Haven, CT: Yale University Press.

Figallo, C., & Rhine, N. (2001). *Building the knowledge management network*. Hoboken, NJ: Wiley.

Friedman, T. (2005). *The world is flat*. New York: Farrar, Straus and Giroux.

Gardner, H. (2004). *Changing minds*. Boston: Harvard Business School Press.

Garreau, J. (2005). *Radical evolution: The promise and peril of enhancing our minds, our bodies—and what it means to be human*. New York: Doubleday.

Gazzaniga, M. (2000). *The mind's past*. Berkeley: University of California Press.

Gee, J. P. (2004). *What video games have to teach us about learning and literacy*. New York: Palgrave Macmillan.

Gelernter, D. (1994). *The muse in the machine: Computerizing the poetry of human thought*. New York: Free Press.

Gell-Mann, M. (1994). *The quark and the jaguar: Adventures in the simple and complex*. New York: Freeman.

Hagel, J. (2001). *Out of the box: Strategies for achieving profits today and growth tomorrow through Web services*. Boston: Harvard Business School Press.

Hallowell, E. (1995). *Driven to distraction: Recognizing and coping with attention deficit disorder from childhood through adulthood*. New York: Touchstone.

Hartmann, T. (1993). *Attention deficit disorder: A different perception*. Nevada City, CA: Underwood Books.

Harvard Business School Working Knowledge. (2005, September 12). *Why office design matters*. Boston: Harvard Business School.

Honore, C. (2004). *In praise of slowness*. San Francisco: Harper.

Horn, R. (1972). *In pursuit of the e-objectives*. Unpublished paper.

Horton, B. (2000). *Designing Web-based training: How to teach anyone anything anywhere anytime*. Hoboken, NJ: Wiley.

Hubbard, B. M. (1998). *Conscious evolution: Awakening the power of our social potential*. New York: New World Library.

Hutchins, E. (1996). *Cognition in the wild*. Cambridge, MA: MIT Press.

IDEO. *IDEO method cards*. Palo Alto, CA: Author.

Illich, I. (1999). *Deschooling society*. London: Marion Boyars Publishers.

IBM. (2005). *IBM executive brief: Learning governance—aligning strategy with organizational outcomes*. Armonk, NY: Author.

Johnson, S. (1997). *Interface culture: How new technology transforms the way we create and communicate*. San Francisco: HarperSanFrancisco.

Johnson, S. (2001). *Emergence: The connected lives of ants, brains, cities, and software*. New York: Scribner.

Kahan, S. (2005, May–June). Conversation with Seth Kahan. *IHRIM Journal*, p. 3.

Kaniger, R. (1999). *The one best way: Frederick Winslow Taylor and the enigma of efficiency*. New York: Penguin.

Kaye, D. (2003). *Loosely coupled: The missing pieces of Web services*. San Rafael, CA: RDS Associates.

Keirsey, D. (1998). *Please understand me II: Temperament, character, intelligence*. Del Mar, CA: Prometheus Nemesis Book Company.

Kelly, K. (1995). *Out of control: The new biology of machines, social systems and the economic world*. Cambridge, MA: Perseus Books.

Kelly, K. (1999). *New rules for the new economy: Ten radical strategies for a connected world*. New York: Penguin Books.

Kelly, T., & Nanjiani, N. (2005). *The business case for eLearning*. San Jose, CA: Cisco Press.

Kleiner, A. (1996). *The age of heretics: Heroes, outlaws, and the forerunners of corporate change*. New York: Currency.

Knowles, M. (1973). *The adult learner: A neglected species*. Houston, TX: Gulf Publishing.

Koster, R. (2004). *A theory of fun*. Scottsdale, CA: Paraglyph.

Krug, S. (2000). *Don't make me think: A common sense approach to Web usability*. Berkeley, CA: New Riders Press.

Langer, E. (1998). *The power of mindful learning*. Cambridge, MA: Perseus Books.

Langer, E. (2005). *On becoming an artist: Reinventing yourself through mindful creativity*. New York: Ballantine Books.

Leonard, G. (1968). *Education and ecstasy*. New York: Delacorte Press.

Leonard, G. (1992). *Mastery: The keys to success and long-term fulfillment*. New York: Plume Books.

Leonard, G., & Murphy, M. (1995). *The life we are given*. New York: Tarcher.

Lesser, E., & Prusak, L. (2003). *Creating value with knowledge: Insights from the IBM Institute for Business Value*. New York: Oxford University Press.

Lidwell, W., Holden, K., & Butler, J. (2003). *Universal principles of design: 100 ways to enhance usability, influence perception, increase appeal, make better design decisions, and teach through design*. Gloucester, MA: Rockport Publishers.

MacKenzie, G. (1998). *Orbiting the giant hairball: A corporate fool's guide to surviving with grace*. New York: Viking.

Madson, P. R. (2005). *Improv wisdom: Don't prepare, just show up*. New York: Harmony/Bell Tower.

Mager, R. (1992). *What every manager should know about training*. Atlanta, GA: CEP Press.

Masie, E. (Ed.). (2005). *Learning rants, raves, and reflections*. San Francisco: Jossey-Bass/Pfeiffer.

Mitchell, W. (1996). *City of bits*. Cambridge, MA: MIT Press.

Moore, G. (1991). *Crossing the chasm*. New York: HarperCollins.

Moore, G. (1998). *The gorilla game*. New York: HarperCollins.

Moore, G. (1999). *Inside the tornado*. New York: HarperCollins.

Moore, G (2000). *Living on the fault line*. New York: HarperCollins.

Morville, P., & Rosenfeld, L. (2001). *Information architecture II*. Sebastopol, CA: O'Reilly Media.

Norman, D. (1994). *Things that make us smart*. Reading, MA: Addison-Wesley.

Norman, D. (1998). *The design of everyday things*. New York: Doubleday.

Norman, D. (2003). *Emotional design: Why we love (or hate) everyday things*. New York: Basic Books.

Norris, D., et al. (2003). *Transforming eKnowledge: A revolution in the sharing of knowledge*. Ann Arbor, MI: Society for College and University Planning.

O'Driscoll, T. (1999). *Achieving desired business performance*. Silver Spring, MD: International Society for Performance Improvement.

Palin, P., & Sandhaas, K. (2000). *Architect for learning*. Ruckersville, VA: St. Thomas Didymus Corp.

Pink, D. (2001). *Free agent nation: The future of working for yourself*. New York: Warner.

Pink, D. (2005). *A whole new mind: Moving from the information age to the conceptual age*. New York: Riverhead.

Postrel, V. (2004). *The substance of style: How the rise of aesthetic value is remaking commerce, culture, and consciousness*. New York: HarperCollins.

Prensky, M. (2004). *Digital game-based learning*. New York: McGraw-Hill.

Pryor, K. (1999). *Don't shoot the dog! The new art of teaching and training*. New York: Bantam.

Rosenberg, M. (2000). *eLearning: Strategies for delivering knowledge in the digital age*. New York: McGraw-Hill.

Rosenberg, M. (2005). *Beyond eLearning: Approaches and technologies to enhance organizational knowledge, learning, and performance*. San Francisco: Jossey-Bass/Pfeiffer.

Rossett, A. (2001). *Beyond the podium: Delivering training and performance to a digital world*. San Francisco: Jossey-Bass/Pfeiffer.

Rummler, G., & Brache, A. (1995). *Improving performance: How to manage the white space on the organization chart*. San Francisco: Jossey-Bass.

Russell, T. (1999). *The no significance difference phenomenon: A comparative research annotated bibliography on technology for distance education*. Montgomery, AL: International Distance Education Certification Center.

Schank, R. (1991). *Tell me a story: A new look at real and artificial memory*. New York: Atheneum.

Schank, R. (2005). *Lessons in learning, elearning, and training: Perspectives and guidance for the enlightened trainer*. San Francisco: Jossey-Bass/Pfeiffer.

Seligman, M. (1995). *What you can change and what you can't: The complete guide to successful self-improvement learning to accept who you are*. New York: Ballantine Books.

Senge, P. M., et al. (1994). *The fifth discipline fieldbook: Strategies for building a learning organization*. New York: Nicholas Brealey.

Senge, P., et al. (2000). *Schools that learn*. New York: Currency.

Senge, P., et al. (2005). *Presence: An exploration of profound change in people, organizations, and society*. New York: Currency.

Shneiderman, B. (2001). *Leonardo's laptop: Human needs and new computing technologies*. Cambridge, MA: MIT Press.

Stafford, T., & Webb, M. (2005). *Mind hacks*. Sebastopol, CA: O'Reilly Media.

Stewart, T. (2001). *The wealth of knowledge: Intellectual capital and the twenty-first century organization*. New York: Currency.

Stott, B. 1991. *Write to the point*. New York: Columbia University Press.

Tapscott, D. (1997). *The digital economy: Power and peril in the age of networked intelligence*. New York: McGraw-Hill.

Tapscott, D. (1999). *Blueprint for the digital economy: Creating wealth in the era of e-Business*. New York: McGraw-Hill.

Tapscott, D. (2000). *Digital capital: Harnessing the power of business webs*. Boston: Harvard Business School Press.

Taylor, M. (2003). *The moment of complexity. emerging network culture*. Chicago: University of Chicago Press.

Tobin, D. (2000). *All learning is self-directed*. Alexandria, VA: ASTD.

Vaill, P. (1996). *Learning as a way of being: Strategies for survival in a world of permanent white water*. San Francisco: Jossey-Bass.

Warshawsky, J., Hardaway, C., & Fugere, B. (2005). *Why business people speak like idiots*. New York: Free Press.

Watts, A. (1968). *The wisdom of insecurity*. New York: Vintage.

Watts, D. (2003). *Six degrees: The science of a connected age*. New York: Norton.

Weinberger, D. (2001). *Small pieces loosely joined: A unified theory of the Web*. Cambridge, MA: Perseus Books.

Wenger, E., McDermott, R., & Snyder, W. M. (2001). *Cultivating communities of practice*. Boston: Harvard Business School Press.

Wheatly, M. (2005). *Finding our way: Leadership for an uncertain time*. San Francisco: Berrett-Koehler.

Wheatly, M., & Kellner-Roberts, M. (1996). *A simpler way*. San Francisco: Berrett-Koehler.

Zinsser, W. (1986). *On writing well*. New York: HarperCollins.

Zinsser, W. (1993). *Writing to learn*. New York: HarperCollins.

Zuboff, S., & Maxmin, J. (2001). *The support economy: Why corporations are failing individuals and the next episode of capitalism*. New York: Viking.

WEB SITES

For a list of relevant Web sites, go to http://informL.com.

PEOPLE AND ORGANIZATIONS

Advanced Human Technologies, Ross Dawson; http://www.ahtgroup.com.

Dawson is the author of *Living Networks: Leading Your Company, Customers, and Partners in the Hyper-Connected Economy* and *Developing Knowledge-based Client Relationships*. Organizations must continually explore the future, or risk falling by the wayside. AHT assists senior executive teams to integrate the immediate implications of ongoing technological, social, and economic developments into strategy.

Ageless Learner, Marcia Conner; http://agelesslearner.com/, http://agelesslearner.com/intros/informal.html.

These Web sites provide terrific resources and the best information to help you get more from life whether you're four or ninety-four. Ageless Learning focuses on how learning and curiosity influence everything you do in life, no matter your age, education, or occupation.

Verna Allee Associates, Verna Allee; http://vernaallee.com.

Allee shares the wisdom of value networks, a great way to understand any business: "Today's business relationships encompass much more than the tangible flows of products, services, and revenue that we have focused on in the past. As we come to depend more and more on exchanges of knowledge and other intangibles with our customers and business partners, success depends on building a rich web of value creating relationships. New approaches and methods are needed to understand the reality of value creation."

Altus Learning Systems, Ted Cocheu; http://www.altuscorp.com/

Altus brings the powers of rapid eLearning to businesses that need to communicate quickly and effectively with large, geographically dispersed audiences. It integrates professional services with methods, tools, and technology to make it simple for companies to transfer mission-critical knowledge to field staff, channel partners, and customers. Altus technology empowers the Cisco Virtual Team project.

Appreciative Inquiry Commons, David Cooperrider; http://appreciative inquiry.case.edu/intro/whatisai.cfm.

Appreciative Inquiry (AI) is about the co-evolutionary search for the best in people, their organizations, and the relevant world around them. In its broadest focus, it involves systematic discovery of what gives life to a living system when it is most alive, most effective, and most constructively capable in economic, ecological, and human terms. AI involves, in a central way, the art and practice of asking questions that strengthen a system's capacity to apprehend, anticipate, and heighten positive potential.

Berkana Institute, Margaret Wheatley; http://www.margaretwheatley.com/ http://www.berkana.org/index.html.

"We are a worldwide community of people who recognize the need for change in our communities, organizations and nations. We are offering our leadership to help resolve our most pressing local problems. We define a leader as anyone who wants to help, who is willing to step forward to make a difference in the world. We know that the world is blessed with an abundance of these leaders."

Beyond Bullets, Cliff Atkinson; http://www.beyondbullets.com/.

Atkinson is the fellow who helped win the multimillion dollar judgment against Merck. The site provides advice and examples of persuasive presentations.

Coaching Platform, Gunnar Bruckner; http://coachingplatform.com/.

"This Web site enables business activities in which collaboration is the key to creating solutions or services. The software was designed by observing how the best coaches and most responsible consultants communicate with each other and with their clients. It is a dynamic, flexible system that supports the entire range of roles and actions required for information sharing and collaboration."

Cognitive Edge, Dave Snowden; http://www.cynefin.net/.

Cognitive Edge (formerly The Cynefin Centre) is an international network that focuses on the application of complexity science to management and organizational practice. At its heart is "a distinction between ordered and unordered systems and the consequent recognition that systems with fundamentally different qualities require the application of contextually differentiated methods for both diagnosis and intervention."

eLearning Centre; http://www.e-learningcentre.co.uk/.

"The eLearning Centre provides independent eLearning advice and consultancy to businesses and education and maintains a large collection of links to eLearning resources in its Information section." It is my first stop when I'm searching for anything in the eLearning arena.

eLearning Forum, Eilif Trondsen; http://www.elearningforum.com.

The eLearning Forum is a noncommercial, global community of people who make decisions at the intersection of learning, technology, business, and design. Founded in 1999 as the Silicon Valley eLearning Network, eLearning Forum has gained a reputation as the thought leader on eLearning trends, best practices, and advice on the industry. Members of the community of practice include corporate chief learning officers, eLearning marketing executives, investment analysts, and researchers and developers.

EPSS Central, Gary Dickelman; http://www.epsscentral.info/.

EPSScentral.INFO is a set of free resources on the many disciplines that comprise performance-centered design: cognitive science, usability engineering, agile development, information engineering and architecture, knowledge management, hypermedia engineering, content management, learning technologies, and human factors engineering. Dickelman is a thought leader in performance-centered design.

Global Learning Resources, Kevin Wheeler; http://www.glresources.com/.

Companies that need leading-edge strategies, fresh mind-sets, and cost-effective processes to win the competition for top talent find Global Learning Resources to be a remarkable partner. Its clients get ahead of business, demographic, and organizational trends due to its research and focus on identifying emerging issues and best practices.

The Grove Consultants, David Sibbet; http://www.grove.com/.

For more than twenty-five years, The Grove Consultants International has taken its pioneering work in visual planning and organization change and seeded it worldwide. It believes that people and organizations are more vital and empowered when working creatively with one another, much like living things in nature. This orientation is the soil from which all of Grove's products, consulting, and design processes grow.

Gurteen Knowledge Center, David Gurteen; http://www.gurteen.com/.

The Gurteen Knowledge Community is a global learning community of over twelve thousand people in 138 countries. The community is for people who are committed to making a difference: people who wish to share and learn from each other and who strive to see the world differently, think differently, and act differently. Membership is free. The main themes of this site are knowledge management, learning, creativity, innovation, and personal development. The site contains over four thousand pages of material on books, people, other Web sites, blogs, articles, events, courses, quotations, and much more.

HeartMath, Bruce Cryer; http://heartmath.com
Institute of HeartMath, Sara Paddison; http://www.heartmath.org/.

"A change of heart changes everything." Research and cases of reducing stress and increasing longevity by focusing on emotions.

Informal Learning Blog and Informal Learning Book site,
Jay Cross; http://informL.com.

This is the hub of the informal learning community. Sign up for Unworkshops. Read extensions to this book.

Integral Transformative Practice, George Leonard; http://www.itp-life.com/main.html.

"Integral Transformative Practice is a long-term program for realizing the potential of body, mind, heart, and soul. It is integral in that the various aspects of the self are seen as separate windows to an underlying wholeness. It is transformative in that it aims at significant positive change, the manifestation of unrealized potential. And it is a practice in that it involves long-term, positive activities that, above and beyond any specific external rewards, are of value in and of themselves."

Internet Time Group, Jay Cross; http://internettime.com.
This site presents articles, presentations, pointers, feeds, and commentary about learning and performance.

IT Conversations, The Conversations Network, Doug Kaye; http://www.itconversations.com/.
This provides great presentations downloaded from information technology conferences and more.

Master New Media, Robin Good; http://www.masternewmedia.org/, http://www.masterviews.com/.
Master New Media provides what you need to know about collaboration, free telephone calls, instant messaging, virtual classrooms, Web tricks, free images, or any other aspect of computer-based communication. Incredible scope.

Meta-Learning Lab, Jay Cross, Clark Quinn, Claudia L'Amoreaux, Claudia Welss, and Bill Daul; http://www.meta-learninglab.com/.
The Meta-Learning Lab is dedicated to increasing people's capacity to learn and improving the performance of individuals and organizations. Learning has become the ultimate competitive advantage in our dynamic, knowledge-based society.

MindJet LLC; http://www.mindjet.com/us/.
Maker of my mind-mapping software. Free trial available.

Network Roundtable at the University of Virginia, Rob Cross; https://webapp.comm.virginia.edu/networkroundtable/.
"By applying network analysis to business imperatives such as innovation, revenue growth, cost containment, and talent management, the Network Roundtable is demonstrating how a relational view of work can improve organizational and individual performance. This group of top organizations has two primary objectives. The first is to teach members how to apply network analysis to critical business issues. Online tutorials, quarterly hands-on workshops, biweekly webinars, free use of a proprietary software, and access to training material enable members to undertake successful projects in their own organizations. The second objective is to conduct research demonstrating how

network analysis yields actionable insights and measurable business impact. Current programs of research on innovation and top-line revenue growth, client connectivity and sales force effectiveness, large-scale change and post-merger integration, talent management and leadership development, and strategy execution and alignment are extending the application of network analysis to a range of business imperatives."

Org.net, Valdis Krebs;
http://www.orgnet.com/.

Valdis is a top expert in social network analysis. His InFlow software is considered state of the art.

Positive Psychology Center, University of Pennsylvania, Marty Seligman;
http://www.authentichappiness.sas.upenn.edu/.

Positive psychology includes the study of positive emotion, positive character traits, and positive institutions. Seligman is now turning his attention to training positive psychologists, individuals whose practice will make the world a happier place, parallel to the way clinical psychologists have made the world a less unhappy place. Take the VIA Signature Strengths Questionnaire to identify the pursuits that will bring you happiness.

Quinnovation, Clark Quinn; http://www.quinnovation.com/.

Quinn is a pragmatic generalist whose work includes games, mobile learning, performance support, content models, and intelligent systems. Combining a deep cognitive background and strong technology experience with creativity and strategic business experience, Quinnovation takes a broad perspective toward meeting real needs, including organizational, learning, performance, and knowledge perspectives.

Stephen Denning; http://www.stevedenning.com/.

Denning is the master storyteller who helped turn World Bank around by telling a compelling story. Read his latest book, *The Leader's Guide to Storytelling*.

Weber Consulting Group, Craig Weber; weberconsulting@earthlink.net.

Weber designed the Courageous Conversations program at Pfizer and elsewhere.

Work-Learning Research, Will Thalheimer; http://www.work-learning.com.

Thalheimer is a research psychologist specializing in learning, cognition, memory, and performance. The site provides the data about what really works.

World Café, Juanita Brown; http://www.theworldcafe.com/

Based on living systems thinking, the World Cafe is a proven approach for fostering authentic dialogue and creating dynamic networks of conversation around your organization or community's real work and critical questions—improving both personal relationships and people's capacity to shape the future together.

XPLANE, the Visual Thinking Company, Dave Gray; http://www.xplane.com/.

XPLANE is an information design firm that develops visual maps and stories to make complex business issues easier to understand. Put Dave's blog, Communication Nation, on your reading list: http://communicationnation. blogspot.com/.

REFERENCES

Adkins, S. (2003, November 16). We are the problem. We are selling snake oil. *Learning Circuit Blog.* Available at http://www.internettime.com/lcmt/archives/001014.html.

Allee, V. (1997). *The knowledge evolution: Expanding organizational intelligence.* Burlington, MA: Butterworth-Heinemann.

Argyris, C. (1991, May). Teaching smart people how to learn. *Harvard Business Review.*

ASTD & Masie, E. (2001, June). *eLearning: If we build it, will they come?* Alexandria: ASTD.

Atkinson, C. (2005). *Beyond bullet points: Using Microsoft PowerPoint to create presentations that inform, motivate, and inspire.* Redmond, WA: Microsoft Press.

Baldwin, T. T., & Ford, K. J. (1988). Transfer of training: A review and directions for future research. *Personnel Psychology, 41,* 63–105.

Baum, D. (2005, January 17). Battle lessons: What the generals don't know. *New Yorker.* Available at http://www.newyorker.com/fact/content/articles/050117fa_fact.

Berensson, A. (2005, August 18). Jurors in the Vioxx trial hear closing arguments. *New York Times.*

Berman, M. (2001). *The twilight of American culture.* New York: W.W. Norton.

The best of 2005. (2005, December 19). *Business Week.* Available at http://www.businessweek.com/magazine/content/05_51/b3964401.htm?chan=search.

Blakeslee, S. (June 28, 2005). What other people say may change what you see. *New York Times,* Section F, p. 3, column 1.

Bolles, R. N. (2005). *What color is your parachute 2006: A practical manual for job-hunters and career-changers*. Berkeley, CA: Ten Speed Press.

Bonk, C., & Graham, C. (2005). *The handbook of blended learning*. San Francisco: Jossey-Bass/Pfeiffer.

Bourdain, A. (2001). *Kitchen confidential: Adventures in the culinary underbelly*. New York: HarperCollins.

Boyatzis, R. & McKee, A. (2005). *Resonant leadership: renewing yourself and connecting with others through mindfulness, hope, and compassion*. Boston: Harvard Business School Press.

Brand, S. (1994). *How buildings learn*. New York: Viking Adult.

Bransford, J. (ed). (2000). *How people learn: Brain, mind, experience, and school*. Washington, DC: National Academic Press. Available at http://newton.nap.edu/html/howpeople1/.

Brinkerhoff, R. O., & Gill, S. J. (1994). *The learning alliance: Systems thinking in HRD*. San Francisco: Jossey-Bass.

Broad, M. L., & Newstrom, J. W. (1992). *Transfer of training*. Reading, MA: Addison-Wesley.

Brown, J., & Isaacs, D. (2005). *The world café*. San Francisco: Berrett-Koehler.

Brown, J. S., & Hagel, J. (2005). *The only sustainable edge*. Boston: Harvard Business School Press.

Buchanan, L. (1994, December 1). Getting your ducks online. *CIO*. Available at http://www.cio.com/archive/120194/intro.html.

Capra, F. (2002). *The hidden connections: Integrating the biological, cognitive, and social dimensions of life into a science of sustainability*. New York: Doubleday.

Collins, J. C. (2001). *Good to great*. New York: HarperBusiness.

Company Command (2005). Available at http://companycommand.army.mil.

Conner, M. (2001, Winter). Our shared playground: An interview with Michael Schrage. *LiNEzine*.

Conner, M. (2005). *Informal learning: Ageless learner, 1997–2005*. Available at http://agelesslearner.com/intros/informal.html.

Cooperrider, D., & Whitney, D. (2004). *A positive revolution in change: Appreciative inquiry*. Case Western Reserve Institute. White paper. *The appreciative inquiry commons at Case Western Reserve Institute*. Unpublished white paper, Case Western Reserve Institute, Cleveland, OH.

CPSquare (January 2006). (Online conference on building communities of practice). Available at http://www.cpsquare.org/News/archives/000060.html.

Cross, J. (2003). *Informal learning: The other 80%*. Available at http://internettime.com.

Cross, J., & O'Driscoll, T. (2005, September). Gloria Gery in her own words. *Performance Improvement Quarterly.* Available at http://www.ispi.org/publications/pitocs/piSept2005.htm.

Cross, R. (2005a). *Network roundtable at the University of Virginia.* Available at https://webapp.comm.virginia.edu/networkroundtable/.

Cross, R. (2005b). Organizational network analysis. Available at http://www.robcross.org/.

Cross, R., Laseter, T., Parker, A., & Velasquez, G. (2005). *Assessing and improving communities of practice with organizational network analysis.* Unpublished white paper, University of Virginia Network Roundtable.

Cross, R., & Parker, A. (2004). *The hidden power of social networks: Understanding how work really gets done in organizations.* Boston: Harvard Business School Press.

Csikszentmihalyi, M. (1991). *Flow: The psychology of optimal experience.* New York: HarperCollins.

Damasio, A. (1999). *The feeling of what happens: Body and emotion in the making of consciousness.* New York: Harvest Books.

Davenport, T. (2005). *Thinking for a living: How to get better performances and results from knowledge workers.* Boston: Harvard Business School Press.

Davis, E. (2005). *Lessons for tomorrow.* Northport, MI: Orgone Press.

Denning, S. (2005). *The leader's guide to storytelling: Mastering the art and discipline of business narrative.* San Francisco: Jossey-Bass.

Dobbs, K. (2000, January). From simple moments of learning. *Training, 37*(1), 52–54, 56, 58.

Drucker, P. (1993). *Managing for results.* New York: Collins.

Ford, J. R., & Weissbein, D. H. (1997). Transfer of training: An updated review and analysis. *Performance Improvement Quarterly, 10*(2), 22–41.

Friedman, M., & Rosenman, R. (1974). *Type A behavior and your heart.* New York: Knopf.

Gatto, J. (2000). *The underground history of American education.* Gilsum, NH: Pathway Books.

Gelernter, D. (1998). *Machine beauty: Elegance and the heart of technology.* New York: Basic Books.

Gery, G. (1991). *Electronic performance support systems.* New York: Ziff Institute.

Gladwell, M. (2004). *Blink: The power of thinking without thinking.* New York: Little, Brown.

Goldberg, N. (1986). *Writing down the bones.* Boston: Shambhala.

Goleman, D. (1995). *Emotional intelligence: Why it can matter more than IQ*. New York: Bantam.

Goleman, D. (2000). *Working with emotional intelligence*. New York: Bantam.

Goleman, D. (2001). *The emotionally intelligent workplace: How to select for, measure, and improve emotional intelligence in individuals, groups, and organizations*. San Francisco: Jossey-Bass.

Grady, S., & Gamez, J. (2005, November 30). *Podcasting@Cisco: A case study*. Presentation at eLearning Forum. Available at http://elearningforum.vportal. net.

Hallowell, E., & Ratey, J. (2005). *Delivered from distraction: Getting the most out of life with attention deficit disorder*. New York: Ballantine Books.

Hartmann, T. (2005). *The gift of ADHD*. Available at http://www.thomhartmann.com/healing.shtml.

Heinlein, R. (1961). *Stranger in a strange land*. New York: G.P. Putnam's Sons.

Henschel, P. (2001). Understanding and winning the never-ending search for talent. *Linezine*.

Hill, N. (1937). *Think and grow rich*. San Diego, CA: Aventine Press.

Honoré, C. (2004). *In praise of slowness*. San Francisco: HarperSanFrancisco.

Horn, R. (1990). *Mapping hypertext: The analysis, organization, and display of knowledge for the next generation of on-line text and graphics*. Lanham, MD: Lexington Books.

Horn, R. (1998). *Visual language: Global communication for the 21st century*. Bainbridge Island, WA: Macrovu Press.

Illinois Trial Practice Weblog. (July 29, 2005). *Plaintiffs' lawyer Mark Lanier received special PowerPoint training before first Vioxx trial*. Available at http://www.illinoistrialpractice.com/2005/07/plaintiffs_lawy.html.

Institute for Play. (2000). Available at http://www.instituteforplay.com. homepage/.

Institute for Research on Learning. (1999). *Seven principles of learning*. Carmel Valley, CA: Author.

Institute of HeartMath. (2004). *The science of the heart*. Available at http://www.heartmath.org/research/science-of-the-heart/.

Jonsson, B. (2001). *Unwinding the clock: Ten thoughts on our relationship to time*. New York: Harvest Books.

Kahan, S. (2004). *Building beehives: A handbook for creating communities that generate returns*. Wayne, PA: Performance Development Group.

Kahan, S. (2005, May–June) Conversation with Seth Kahan. *IHRIM Journal*, p. 3.

Kahn, T. (2001). *Social "know-who" for building virtual communities: It's both what you know and who you know that count!* Available at http://www.designworlds.com/articles/KnowWho.html.

Kiuchi, T., & Shireman, W. (2002) *What we learned in the rainforest: Business lessons from nature.* San Francisco: Berrett-Koehler.

Klein, G. (2004). *The power of intuition: How to use your gut feelings to make better decisions at work.* New York: Currency.

Kleiner, A. (2003). *Who really matters: The core group theory of power, privilege, and success.* New York: Currency.

Kurzweil, R. (2005). *The singularity is near: When humans transcend biology.* New York: Viking.

Langer, E. (1990). *Mindfulness.* Reading, MA: Addison-Wesley.

Lamott, A. (1995). *Bird by bird.* New York: Anchor.

Leonard, D., & Snap, W. (2004). *Deep smarts, how to cultivate and transfer enduring business wisdom.* Boston: Harvard Business School Publishing.

Leonard, G. (1968). *Ecstasy and education.* Berkeley: North Atlantic Books.

Leonard, G. (1991). *Mastery.* New York: Dutton.

Leonard, G. (1999). *The way of aikido.* New York: Dutton.

Leonard, G., & Murphy, M. (1993). *The life we are given: A long-term program for realizing the potential of body, mind, heart, and soul.* New York: Tarcher/Penguin.

Lesser, E., & Prusak, L. (2003). *Creating value with knowledge: Insights from the IBM Institute for Business Value.* New York: Oxford University Press USA.

Lloyd, R. (2000, November). Informal learning most effective. *Knowledge Management.* Available at http://www.kmmagazine.com.

Locke, C., Weinberger, D., Levine, R., & Searles, D. (2000). *The cluetrain manifesto: The end of business as usual.* Cambridge, MA: Perseus Books.

Maister, D. (1997). *Managing the professional service firm.* Detroit: Free Press.

Malone, T. (2004). *The future of work: How the new order of business will shape your organization, your management style and your life.* Boston: Harvard Business School Press.

McDonald, W. (1983). *An old guy who feels good.* Berkeley: Ol'McDonald Press.

Mehrabian, A. (1972). *Nonverbal communication.* Ossining, NY: Walter De Gruyter.

Naiman, L. (2000, February). Ideas are the currency of the new economy. *Creativity at Work Newsletter.* Available at http://www.creativityatwork.com/articlesContent/Currency.html.

Norman, D. (2004). *Defense of PowerPoint*. Available at http://www.jnd.org/dn.mss/in_defense_of_powerp.html.

Peters, T., & Waterman, R. (1982). *In search of excellence*. New York: Warner Books.

Pitt, L. (2002). *Paris disparu. Un voyage dans le temps au coeur du Paris historique*. Paris: Editions Parigramme.

Quinn, C. (2005). *Engaging learning*. San Francisco: Jossey-Bass/Pfeiffer.

Raybould, B. (2000). Performance support engineering: An emerging development methodology for enabling organizational learning. *Performance Improvement Quarterly*, 8(1), 7–22.

Raymond, E. (2001). *How to ask questions the smart way*. Available at http://www.catb.org/~esr/faqs/smart-questions.html.

The real reason you're working so hard. (2005, October 3). *Business Week*. Available at http://www.businessweek.com/magazine/content/05_40/b3953601.htm?chan=search.

Rosenberg, M. (2000). *eLearning: Strategies for delivering knowledge in the digital age*. New York: McGraw-Hill.

Rosenberg, M. (2005). *Beyond eLearning*. San Francisco: Pfeiffer.

Rummler, G., & Brache, A. (1995). *Improving performance: How to manage the white space on the organization chart*. San Francisco: Jossey-Bass.

Rushkoff, D. (2005). *Get back in the box*. New York: HarperCollins.

Santosus, M. (2004, March). Cisco on video. *CIO magazine*.

Sapolsky, R. (2004, March 1–3). *Why zebras don't get ulcers*. Paper presented at Training 2004 conference, Atlanta, GA.

Sarnoff, D. (1989). *Never be nervous again*. New York: Ivy Books.

Schrage, M. (2000). *Serious play*. Boston: Harvard Business School Press.

Seligman, M. (1991). *Learned optimism: How to change your mind and your life*. New York: Free Press.

Seligman, M. (2002). *Authentic happiness: Using the new positive psychology to realize your potential for lasting fulfillment*. New York: Free Press.

Senge, P., Kleiner, A., Roberts, C., Ross, R., & Smith, B. (1994). *The fifth discipline fieldbook*. New York: Currency.

Stewart, T. (2003). *The wealth of knowledge: Intellectual capital and the twenty-first century organization*. New York: Currency.

Stolovitch, H., & Keeps, E. (2002, June). Stop wasting money on training. *Performance eXpress*, 1.

Stott, B. (1991). *Write to the point*. New York: Columbia University Press.

Sugrue, B., O'Driscoll, T., & Vona, M. (2005, October). The C-level and the value of learning. *T+D magazine*, pp. 69–78.

Thalheimer, W. (2006, February). *Spacing learning events over time: What the research says*. http://www.work-learning.com/catalog.

Thompson, C. (2005, October 16). Meet the life hackers. *New York Times*. Available at http://query.nytimes.com/gst/fullpage.html?res=9804E1DA103 FF933A05753C1A9639C8B63.

Tognazzini, B. (1995). *Tog on software design*. Reading, MA: Addison-Wesley.

Tooher, N. (2006, July). Texas jury awards $253 million in first Vioxx trial. *Lawyers USA*.

Tufte, E. (2003). *The cognitive style of PowerPoint*. Cheshire, CT: Graphics Press.

Vader, W. (1998). *Informal learning*. Available at http://www.ontariohome school.org/informallearning.html.

Weber, M. (1904). *The Protestant ethic and the spirit of capitalism*. New York: Routledge.

Wenger, E. (2005). *Learning for a small planet: A research agenda*. Unpublished paper.

Wheatley, M. (2002). *Turning to one another: Simple conversations to restore hope to the future*. San Francisco: Berrett-Koehler.

Zinsser, W. (1976). *On writing well*. New York: Collins.

INDEX

I

IBM: *Blue Pages* directory of, 61–62; culture of, 230; learning space problem at, 43; UAE presence of, 133; *world jam* community of, 162

Illinois Trial Practice Weblog, 104

Impromptu meetings, informal learning during, 28

In Praise of Slowness (Honoré), 11

In Search of Excellence (Peters & Waterman), 51

Informal learning: as alternative to training, 222–223; business benefits/results of, 25–29, 232; coaching as form of, 127; comparing outcomes of formal and, 31–34; described, 16–17; developing platform supporting, 223; dimensions of, 127t; as freedom from learning "games," 225–226; lessons of experience on, 227–232; spending-outcomes paradox of formal and, 17; three gravitational forces for, 18–19. *See also* Formal learning; Learning

Informal learning lessons: culture matters, 230–231; do the possible, 228; envision opportunity, 229–230; examining your organization readiness, 231–232; keep it simple, 227–228

Informal organization: described, 65–66; mapping connections in, 66–67; ONA used to pinpoint vulnerability in, 71fig. *See also* Networks

Information sources: Cisco's approach to, 154–158; discovering the most valuable, 66–67; finding the right information through, 62–63; importance of developing, 61–62; knowledge management (KM) and, 63–64; optimizing informal, 64–66

Information technology: informal learning to increase flexibility of, 26; Internet as, 55–57, 177–182, 187–192

Innovation: evaluating, 29–30; informal learning to facilitate, 26

Institute for the Future, 144

Institute of HeartMath, 108, 109–110, 111

Institute of Noetic Sciences, 76

Institute for Play report (2000), 53

Institute for Research on Learning, 17, 223

Intel, 121, 133

Internet: blogging and the, 179–182; CGI use of the, 187–192; connections through, 177; cultural impact of, 178–179; emergent learners and the, 55–57; learning applications using the, 187t; unworkshops connected using the, 186fig; Web 2.0, 184–186. *See also* Networks; Web sites

Internet culture, 178–179

Internet Time Blog, 179, 180fig

Internet Time Group Command Center (Microsoft), 46–47fig

Intuition, 86–89

Isaacs, D., 135, 136

J

Jobs, S., 91, 121, 126, 213

Jonsson, B., 11

Joy, B., 3

K

K–12 educational revolution, 134

Kahan, S., 132, 151

Kahn, T., 64

Kaye, D., 209

Keeping up, 29

Keeps, E., 33

Keller, H., 4

Kelly, K., 221

Kelly, T., 158

Kierkegaard, S., 11

Kitchen Confidential (Bourdain), 151

Klein, G., 88

Kleiner, A., 65, 77

Know "What-if . . . ?," 64

Know-/Care-why, 64

Know-what/Know-not, 64

Know-when, 64

Know-where, 64

Know-who, 64

Knowledge Campus (Novartis), 49–50

Knowledge management (KM), 63–64

Knowledge work: future of, 8–10; innovative, 9. *See also* Work

Knowledge workers: changes experienced by modern, 9–10; delusions of control over, 17–18; description of, 8; empowering, 91; improving morale of, 28; informal learning to unlock potential of, 27; information sources used by, 61–67; learning lifecycle of, 81–83; "wants" of, 30–31. *See also* Learners; Work

Kofman, F., 148

Krebs, V., 66

Kurzweil, R., 1, 3

L

L'Amoreaux, C., 75

Lamott, A., 101

Langer, E., 226

Lanier, M., 103–104

Lave, J., 152

The Leader's Guide to Storytelling (Denning), 132

Learned helplessness, 97

Learners: aiming for breakthrough performance, 96fig; belief in positive future, 96–97; feelings of, 94–96; finding your calling, 93; finding-yourself, 92–93; focusing on your interest, 114–115; happy attitude by, 111–114; health factor and, 108–111; reflection by, 79, 106–108; system check by, 93–94; written communication by, 100–106. *See also* Knowledge workers

Learning 2005, 206, 215–218

Learning: as adaptation, 15fig–16; benefits of, 15; blending good work with good, 226–227; continuum of yes to no, 16fig; decisions on what to include in, 80–81; definition of, 15, 18; differences between training and, 37; eLearning approach to, 166–175; evolution of, 7fig–8; human potential for, 21–22; impact on human networks, 7–8; Internet culture impact on, 178–179; neck-up versus neck-down, 108; role of reflection in, 79, 106–108, 128; self-service, 28, 39, 83–84; spectrum of, 16–17; spending-outcomes paradox of corporate, 17; three segments of

ABOUT THE AUTHOR

JAY CROSS has been passionate about harnessing technology to improve adult learning since the 1960s. Fresh out of college, he sold mainframes for NCR. He designed the University of Phoenix's first business degree program. He transformed a start-up into an Inc 500 award winner, training a million professionals to make sound decisions and sell services. He has managed software start-ups. A self-avowed "Web fanatic," he has been marrying training to the Net since 1996.

Jay founded Internet Time Group in 1998 to help organizations learn. Cisco, IBM, and Smartforce are among his clients. His five-year scenario plan, the Internet Time Machine, was a pioneering description of eLearning. He delivered the inaugural keynote on Web marketing to the first meeting of the Online Banking Association. He has spoken at conferences around the world and is the author of numerous articles and white papers on learning and business effectiveness.

Jay is coauthor (with Lance Dublin) of *Implementing eLearning*, and he contributed a chapter to ASTD's *Implementing E-Learning Solutions*. He assisted the Institute for the Future in building scenarios for global corporate learning circa 2008. He writes the Effectiveness column for *Chief Learning Officer* magazine.

Jay's interests include design, photography, conceptual art, hiking, and the nature of time. Jay was on the Web before Mosaic changed its name to Netscape, and gave up television for Web surfing long ago.

Jay was born in Hope, Arkansas, and grew up in Virginia, Texas, Rhode Island, France, and Germany. He lives with his wife, Uta, and two miniature longhaired dachshunds in the hills of Berkeley, California. He is a graduate of Princeton University and Harvard Business School, with additional study in design, systems analysis, programming, leadership, information architecture, decision making, direct marketing, and languages.

You may reach him at http://internettime.com.

Pfeiffer Publications Guide

This guide is designed to familiarize you with the various types of Pfeiffer publications. The formats section describes the various types of products that we publish; the methodologies section describes the many different ways that content might be provided within a product. We also provide a list of the topic areas in which we publish.

FORMATS

In addition to its extensive book-publishing program, Pfeiffer offers content in an array of formats, from fieldbooks for the practitioner to complete, ready-to-use training packages that support group learning.

FIELDBOOK Designed to provide information and guidance to practitioners in the midst of action. Most fieldbooks are companions to another, sometimes earlier, work, from which its ideas are derived; the fieldbook makes practical what was theoretical in the original text. Fieldbooks can certainly be read from cover to cover. More likely, though, you'll find yourself bouncing around following a particular theme, or dipping in as the mood, and the situation, dictate.

HANDBOOK A contributed volume of work on a single topic, comprising an eclectic mix of ideas, case studies, and best practices sourced by practitioners and experts in the field.

An editor or team of editors usually is appointed to seek out contributors and to evaluate content for relevance to the topic. Think of a handbook not as a ready-to-eat meal, but as a cookbook of ingredients that enables you to create the most fitting experience for the occasion.

RESOURCE Materials designed to support group learning. They come in many forms: a complete, ready-to-use exercise (such as a game); a comprehensive resource on one topic (such as conflict management) containing a variety of methods and approaches; or a collection of like-minded activities (such as icebreakers) on multiple subjects and situations.

TRAINING PACKAGE An entire, ready-to-use learning program that focuses on a particular topic or skill. All packages comprise a guide for the facilitator/trainer and a workbook for the participants. Some packages are supported with additional media—such as video—or learning aids, instruments, or other devices to help participants understand concepts or practice and develop skills.

- *Facilitator/trainer's guide* Contains an introduction to the program, advice on how to organize and facilitate the learning event, and step-by-step instructor notes. The guide also contains copies of presentation materials—handouts, presentations, and overhead designs, for example—used in the program.

- *Participant's workbook* Contains exercises and reading materials that support the learning goal and serves as a valuable reference and support guide for participants in the weeks and months that follow the learning event. Typically, each participant will require his or her own workbook.

ELECTRONIC CD-ROMs and Web-based products transform static Pfeiffer content into dynamic, interactive experiences. Designed to take advantage of the searchability, automation, and ease-of-use that technology provides, our e-products bring convenience and immediate accessibility to your workspace.

METHODOLOGIES

CASE STUDY A presentation, in narrative form, of an actual event that has occurred inside an organization. Case studies are not prescriptive, nor are they used to prove a point; they are designed to develop critical analysis and decision-making skills. A case study has a specific time frame, specifies a sequence of events, is narrative in structure, and contains a plot structure— an issue (what should be/have been done?). Use case studies when the goal is to enable participants to apply previously learned theories to the circumstances in the case, decide what is pertinent, identify the real issues, decide what should have been done, and develop a plan of action.

ENERGIZER A short activity that develops readiness for the next session or learning event. Energizers are most commonly used after a break or lunch to stimulate or refocus the group. Many involve some form of physical activity, so they are a useful way to counter post-lunch lethargy. Other uses include transitioning from one topic to another, where "mental" distancing is important.

EXPERIENTIAL LEARNING ACTIVITY (ELA) A facilitator-led intervention that moves participants through the learning cycle from experience to application (also known as a Structured Experience). ELAs are carefully thought-out designs in which there is a definite learning purpose and intended outcome. Each step—everything that participants do during the activity— facilitates the accomplishment of the stated goal. Each ELA includes complete instructions for facilitating the intervention and a clear statement of goals, suggested group size and timing, materials required, an explanation of the process, and, where appropriate, possible variations to the activity. (For more detail on Experiential Learning Activities, see the Introduction to the *Reference Guide to Handbooks and Annuals*, 1999 edition, Pfeiffer, San Francisco.)

GAME A group activity that has the purpose of fostering team spirit and togetherness in addition to the achievement of a pre-stated goal. Usually contrived—undertaking a desert expedition, for example—this type of learning method offers an engaging means for participants to demonstrate and practice business and interpersonal skills. Games are effective for team building and personal development mainly because the goal is subordinate to the process—the means through which participants reach decisions, collaborate, communicate, and generate trust and understanding. Games often engage teams in "friendly" competition.

ICEBREAKER A (usually) short activity designed to help participants overcome initial anxiety in a training session and/or to acquaint the participants with one another. An icebreaker can be a fun activity or can be tied to specific topics or training goals. While a useful tool in itself, the icebreaker comes into its own in situations where tension or resistance exists within a group.

INSTRUMENT A device used to assess, appraise, evaluate, describe, classify, and summarize various aspects of human behavior. The term used to describe an instrument depends primarily on its format and purpose. These terms include survey, questionnaire, inventory, diagnostic, survey, and poll. Some uses of instruments include providing instrumental feedback to group members, studying here-and-now processes or functioning within a group, manipulating group composition, and evaluating outcomes of training and other interventions.

Instruments are popular in the training and HR field because, in general, more growth can occur if an individual is provided with a method for focusing specifically on his or her own behavior. Instruments also are used to obtain information that will serve as a basis for change and to assist in workforce planning efforts.

Paper-and-pencil tests still dominate the instrument landscape with a typical package comprising a facilitator's guide, which offers advice on administering the instrument and interpreting the collected data, and an initial set of instruments. Additional instruments are available separately. Pfeiffer, though, is investing heavily in e-instruments. Electronic instrumentation provides effortless distribution and, for larger groups particularly, offers advantages over paper-and-pencil tests in the time it takes to analyze data and provide feedback.

LECTURETTE A short talk that provides an explanation of a principle, model, or process that is pertinent to the participants' current learning needs. A lecturette is intended to establish a common language bond between the trainer and the participants by providing a mutual frame of reference. Use a lecturette as an introduction to a group activity or event, as an interjection during an event, or as a handout.

MODEL A graphic depiction of a system or process and the relationship among its elements. Models provide a frame of reference and something more tangible, and more easily remembered, than a verbal explanation. They also give participants something to "go on," enabling them to track their own progress as they experience the dynamics, processes, and relationships being depicted in the model.

ROLE PLAY A technique in which people assume a role in a situation/scenario: a customer service rep in an angry-customer exchange, for example. The way in which the role is approached is then discussed and feedback is offered. The role play is often repeated using a different approach and/or incorporating changes made based on feedback received. In other words, role playing is a spontaneous interaction involving realistic behavior under artificial (and safe) conditions.

SIMULATION A methodology for understanding the interrelationships among components of a system or process. Simulations differ from games in that they test or use a model that depicts or mirrors some aspect of reality in form, if not necessarily in content. Learning occurs by studying the effects of change on one or more factors of the model. Simulations are commonly used to test hypotheses about what happens in a system—often referred to as "what if?" analysis—or to examine best-case/worst-case scenarios.

THEORY A presentation of an idea from a conjectural perspective. Theories are useful because they encourage us to examine behavior and phenomena through a different lens.

TOPICS

The twin goals of providing effective and practical solutions for workforce training and organization development and meeting the educational needs of training and human resource professionals shape Pfeiffer's publishing program. Core topics include the following:

Leadership & Management

Communication & Presentation

Coaching & Mentoring

Training & Development

e-Learning

Teams & Collaboration

OD & Strategic Planning

Human Resources

Consulting

What will you find on pfeiffer.com?

- The best in workplace performance solutions for training and HR professionals

- Downloadable training tools, exercises, and content

- Web-exclusive offers

- Training tips, articles, and news

- Seamless online ordering

- Author guidelines, information on becoming a Pfeiffer Affiliate, and much more

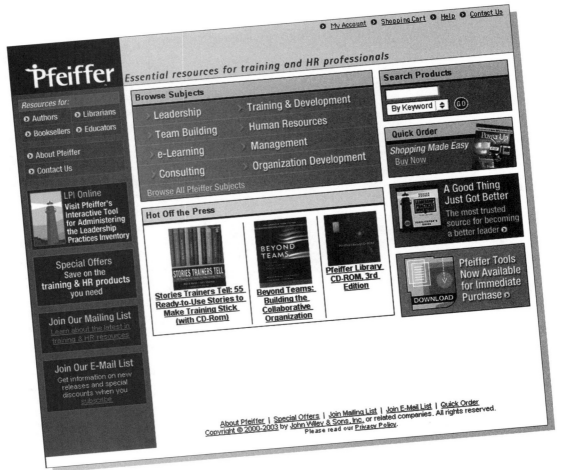

Discover more at www.pfeiffer.com